PRAISE FOR *MOVING MOUNTAINS*

'*Moving Mountains* is a rich gift of much-needed stories and cosmologies that help us see the earth, our world and interdependence, and our ideas of "nature" and the "natural" with greater clarity. I found each of the narratives uniquely compelling, dynamic and powerful. Beautifully curated and edited with a moving introduction by Louise Kenward, *Moving Mountains* is a generative and profound anthology that I know I will return to – and it will help us untangle ourselves from many of the modern myths which separate and sever'

– LUCY JONES

'Bringing together startlingly original voices, *Moving Mountains* invites us not only to look at nature, but to live alongside it in community and collaboration. Privileging the experiences, perceptions, and perspectives of disabled and chronically ill writers and poets, this anthology is both an urgent call for justice, and an endlessly moving exploration of what it means to be human. Compelling, challenging, contemplative and curious, *Moving Mountains* is an anthology to treasure and return to'

– ELINOR CLEGHORN

'A stunning anthology that promises to change the landscape of nature writing. Challenging who gets to write about nature, *Moving Mountains* is an ambitious, beautiful collection of work'

– LIZZIE HUXLEY-JONES

'Some of my favourite writers and artists are collected here. Together they present a strong argument for the expansion of nature writing into the realm of illness and disability – whether from bed, chair, balcony or close neighbourhood. What if your illness and/or disability – or for that matter ableism and lack of access – restricts your capacity to "immerse" yourself in nature? What can experiencing nature through an unsteady, uneven body reveal? In Eli Clare's words, a world that "relishes crookedness, wholeness and brokenness"'

– ALICE HATTRICK

'Personal involvements with nature are exposed in this deeply affecting collection, which will stay with you'

– TOM SHAKESPEARE

'An important, vital, questing collection of words, stories and experiences of wild green space which asks what it means to lose oneself in nature

and explores how acquaintance with living landscapes both urban and rural can earth, galvanise and inspire. An anthology to open eyes, minds and hearts, I loved it'
— DAN RICHARDS

'Nature and pain have always been caught up together; in this lively anthology, nature and pain shine light on one another and both come out transformed'
— NOREEN MASUD

'This polyphonic exploration of bodies, minds and the natural world brings together fascinatingly diverse writing to create something magical. A collection that fuses fierce strength with lyricism, vulnerability with exciting prose, it's a moving testament to resilience and hope, and to celebrating joy wherever we can find it'
— LULAH ELLENDER

'*Moving Mountains* is a stunning book that captures the experience of living with a disability or chronic illness. Through the beautifully described narratives I felt seen, known and far less alone. *Moving Mountains* raises the voices of disabled authors, but it offers insights to everyone, because illness impacts us all'
— CLAIRE WADE

'Nature might not heal disabled bodies, but it does connect and soothe. Just like this beautiful, raw book did for me'
— RACHEL CHARLTON-DAILEY

'This is a beautiful collection of stories and poems by a variety of authors. The authors will feel like they are old friends sharing their deepest thoughts with you. As someone living with chronic illness, it was comforting and validating to be heard through these stories too'
— JEANNIE DI BON

MOVING MOUNTAINS

Edited by
LOUISE KENWARD

FOOTNOTE

First published in 2023 by
Footnote Press

www.footnotepress.com

Footnote Press Limited
4th Floor, Victoria House, Bloomsbury Square, London WC1B 4DA

Distributed by Bonnier Books UK, a division of Bonnier Books
Sveavägen 56, Stockholm, Sweden

First printing
1 3 5 7 9 10 8 6 4 2

Introduction and Selection Copyright © Louise Kenward 2023
Foreword © Samantha Walton 2023

'Abi Palmer Invents the Weather' Copyright © Abi Palmer 2023. Produced and commissioned by Artangel. Courtesy The Artangel Collection

'Foraging and Feminism: Hedge-Witchcraft in the 21st Century' Copyright © Alice Tarbuck 2017. First published in the anthology *Nasty Women*, published by 404 Ink

All other contributions Copyright © the Individual Contributors 2023

The right of Louise Kenward to be identified as the author of this work has been asserted in accordance with the Copyright, Designs and Patents Act 1998

The right of the contributors to be identified as the creators of the contributions within this work has been asserted in accordance with the Copyright, Designs and Patents Act 1998

No part of this publication may be reproduced, stored in a retrieval system, or transmitted in any form or by any means without the written permission of the publisher, nor be otherwise circulated in any form of binding or cover other than that in which it is published and without a similar condition being imposed on the subsequent purchaser

A CIP catalogue record for this book is available from the British Library

ISBN (hardback): 978 1 804 44053 7
ISBN (trade paperback): 978 1 804 44054 4
ISBN (ebook): 978 1 804 44055 1

Printed and bound in Great Britain
by Clays Ltd, Elcograf S.p.A.

Dedicated to everyone living with chronic illness and disability,
in celebration of the myriad of ways in which
you engage with the world around you, whatever
scale or speed that might be.

In memory of Marcus Sedgwick (1968–2022)

'Considering how common illness is, how tremendous the spiritual change that it brings, how astonishing, when the lights of health go down, the undiscovered countries that are then disclosed, what wastes and deserts of the soul a slight attack of influenza brings to light, what precipices and lawns sprinkled with bright flowers a little rise of temperature reveals, what ancient and obdurate oaks are uprooted in us in the act of sickness, how we go down into the pit of death and feel the waters of annihilation close above our heads and wake thinking to find ourselves in the presence of the angels and the harpers when we have a tooth out and come to the surface in the dentist's arm chair and confuse his "Rinse the mouth – rinse the mouth" with the greeting of the Deity stooping from the floor of Heaven to welcome us – when we think of this and infinitely more, as we are so frequently forced to think of it, it becomes strange indeed that illness has not taken its place with love, battle, and jealousy among the prime themes of literature.'

Virginia Woolf, 'On Being Ill', 1926

Contents

Image Descriptions ... ix
Foreword ... xiii
Introduction ... xvii

Water
Field Notes by Sally Huband ... 3
Not Healthy, Never Healed by Isobel Anderson ... 13
Sequences of the Body by Jane Hartshorn ... 23
On Becoming Ocean by Victoria Bennett ... 36

Air
An Ode to Climbing Over Fences Instead of Needing Them Open by Hannah Hodgson ... 47
712 Stanza Homes For The Sun by Cat Chong ... 49
This is Not Just Tired by Louisa Adjoa Parker ... 64
Under a Wide Blue Sky: Chronic Illness, Nature and Me by Louisa Adjoa Parker ... 66
Things in Jars by Louise Kenward ... 80
my body is not my country by Dillon Jaxx ... 87

Weather
Abi Palmer Invents the Weather by Abi Palmer ... 93

Threatening Rain: On Bodies, Bad Weather and
    Bad Clothing by Polly Atkin   104
The Thing I Fear Has Found Me by Carol Donaldson   115

Trees
The Clocktower and the Canopy by Khairani Barokka   127
Foraging and Feminism: Hedge-Witchcraft in the
    Twenty-First Century by Alice Tarbuck   137
A Quince in the Hand by Nic Wilson   147

Moorland
Climbing Against Gravity: on Mountaineering and
    Genetic Haemochromatosis by Kerri Andrews   157
Endometriosis and the Female Trinity in the Peak
    District by Rowan Jaines   166
Beats Per Minute by Feline Charpentier   177

Earth
Moving Close to the Ground: A Messy Love Song
    by Eli Clare   189
A Natural Force by Jamie Hale   198
the poet limps in words as a balance for worlds
    by Alec Finlay   203
this is my body by Kate Davis   228

Acknowledgements and thanks   235
Contributors   237

Resources   245
Endnotes   247

Image descriptions

Artificacaea by Dawn Cole

Physalis Protectus Serificium I p. xi
Physalis Protectus Serificium II p. 233
'Artificacaea' is a series of engravings, inspired by antique botanical illustrations, documenting various flowers and breaking them down into their component parts. The prints which open and close *Moving Mountains* are of Chinese Lanterns, Physalis Alkekengi, renamed for their artificial version Physalis Protectus Serificium, the project title 'Artificaceae' being the family name for all the artificial flowers.

Birdwoman by Lorna Crabbe

Birdwoman I p. 12
Black and white line drawing of a woman dressed like an eighteenth-century maid wearing a dark dress and white apron. A dark mask covers the lower face. One arm holds out a crude, dark puppet, shaped like a bird.

Birdwoman II p. 44
Black and white line drawing of a woman in dark clothing, from behind. Her arms are stretched out with crude bird-head puppet gloves.

Birdwoman III   p. 63
    Black and white line drawing of a woman dressed in black, with a bird shape emerging from her clothing, across her body.

Birdwoman IV   p. 90
    Black and white line drawing, showing four pairs of theatrical legs in black hose, with black pointed shoes.

Birdwoman V   p. 146
    Black and white line drawing of a woman's head and shoulders in a full, dark coloured dress, with a dainty white collar. Five bird shapes emerge from her dark hair, as a kind of headdress.

Birdwoman VI   p. 153
    Black and white line drawing of featureless female figure, with arms raised and broken puppet-like strings.

Birdwoman VII   p. 186
    Black and white line drawing of a young woman in a dark belted dress, with simplistic wing forms instead of arms.

Birdwoman VIII   p. 197
    Black and white line drawing of a woman's head and shoulders. A beak-type mask covers the nose and mouth. From the shoulders and chest, seven forms like long bird necks point downwards.

Physalis Protectus Senfucuon

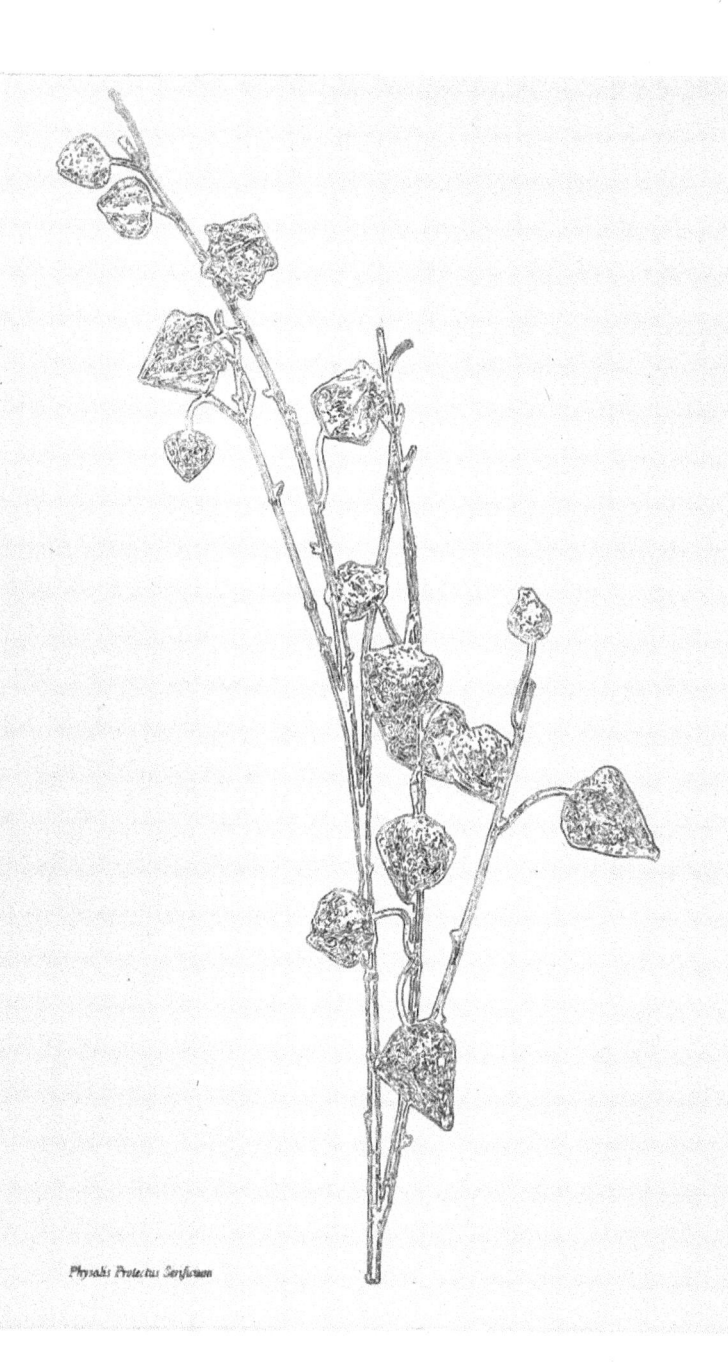

Foreword

Samantha Walton

In periods of illness or pain, the body's silence would be the greatest release. To invert William Wordsworth's lines, it is not the world but the body that is too much with us. This may partly explain illness's absence from what Virginia Woolf calls 'the prime themes of literature'. It makes sense that writers might turn their attention away from the flesh when they experience respite – to suppress the body textually, even when it screams to be heard.

Of course, there are other reasons why chronically ill and disabled voices have been suppressed in literature. Many conditions are grossly under-researched, meaning sufferers have to fight to receive treatment, if treatments even exist. Capitalism prizes productivity, while those who fall outside its temporalities of wellness are ruthlessly stigmatised. Writing under such circumstances is a drain on precious time and energy.

Producing work that dwells with pain, discomfort and struggle also demands that readers are willing to go to those places and to confront the reality that we are all only temporarily able-bodied. This willingness isn't always guaranteed. Nature writing in particular has celebrated stories of demanding physical feats instead of quotidian reflections on bodies and landscapes in processes of difficult, slow and sometimes mysterious change.

Moving Mountains shows what literature can achieve when writers have the space, support and fellowship to turn their attention to the body in states of illness, pain and disability. Exploring 'the undiscovered countries' that illness discloses has inspired startlingly original writing: penetrating, tender, inventive, intertextual, iconoclastic, rich in surprising metaphor and experimental in form.

In her classic work *The Body in Pain* (1988), Elaine Scarry suggests that pain is not only difficult to articulate, but is also actively destructive to language, reducing the sufferer to moans and wails. This anthology innovates by thinking and feeling with nature to create a bold new lexicon to describe the supposedly indescribable. In 'Field Notes', Sally Huband realises that having been silenced by the medical profession, she had 'already dismissed the symptoms of autoimmune disease to the point that I had started to lose words'. Yoking sensations of pain to observed natural phenomena like a hooked kittiwake or washed up by-the-wind sailors, she shows up the weakness of medical vocabulary and produces arresting new language, culturing empathy with suffering human and animal bodies alike.

Metaphors that are deeply entangled in nature and the corporeal emerge across this anthology. Sayings like 'under the weather' take on new meaning when the body feels like 'a giant barometer, flexing and shifting with the weather like a great big pine cone', in Carol Donaldson's words. In Polly Atkin's dialogue with Dorothy Wordsworth, old nature writing tropes linking weather and the mind are upturned, and the body thrums like an aeolian harp responsive to changes in climate and temperature. Heightened sensitivity brings with it an awareness that, to Atkin, reveals that the 'the skin is not a dome habitat, sealed by climate. The weather outside alters the weather within.' 'It reminds me that I am part of a web I do not understand,' Donaldson writes, precipitating a precious and revelatory intimacy with the more-than-human.

Of course, this intimacy is not always comfortable. Many of these writers ask what it means to love nature when it causes pain. Running counter to nature writing's traditional celebration of discomfort and extremes, Atkin notes that one can often best appreciate bad weather by staying inside. It is possible, too, to 'bring / the outside in', as Jane Hartshorn and Louise Kenward describe in their tender records of things gathered in jars, and Abi Palmer in her extraordinary account of creating weather for her indoor cats. Miraculous, alchemical processes produce the scent of petrichor and the quality of light. Permeated by love, these animated theatres blur boundaries between the microcosm of the terrarium and the vast web of living nature.

As this anthology shows, experiences of disability and illness trouble distinctions between the body and the mind, nature and the human. The kind of intelligence this produces, rooted in the bodymind, is a precious discovery in the midst of a climate and ecological crisis. Modernity and capitalism have forced a separation between people and nature, a closing down of care and severing of the ties that bind. Against this colonial trajectory, Khairani Barokka offers Indigenous frameworks and medicines of Deep Peace. Beyond the ravages of extractivism, she explains, disabled people have been held and cherished by communities and calmed by flourishing ecosystems. Her contribution – like many others collected here – demands a transformation of the social and a recognition of the wisdom and power of disabled people. 'I do not want to be undisabled at this point: it has taught me too much, given me too much,' she writes.

In 'On Being Ill' (1926), Woolf writes that illness brings about a spiritual change, but it does this and more. *Moving Mountains* shows how rich, various and new the world can look and feel through different bodyminds. These pages are a delight in themselves, and an invitation for others to report back from those 'undiscovered countries' – to transform language and shed fresh light on hidden and vital relations between the body, mind and the living world.

Introduction

Over the last ten years my connection with nature and the world around me has altered markedly. Growing up in the 'Garden of England' of rural Kent in the '70s and '80s, I climbed trees and made dens, unaware of the vulnerability of the place I inhabited and of my own physical form. When I recovered, well enough, from my first prolonged period of illness, I travelled. Unable to return to work, those longed-for hopes and wonderings of youth became all the more prescient faced with the reality of life as finite, and the visceral knowledge that my body was fallible and prone to falling and failing. It is through this period of travel that I reconnected with the world around me and developed a renewed relationship with 'nature'.

I embarked on a great adventure, taking the train as far as I could and travelled eastwards. I was neither an exuberant student on a gap year, nor a retired person of means, so found my own way, cheaply and slowly, connecting with conservation projects and learning to dive. Returning to the UK almost a year later, I trained to be a Marine Mammal Medic with the British Divers Marine Life Rescue (BDMLR) and studied the intertidal zone with citizen science projects on the south coast of England, before travelling to Spain to work as a diver on a seahorse project in the Bay of Roses. I thought I had found a new life that my sick body could sustain.

What I hadn't bargained for was that I could lose it all again so easily. Second time around I have been landlocked, looking instead out of a stationary window and watching cobwebs gather in corners. As travel reconnected me with nature, prolonged illness led me to writing.

I have since been learning to live in this body anew, grateful to have travelled when I did and more knowledgeable than I ever thought possible about my body and medicine's failings. I have come to see society and healthcare from a different perspective than the one I believed in when working as a psychologist with the NHS. I continue my quest for change, however, for greater understanding of chronic illness, complex health issues and disability, and with hope for shame and stigma to be burdens that we do not have to carry when our bodies fall from under us.

Nature cure?

The term 'nature cure' is often used to suggest a correlation between spending time in green spaces, and a recovery of some kind, be it from mental or physical ill health, for example. Taken from the title of Richard Mabey's 2007 book of the same name, 'nature cure' has since been adopted more broadly to encompass (and imply) that our ills may be resolved through time spent in nature, and a genre of writing has sprung up around these themes in different and wonderful forms. Yet this is not a solution for everyone. Being in nature is not always accessible or desirable, those of us with genetic conditions and chronic illness, aren't and can't be 'cured'. The notion of 'cure' in itself has complicated ties with eugenics, when 'at the centre of cure lies eradication'.[1] What is easy to forget is that we are very much a part of nature and cannot separate ourselves from it. Time spent in and with nature can be enormously valuable despite, and because of, all these things and more.

This may be particularly pertinent for chronically ill and disabled people, as we experience the impact of the world around us – from weather systems to rough terrain – more acutely than people who do not need to be so conscious of their bodies as they move through the landscape.

There is a much-denied fact – that illness and disability are a normal part of life, and not some aberration or fault of the individual. This denial and the connection of the 'nature cure' risks harm twofold. Firstly, a perpetuation of the sentiment that access to the natural world is a human right. The increase seen in recent years of green spaces 'on prescription', while being of value to many, risks continuing a view of nature as being another commodity for our benefit, with the additional expectation that we would be cured if only we went forest bathing/sea swimming/some other activity involving physical exertion and the outdoors. Secondly, while many of these things may be beneficial and enjoyable for some, green spaces do not have the same effect on everyone, and this is not always considered. In addition, the expectation of recovery or cure can be harmful for those who do not seek cure from a key aspect of their identity, or when recovery is not possible. Such schemes often also exclude disabled people, consciously or unconsciously, who cannot access these spaces.

For those of us who live with poorly understood chronic illness, the challenges also include significant and persistent underfunding and a lack of research and understanding of debilitating conditions. A lack of access to assessment and treatment of complex illness is a more pressing barrier than accessing green spaces. Suggestions of a 'nature cure' can undermine and distract from the need for adequate healthcare.

The 'natural'?

An idealised body, as idealised landscapes, can be focus for celebration and nostalgia. Protecting and valuing the 'pristine' and ignoring the poisoned and neglected can be paralleled in place and in bodies. 'Natural' has become a word to indicate 'good' and 'healthy', with all its complications. Shame and stigma can stem from much that seeks to distinguish between the 'natural' and 'unnatural'. Derelict sites and run-down urban spaces can be a refuge for the more-than-human. These will always be different in biodiversity to the landscapes of ancient woodlands and open undisturbed moorland, but are not valueless sites worthy only of abandonment.

In Eli Clare's powerful essay 'Notes on Natural Worlds', he relates the sick and disabled human body to the ecological loss of monocultures and destruction of habitats:

> Sometimes viable restoration is not possible. Sometimes restoration is a bandage trying to mend a gaping wound. Sometimes restoration is an ungrounded hope motivated by the shadows of <u>natural</u> and <u>normal</u>. Sometimes restoration is pure social control. I want us to tend the unrestorable places and ecosystems that are ugly, stripped down, full of toxins, rather than considering them <u>unnatural</u> and abandoning them. I want us to respect and embrace the bodies disabled through environmental destruction, age, war, genocide, abysmal working conditions, hunger, poverty, and twists of fate, rather than deeming them <u>abnormal</u> bodies to isolate, fear, hate, and dispose of.[2]

Disability and climate crisis

Just as human beings have polluted and created sickness in the environment, increasing levels of chronic health difficulties are impacting us now. The effects of pollution, destruction and extraction are impacting on us too, with greater levels of sickness in allergies and autoimmune conditions since the Industrial Revolution.[3] We cannot poison one without also poisoning the other. The two are inextricably entwined, we cannot talk about climate crisis or environmental destruction without talking also of illness and disability.

The climate crisis is already having, and will continue to have, the most significant impact on those most vulnerable in society, and multiply marginalised communities more so: those of the Global South, in poverty, LGBTQ+ and disabled people, for example. People with disabilities are particularly at risk from escalating temperatures, and climate change will cause further pandemics too, creating increased levels of disability. Yet disaster-planning for incidents such as floods and heatwaves excludes disabled people.

In 2021, the organisers of the United Nations Climate Change Conference (COP26) in Glasgow had not even considered the access needs for the Israeli energy minister, Karine Elharrar, a wheelchair user, who was shut out of proceedings because the venue wasn't accessible.

Getting sick and acquiring a disability is not as unusual as you might think; it is simply that these stories are not embraced in society as much as the recovery tales of survival and overcoming are. Indeed, with them, also comes value, as Alison Kafer writes, 'the experience of illness and disability presents alternative ways of understanding ourselves in relation to the environment, understandings which can generate new possibilities for intellectual connections and activist coalitions'.[4] The power of storytelling is crucial in opening up discussions about illness and effecting change in and across society, in order that marginalised voices are centred and amplified[5] as well as engaging with the public on the climate crisis.[6]

Covid-19 pandemic

In many ways, it is thanks to the online access and sense of community the pandemic brought that this book came to being as it did. With more online events and conversations on social media, access to people and engagement was easier. The pandemic brought the themes of *Moving Mountains* to the fore: bird song was noticed for the first time by many, as rush hour traffic ceased, and the general population became more conscious of the risk of illness and its impacts. *Moving Mountains* grew in fertile soil. Well used to the isolation that disability and long-term illness often bring, the pandemic, and periods of lockdown were, for some of us, periods of time where we could flourish.

However, the development of this anthology at a time of Covid-19 is all the more pertinent when we remember that 60 per cent of Covid-19 deaths in the UK have been of disabled people.

While chronically ill and disabled people make up 26 per cent of the population, the pandemic highlighted a disregard for this group and the removal of health and safety precautions continues to risk further numbers. It has also highlighted the importance of clean air, just as the necessity for clean water was learned following the epidemic of cholera in nineteenth-century Europe. Many chronically ill and disabled people have returned to, or continued with, shielding strategies as the Covid-19 pandemic continues to pose a risk to health, with persistent death rate figures and rising disability. Despite being downgraded from the highest alert level by the World Health Organization (May, 2023), this is not a declaration that the pandemic is now over, as has been interpreted by some media outlets. Rather, the WHO statement says the pandemic is no longer an 'unusual or unexpected event', but is ongoing and remains a global health risk.[7]

Nature writing and disabled and chronically ill authors

This anthology's story began in April 2021, when, at the end of an online book launch of *Disturbing the Body* with Five Leaves Bookshop in Nottingham, Deirdre O'Byrne asked me 'so what's next?' and for the first time I heard myself say, 'a nature writing book by people with chronic illness and physical disability'. While it was the first time such a thought had consciously occurred to me, looking back, I had been unconsciously preparing for such a thing for a long time, and other people had been considering similar themes too.

The launch of the Nan Shepherd Prize for nature writing was the first (and still only) literary prize for underrepresented voices in nature writing. Not only looking for 'the next voice in nature writing', the Nan Shepherd also seeks to 'provide an inclusive platform for new and emerging writers from underrepresented backgrounds.' Created and developed by Kate Davis, Polly Atkin and Anita Sethi, Open Mountain was also established with the intention of 'redefining mountain literatures and cultures to include voices and experiences often excluded or invalidated'. The launch of the Barbellion Prize in 2019 by Jake Goldsmith, marked the first celebration of the writing of disabled authors and/or those with chronic illness. *Stairs and Whispers: D/deaf and Disabled Poets Write Back*, edited by Sandra Alland, Khairani Barokka and Daniel Sluman (Nine Arches Press) in 2017, 'a ground breaking anthology examining UK disabled and D/deaf poetics', was another influence on me in considering this project too.

The work of *Moving Mountains* was long overdue and contributes to a growing field of nature writing, and writing about place and landscape, that is seeing more inclusive and representative voices in our society. Highlighted by the oft-quoted essay by Kathleen Jamie who pointedly notes the prevail of the 'Lone Enraptured Male' dominating the New Nature Writing: a middle-class white English able-bodied man '[h]ere to boldly go, "discovering"'.[8] As Polly Atkin says: '[t]here is nothing wrong in itself with being a lone enraptured male... it becomes a problem when the only voices we hear repeat the same messages, over and over again.'[9]

Moving Mountains seeks to expand and develop the increasingly popular field of nature writing, to highlight the marginalised voices of those of us who live with chronic illness and disability. The range of voices that have gone unheard, or indeed, been silenced, have valuable and important contributions to make. And so, in that short sentence I spoke to Deirdre, was embedded the groundwork of poets and writers before me who enabled the seed of *Moving Mountains* to be sown, such that the field of nature writing grows to become more inclusive, and with it stronger and richer.

In the months that followed, through 2021 and 2022, the project gathered pace and grew through conversations and emails. Many wonderful authors and artists agreed to contribute, and from there, and with huge support from an Arts Council England (ACE) grant, it has fruited into this beautiful book.

Limitations and current narratives

While barriers to access are often external, they can be carried within us too. Constructs of ableism, born from the same ideas and ideals that create societal barriers can influence also our own internal ones – our own sense of shame, feeling a burden to others and feeling that we are being difficult simply for asking for access and accommodations. In addition to these internal barriers are also the impact of health conditions that limit levels of energy and raise levels of pain, which can often make leaving the house impossible, let alone climbing mountains or hiking rough terrain.

Complex and poorly understood conditions lack effective treatment as well as limited tools of assessment. Pain and fatigue are the most common symptoms of so many illnesses and disabilities and yet remain without clear understanding or effective treatment regimes. Autoimmune conditions are more likely to be experienced in women than men, but in a misogynistic medical system trained to dispute the views of women's accounts of their own bodies, it leaves many misdiagnosed or undiagnosed for years. Black people's pain is routinely disbelieved, a colonial backdrop to medicine perpetuating myths that support unconscious bias and systemic racism. This all means that marginalised people remain so, with additional insurmountable hurdles to accessing healthcare. The medical model is deeply flawed.

While we may be limited by our bodies' capabilities, the social model of disability turns this notion on its head, framing society as holding the barriers to our full engagement with the world around us. This is a long-fought and valuable model. The online access, for example, that opened up working from home options during lockdown, is a prime example of something disabled people had asked for for years, and that made life easier, more accessible, but had not happened as a matter of routine until people without disabilities needed it. A call from the UK government for workers to return to the office, and online events closing, a return to in person only, marks a sad loss and a return to an inaccessible world for millions. There remain limitations too, as (while vital in many areas and for many people) no amount of adjustments or accommodations can address debilitating pain and energy levels, or poorly treated and misunderstood illness.

Themes of 'conquering' permeate through illness as well as the natural world, a nod to colonialism and species supremacy.

Similar drivers contribute to tired and outdated regards for illness of wars, battles and moral failings. I wonder if a more respectful and reciprocal relationship between the human and more-than-human,[10] and a more compassionate regard for both, is more likely to foster healthier outcomes for us all.

New narratives

Without clear models of understanding and knowledge, we have the capacity to create our own. Rather than seeking a 'nature cure' or offering inspirational and problematic messages of conquering and overcoming, *Moving Mountains* is a collection of stories exploring our connection with, and at times disconnection from, the world around us and the more-than-human. They are explorations of connection from places of dwelling and inhabiting, in bodies that remind us daily of their presence.

I hope that in creating this collection we can demonstrate what an orchestra of voices there are, how much more nuanced and complex the narratives of illness and disability can be, and how much richer the narratives in relation to the more-than-human are when the diversity of experiences that exist are embraced.

Moving Mountains is a collection of nature writing, poetry, prose and all things in between, that connects with those most acutely aware that nature is not always of the 'green and pleasant land' and that the world around us, like our bodies, cannot be returned to what was, following illness, accident and injury.

Themes of time through seasonal change and transformation, of mirrors between the 'before' and 'after', so acutely felt in chronic illness and acquired disability, can all be found in this collection, along with a very clear sense that we are all a part of something much larger than we can ever know or fully appreciate. Communities are referenced throughout this anthology, be them families, friendships, disability communities, wider society or ecosystems. There is a palpable sense of being more than, and a part of, humanity, when living with illness and disability, that makes tangible our interdependence and connectedness with one another.

The intention for this book is to add to the experience of engagement with the more-than-human world which has for too long focused on the physical accomplishments and dexterity and endurance of those who have climbed mountains and come back to share their tales and the views from the top. What is less recorded, but more commonly trodden, is the path around the edge, from the window and on the screen as we watch from our beds and our sofas.

At a time when the world around us is showing us it is sick and at risk, the voices of people who live similarly with risk and vulnerability are able to offer different narratives and new knowledge to those who do not have to regard or question their own bodies in the same way. My hope for this anthology is that it will open up new worlds and connections across landscapes and experience, offering perspectives that invite the reader to look again at the world around them.

A kaleidoscope sits within these pages. This anthology offers a rich world of wild experience. Each contribution is filled with wisdom and vulnerability, insights and fears, losses and treasures. The experience of illness and disability provides a particular lens through which to view the world, but not the same lens for all, for there are as many interpretations of the more-than-human as there are humans from which to perceive it. Each essay and poem in these pages speaks to the uniqueness of the author's experience, while also carrying elements of universality in their explorations of loss and grief, joy and celebration. Indeed, it may be that it is precisely because we are living in bodies that remind us of our own vulnerabilities, of decay and mutability, that identifying with and experiencing the more-than-human can become all the more significant.

Why *Moving Mountains*?

The title of this collection, *Moving Mountains*, comes from my time in Canada, where I spent a month in Saskatchewan, amidst prairie land, one of the flattest landscapes in the world. 'Land of the Skies' it is called on the back of cars on number plates.

The skies are indeed some of the biggest I have seen. This is the land of the First Nations, whose presence prior to colonisation has frequently been erased or buried, as communities were moved on or forced out – for whom there is little archaeological trace aside the rocks that held in place camp sites and those used in fires for cooking. The richness of history comes from the landscape and these rocks, pioneer farmers cursing their presence, for they would work their way up through the soil, the farmers duly moving these rocks to plough fields, only to grow more. The rocks that appear entirely stationary above the ground, beneath the earth are able to move and defy gravity. The rocks that are the debris and sediment of the glaciers, similarly known for their slow movement, that had moved across the centre of Canada, which had been ocean before it was prairie, and prior to that, mountains. In time, geological time, the mountains that were created by the movement of tectonic plates blew and washed away. With enough wind and rain and time, even mountains move. May this anthology be a storm or a hurricane in the change needed for people living with chronic illness and disability, and an invitation to look at the world around us anew.

Water

Field Notes

Sally Huband

Wind

In her essay 'The Pain Scale', Eula Biss writes: 'Wind, like pain, is difficult to capture. The poor windsock is always striving, and always falling short.' In medical terminology, 'exquisite pain' describes pain that is 'extremely intense, sharp'. The word 'exquisite' has the meaning of 'precise' in Late Middle English and 'sought out' in Latin. The east wind is a wind of stealth and always finds, with great accuracy, the places under my skin where pain hides. The west wind is not so cunning. It comes across the ocean in plain sight and uses blunt force to raise pain. I am wary of a north-westerly, the wind that brings Iceland gulls and air so bitterly cold that my limbs lock frozen. But the true north wind is generous, is an icepack on a tender joint. I am fond of the true north wind but despise the meticulousness of a north-easterly. I cower indoors and wait for this scalpel wind to pass. By the end of winter, I long for a south-easterly to carry warm air and migrant passerines to our islands. Most treasured wind of all is a gentle southerly, of any kind – true, east or west – on a sunny summer's day. I lie on the grass under the garden trees and pain becomes airborne, drifts away with the willow down.

Aurora

On a cold winter's night, there is an aurora of rare intensity. Cars fill every passing place along the single-track road. People stay close to their cars as if poised to flee. Everyone stares skywards, heads tilted back. Some watch the aurora with mouths agape, and so they seem to swallow the wild streams of light that pour down from the heavens. The aurora strikes and recoils, appears animate. There is nowhere to hide. I know this game at least, the way that pain can arrive and overwhelm, flit about, fade and then return. I stand in the light troubled dark and hold my nerve. I am used to holding my nerve and sometimes losing it, too. The awe that I feel, when I contemplate my bodymind, is a constant state of flux between fear and wonder.

By-the-wind-sailors

In the community shop, I overhear Adeline say that she has never known the west wind blow for so long. At home, I hang out the washing and hope for the best. If it is not blown off the line, the wind will unpick stitches and tangle the ties of the apron into tight knots that my unpliant fingers cannot free. I leave the washing whip-cracking in the wind and walk down the track to the sea, eager to know if anything of interest has been blown ashore. I hope for a mermaid's purse for my collection, or a fish crate that I can fill with soil and flowers, but find only fresh swathes of sea-torn kelp. It is flecked with small pieces of blue plastic, or so I think. When I reach down, I see that it is not plastic but a mass of tiny violet-blue tentacles. The west wind has wrecked a whole fleet of by-the-wind sailors on the shore. These tentacles hang down from a transparent float, an oval disc, and the upper side of this float is bisected by a transparent 'sail'. They are not so big – each float is the length of my thumb – but they are many: fifty or more. It must have been some sight, this flotilla of small, surface-dwelling creatures adrift in the vastness of the ocean. I pick one up by its sail, but the wind snatches it from me. I pick up another and stick it, viscous tentacles down, to the skin on the back of my hand. It holds fast. I gather more until both hands are gloved in violet-blue. I've read that they do not sting but find that they do, and softly. They reach down through the surface of my skin and turn pain into something more diffuse, beautiful and worn.

Classification

The first time that a rheumatologist, a woman, asked me to describe the different kinds of pain that I encounter, I could not find the words because two rheumatologists, both men, had already dismissed the symptoms of autoimmune disease to the point that I had begun to lose words. It took me a while to find them again. For example, a dead gannet lies on a beach, white feathers immaculate and gleaming. A metal fish-hook has snagged on one of its wings. A length of nylon line dangles from the hook. Imagine one type of pain as a small and sharp metal hook embedded in a joint. Nylon line is also tied to this hook. Some days the line is slack, the hook is felt, but not so much. Other days, the line is taut and there is no ignoring its sharp pull. On rare occasions, the line is reeled in, rendering me immobile. This hook can never be removed. The pain of this hook can be dampened by an injection of steroids in a procedure that provokes its own unique glow of discomfort. Imagine another type of pain as reassuring, the comforting familiarity of a favourite tree. When this pain is present, everything is as it should be. This is in contrast to a cleaving pain, which makes me think of an axe splitting wood along its grain, but slowly. Some pain has no edges, is as smooth as wave tumbled sea glass. Some pain is sharp and sudden, a piece of broken glass hidden in the sand. Aftermath pain is deep and throbbing and fades to a faint persistence and I think of this as infrasound generated by waves colliding in mid-ocean. Fatigue is salt spray on windows and it is also the haar: the kind that weighs heavy, as if silted with sediment, or the kind that is bright and buoyant, a clean sheet of paper, a blank space of possibility.

Noost

Down at the shore and above the high-water mark, there is a boat shaped hollow in the ground, a noost in which to shelter a boat when it is not in use. The prow of the noost points inland and its sunken walls are made of stone. It is lined with grass and comely and makes me want to lie down in its sanctuary, but most days it is occupied by my neighbour's small aluminium boat. He only ever takes his boat out on days of complete calm, when it will not be flipped or swamped by a wave. The next noost along the shore cradles a clinker-built boat, the wooden planks of its hull overlap. This boat can twist and flex along its length in response to the swell. When chronic illness arrived, hot on the tail of pregnancy, it took me time to learn when to set out, and when to remain within shelter. In days past, when wooden boats were hauled up onto boulder beaches in summer months, a temporary boat shelter, a structure of stone called a skordabøl would be built. Each winter, storm waves would destroy these skordabøls and each spring, they would be built again. In an ableist society, this constant rebuilding of shelter is the heavy work of the disabled and chronically ill.

Kittiwake

A kittiwake, a delicate white gull, hangs in the turbulent air, just beyond the break of the waves. The fine movements of its muscles tell of how hard it must work to maintain its position. It forages in the aftermath of a storm and the wind is still violent. I stand on the beach with my feet planted wide and watch the kittiwake plunge down into the sea to take a morsel of food. It disappears underwater and only the tips of its wings reach through the surface. They point skywards, as if the bird is anchoring itself to the air, and bob up and down with the swell. The kittiwake stays submerged for longer than is comfortable to watch. I fear that it is lost, but then both wings begin to rise and when they are clear of the sea, they lower in unison and push down hard on the surface. In this way, the kittiwake frees its body from the hold of the ocean. I sometimes find it difficult to retain a sense of self, and self-respect, when faced with the pity or indifference of ableism. But the memory of the kittiwake's wingtips in a storm-driven sea stays with me. I always make sure to keep a part of myself above the surface.

Brittlestar

I think of brittlestars, the fine and feathery limbed relatives of starfish, as fragile. I only ever meet them dead on the shore. I handle their remains as gently as I can, but inevitably, a limb or two will break away from the body at my touch. But my misconception of their fragility is based on my land-dweller ignorance. When currents are strong enough to scour individuals away, brittlestars link arms and flatten their bodies to the seabed to reduce drag. When currents are not so strong, they still form mats, arms interlinked, because this allows each individual to raise more limbs to feed. I am grateful for friends with chronic illnesses, for the way in which we anchor ourselves to one another.

Hyper-oceanic[1]

I walk the strandline of a beach in gentle rain and sharp pain, find nothing of note and allow myself to consider leaving the island on the afternoon ferry. But I decide to stay and the pain eases. The rain lingers. The holiday house is cold and damp and the pages of my book buckle. In this book, the island is described as hyper-oceanic. The rock here is volcanic, softer and more vulnerable to the wear and tear of the ocean. I've come to visit the island's many sea stacks and caves, but the next morning I wake to a thick mist and it would be foolish to walk along the cliffs. I visit a beach instead, where much storm-driven litter gathers, and find the muscled torso of a doll and an empty vial of rectal diazepam. I pocket a plastic tag labelled Laura Lee, Fire Island, New York. When I pull the length of a curlew skull from a brackish tidal pool, the island feels mine. By the time my beachcomber's lust is sated, the mist has thinned, and the sky has brightened. I set off for the cliffs, my feet as heavy as granite, and walk slowly across ground that has been scalped of its soil. Stones lie flecked with the translucent bones of fish. I find the place where a long sea cave stretches far inland. Part of its roof has collapsed and the land gapes open like a wound. A thin section of cave roof remains intact and bridges the void like a dare. The sea thunders back and forth through the cave. I sense the energy of the burrowing waves through the soles of my feet.

They start to tingle and begin to warm. On the walk back, my feet are nimble and as light as pumice. I talk with a man who asks me where I have walked and when I tell him, and remark on the fragility of volcanic rock in the face of the ocean, he pauses for a moment and then counsels me that it is unwise to walk the island's cliffs alone. I nod in agreement but say nothing. It would take too much energy to explain that it is almost always unwise for me to walk alone.

Sphagnum

In *Microscopic Life in Sphagnum*, Marjorie Hingley explains that '[f]ootprints on the Sphagnum carpet take a long time to disappear.'[2] In summer, I seek out mounds of sphagnum, bog moss, and slip my tender fingers into their moist warmth. My intrusion leaves a gaping hole and I always feel a little guilty. I would like to find an out-of-sight place, somewhere safe where I could lie naked on a carpet of sphagnum and let the warm softness of the moss soothe my aches. Somewhere hidden where I could leave an imprint of my body on the surface of the bog. There are times when I wish I could fold myself into the bog like a guillemot folds itself through the surface of the sea, in a single graceful movement that leaves little trace.

Sillock

In the absence of any wind, the sea lies still. I wish to steal some of its calm, but my wetsuit compresses my wrist and ankle joints and pain sears, warning me that it would be better to stay on land. Through my snorkel mask, I watch a sillock, a young saithe, swim through lofty columns of bladderwrack. I drift closer. The fish halts and does not flee. We regard one another for what seems like an age. For three days afterwards, my hands remain seized up, as if frozen by the cold stare of a fish.

Octopus

At the community fishing competition, people disembark from boats and haul their catch to the weighing scales on the pier. A child holds an olick, a ling, proudly aloft. A pink swim bladder extrudes through its mouth and dangles like a flaccid balloon. In a bucket, a mackerel twitches. A woman crouches down and gently empties the contents of a white plastic carrier bag onto the tarmac. An octopus, as pale as the bag, spills out. Children huddle around the octopus and watch it turn pink and then orange. The woman scoops the octopus up and carries it into the shallows. All the children wait in silence for it to reanimate. It does not move. A child asks if it is dead. An adult fetches an oar and gives it a prod. The octopus rockets away, trailing dark ink. The children shriek. The octopus is the vulnerability of a sedated bodymind on an operating table. The extruded swim bladder is pain removing the ability to speak. The oar is the touch of a hand when no consent has been given. The ink is rage at the transgression of men who work in the medical profession. The twitch of the mackerel is the barely suppressed panic in each waiting room.

Cetacean

After my first child was born, my spine seized up. This still happens, now and then. I don't exactly know why. When I watch the perfect curve of a porpoise's back as it dials through the surface of the sea to breathe, I bend my spine in automatic response. My body is no longer supple. I need more space to manoeuvre. On a visit to the whale hall in the Natural History Museum in London, I find myself unnerved by the tight pack of human bodies. The upper gallery is quieter and there is a bench where I can sit and rest for a while and study a life-size model of a newborn common dolphin. Its spine is gently curved. The model demonstrates how the skin of a dolphin resists the drag force of water. A magnified cross-section illustrates how neat folds of skin anchor down into the subcutaneous layer. The regular spacing of these folds causes small ridges in the dolphin's skin, the same size as those on human fingertips. The model is painted white and the ridges are superimposed in black. They form contour lines that map the flow of water over the newborn's body. If we centred the needs of the chronically ill and disabled, we would create contours of flow for everyone.

Tirrick

Tirricks, (Arctic terns) defend their nests by swooping at intruders. They shriek, or spray shit. Only rarely do they cut the skin of an unprotected human scalp with their blood-red beaks. Too exhausted to retreat from their attention, I lie down on the boggy ground. The terns are instantly appeased by my supine form. I should have thought to offer them this deference long before now. It is peaceful on the ground. Water soaks through my clothes and cools my skin, but the air is warm. Sunlight passes through the terns' feathers and dissolves their edges. I try to forget the nights when I have lain awake in pain and craved the dissolution of morphine. I have a friend who knows what it is like to have steroids injected into inflamed joints. She too fantasises about other islands, places of warmth and light where bodyminds are not always braced against the wind and the cold. But I live in this cold island and in this sore bodymind. I pay attention to the birds that fly between hemispheres and summers. It is said that Arctic terns see more daylight than any other living creature. One summer evening, while visiting a different island in this archipelago, I become immobilised by pain on a shell sand beach far from any human habitation. Two Arctic terns sit on the sand and face the sea. I do not know if the tide is ebbing or flooding. It occurs to me that I might miss the last ferry home, but at this moment, I do not care. The pain that keeps me pinned to the spot has also somehow unleashed all the light that these birds have ever known. I watch the terns with sharpened clarity, see them feather by feather, feel a rare intensity of ecstasy. On a midsummer night, too sore to settle, I give up on sleep and get up from my bed to sit by an open a window in the glow of the *simmer dim*, the twilight that infuses these northern nights with magic. There is movement in the meadow when all should be still. Arctic terns fly low over the long grass. They rise and fall as if to pluck small fish from the sea. But on this midsummer night, they hunt moths, a hatch of ghost moths that sway over the long grass in courtship flight. I have only ever seen this once. Sometimes, the peculiarities of my bodymind bring such gifts.

Birdwoman I

Not Healthy, Never Healed

Isobel Anderson

A path I have walked so many times I cannot count runs through the heart of the town where I grew up. This path clings to the edge of the river Ouse: a gentle river; a quiet river; one could legitimately say a cursed river; a river that reflects back a black, metallic, diffuse version of this world. Sometimes, you might catch yourself wondering how much better it would feel to be dunked under its slippery, mirrored surface, if you only had the guts to dive in. It's a tricky river like that. You can't watch it too long.

Someone walked in once with stones in her pockets, past the Ouse's many twists and bends, out near the small village of Rodmell that nestles at the foot of the South Downs. How many times did that person stare into its shining, murky depths and see a better option? The chance of a quieter, motionless, floating existence, sheltered by the Downs' large, undulating hills, safe under the river's watery threshold? That was once my fantasy too.

Perhaps it seems morbid or foolish or selfish to imagine such things. But in reality, running this submersion – and then floating, and then disappearing – over again and again while I walked beside this river probably saved my life, or was one of the *many* things that kept me alive for another day. Multiple times I wished the river would put me out of my misery. Yes, this chapter won't be one of those uplifting, nourishing, escapist pieces of nature writing. I'm sorry about that. But, if you'll bear with me, it also won't be too despairing or maudlin. I am describing a scar, a memory, and not an open wound; a time I can now see from the sky rather than the river bed. I invite you back there because I hope it shows the power of nature not only to heal, as is so often discussed, but also to accompany us when our bodies, minds and souls stay ill, for my story is one of not being healthy and never being healed.

This is now ten years ago and I am ill. I am ill in ways that doctors can't explain, ways I cannot rationalise myself and other people cannot seem to understand either. As I write this, a decade on, this is still the case. I am just nowhere near as ill as I was. But ten years back, illness had forced me to walk away from my career and entire independent adult life and to reframe what might be possible for my future. I want to add, however, that I had the privilege to do so – many people cannot move back to a part of the UK with access to London hospitals and parents who would take their adult daughter in and help her to not feel totally lost, frightened and alone. Because, that is what most people feel who are ill like I was; strangely, unpredictably and seemingly untreatably ill. And when you don't have an illness that doctors can see on a scan, a test or even in a diagnostic book, people around you can start to feel lost, frightened and alone too. It's not uncommon for this to turn into anger at the illness and at the ill person because it's all too grim and unending. It requires unfathomable amounts of patience, acceptance and hope.

My illness was pain, and pain in a part of my body that made it feel even more frightening and emotionally fraught. I had so much pain in my pelvis and genitals that I couldn't sit down for more than five minutes, just a few limited times a day. My daily existence was a constant alternation between standing and kneeling, and at night I could only lie on one side. If I broke that unspoken agreement with my body, the burning, searing, unrelenting pain would be elevated for days, or even weeks, afterwards. In the initial stages of this illness, I was put on medication, had numerous tests run and after nothing conclusive came back, was even told by one doctor that I had tipped into hypochondria. He told me that, even if this pain was 'real', women have numerous, mysterious, overlapping types of pelvic pain, and that they usually 'fizzle' out by the time they hit middle age. As a very much single twenty-seven-year-old woman, I felt like I was expected to silently accept the fear of never doing normal, everyday seated activities ever again, let alone have an intimate sexual relationship or children. If I still felt this wasn't OK – or simply acknowledged that it petrified me to my very core – I should remember the lab results said this was all in my head; that at the very best, my emotional reaction had made it worse and, at worst, my mind had made it all up in the first place.

This narrative or framing of my illness unfolded over months and years, not days or weeks. It was a slow drip of negative test results, puzzled expressions on doctors' faces, a tone of vacant disappointment in friends' and family members' voices and the gradual realisation that this wouldn't be an illness like you see on the TV or in films. There would be no narrative arc where someone died or was healed, but it would, nevertheless, irreversibly change my experience of generally being alive. And during those months and years of waiting to see more doctors and hoping to find something – maybe just even lots of little things – that would help me to 'heal', I would walk.

I had the privilege that moving back home to 'get better' meant being on the doorstep of East Sussex's South Downs with their swooping, desolate, undulating slopes. Walking became one of the only things I could still do and so I did multiple walks in different directions out of the town each week. The path beside the river Ouse takes you out to Hamsey, and has a different character to the numerous other walks that tumble you over the top of the Downs' cascading slopes and chalky tracks. Down beside the river, you are gently pulled round its many bends and forks. The river almost coaxes you along, hugging you to its side to discover what is round its many twists and turns. Walking beside the river felt more like getting to know a sentient being and walking itself was one of the only times I could trick myself into feeling momentarily well again.

These are some of the things that walking and the river taught me during that time.

Manic propulsion, essential rebellion

I often felt a strange contradiction of energies in my body during this time. It seemed to be largely fuelled by the effects of the heavy doses of medication I had been prescribed, but there was undoubtedly an emotional component too. I would, on the one hand, feel all the more predictable, drug-tinged sensations of sluggishness, sleepiness and even clumsiness. I'd find this would result in a type of stagger at times that would send me bumping into corridor walls or stumbling over steps. It was hard to judge the space around me or react to objects or surfaces with enough time.

On the other hand, surges of energy would sometimes rise, especially while walking: jittery, jagged, ill-judged swells of forward motion would erupt, as if I were an inanimate object conjured into motion by a magician or some other 'higher power'. I sometimes enjoyed how it almost felt like flying and that the whole sensation had a powerful, reckless character to it. Amidst all the hospital visits and pacing, pain management and missed life-experiences, this felt undeniably liberating. I felt like a force of nature; one that didn't care who or what would collide with its propulsion, including my healing 'process'.

These slightly manic, physical surges felt neurological in that they would arise out of nowhere, like I was withdrawing from a chemical of some kind. But once the wave was in full swell, I could tangibly observe the emotional function in the moment. I never fought these surges. Something in me knew they were a much needed rebellion in what had become an ever increasingly shrunken, reduced, but still young, life.

The privilege of 'healing'

One thing that appealed to me about walking beside the river, and in 'nature' in general, was its lack of expectation that I should be 'healed', 'whole', 'in balance' or 'fixed'. Even though many people report these to be the effects of nature on their health and human condition, walking amongst nature was light relief from the expectation that I should be, or even be working towards, 'healing'. While walking beside the Ouse, as well as seeing vibrant, juicy, abundant spring flowers, I'd encounter sodden, smelly, rotting autumn leaves. I'd see trees with fallen branches, grass that was parched and dead and plants that, despite having some kind of disease, were still working their new shoots towards the sunlight. In short, I saw a whole mess of what would be termed 'health' and 'illness' in human terms, in coexistence.

This is a different message to the one chronically ill people often receive; that they are 'still ill' because they just haven't located the root cause, which usually means some type of 'unhealed' trauma. That is not to say I don't believe the mind, body, soul and whatever else are all connected. It's precisely because they are that it's impossible to prescribe a global solution to illness. I have witnessed others genuinely and profoundly 'heal' from addressing past, internalised trauma, both physically and emotionally. As part of my own process of healing or health, I too have seen reflexologists, psychotherapists, sound healers, yoga teachers, life coaches, reiki healers, massage therapists, past-life guides, homoeopaths and more, but none of these, or even the sum of them, has brought my body entirely back into 'health'.

This is simply proof that I haven't tried hard enough, for some. A social media influencer might suggest that I just haven't tried the thing that healed them or believed in the process enough, for example. Therefore, I am still being kept ill by 'unreleased trauma'. But there is a truth I have come to learn: sometimes physical illness and disability is about trauma, sometimes it isn't and sometimes it's about this and more. Expecting everyone to 'heal' or be anything less than 'healthy' shows a privileged, and likely temporary, experience of living in a healthy or healed body. Bodies, minds and souls are always in flux, just like trees, leaves, the sky, the seasons, the river. They change course and not always in ways we would wish. They can 'misbehave'. It's possible to both decay and grow at the same time.

It's for this reason I've given up trying to 'heal'. It's an ideal enforced upon me by an ableist, healthist culture obsessed with immortality and physical and moral purity. I am fine with not being fine. Even when my body has stopped being able to walk, I am not an unreleased trauma waiting to be healed. I am whole. I am changing. I am alive.

The mantra of possibility: What *can* I still do, right *now*?

It's impossible to ignore the raft of things chronic illness takes away from your day-to-day life. In my first few years living with chronic pain this loss was mainly centred around sitting, lying and intercourse: I couldn't sit at the dinner table, meet friends in the pub for a seated drink, sit through a meeting or concert at work or sit down in the evening in front of the telly. I could also only lie on the right side of my body, so this meant sleeping with exact precision (something I got better at and then later took for granted). So this question, 'What can I *still* do, right *now*?' was crucial in me not only having some agency, but also still taking part in normal, everyday activities.

If I couldn't meet friends in the pub as we normally would, sitting down, my *good* friends – my *true* friends – would happily perch on a stool while I stood at the bar. If I couldn't sit down at the cinema, I could lie on the couch on my right side at home with a good film. Nature is similarly creative. Put an obstruction in the river and the water will re-adjust its flow. This same reactive, responsive approach became a vital component to finding a way forward and not stagnating in what had changed or been stripped away from my life and identity. Walking was, thankfully, one thing I could still do.

Walking towards while walking away

As well as walking having a personal significance in my own experience of chronic illness, I had always appreciated the satisfaction and achievement in completing a walk, prior to becoming 'unwell'. This became even more important during a time when I was having to walk away and retract from so much that had given me a sense of identity – and even importance – as a human. I had to walk away from my PhD, something I had worked incredibly hard to secure funding for (or even be in the position to be able to apply for). Likewise, I had to walk away from my music career, which had required a similar level of tenacity to grow and sustain.

But even so, completing a walk gave me both a sense of satisfaction, pride and even creative fulfilment. On these daily walks on the Downs and beside the Ouse, I found myself using new pathways, putting together new routes and exploring new territory. This was a modest, but crucial, form of self-expression at a time where I felt shut out from my own life.

Walking genderless, female fraud

To be near to nature also meant I could momentarily opt out of the usual human performances of both gender and sexuality. The loss or change in both of these identities were one of my most fundamental experiences at this time. Solitary walking offered some respite from the incongruence I felt on a daily basis and the medicalised scrutiny that was slowly eroding both. To walk for hours and not be seen by others helped me to, in some small way, accept the loss I felt around my gender and sexuality.

At the time, I was managing to hold down a shift in one of the town's local pubs. Bar work was physically a great fit because I could stand up the whole night. It was hugely challenging emotionally, however. At twenty-seven-years-old I was seen as 'fair game' by many of the pub's clientele. In fact, I was given the distinct impression that my role was to provide pleasant, mildly educated conversation for older male barflies who normally wouldn't get the chance to shoot the breeze with a young female. But, problematic as that already is, this often tipped over into overtly sexual comments and, on some occasions, even violently sexualised drawings of me on the back of beer mats.

And yet I knew that my vagina wasn't working. In fact, I felt like I didn't have one anymore. Instead, there was a thread of barbed wire tearing through my pelvis that needed to be yanked out. I knew that even if I wanted to 'hook up' with someone at the bar (however unlikely that might have been) they would be doing so with another human in immense pain. There would be no carefree physical exploration, too much pain for me to 'put on a brave face', and I felt guilty that interested strangers didn't know this. Even during my stronger, healthier times, when I acknowledged that I owed their sexual fantasies absolutely nothing, it was still exhausting being seen sexually. Where I had before simply felt unattractive, now I felt like a sexual void. A lie. A deep-fake. I was a female fraud.

It's fair to say a significant part of my sexuality being eroded was the multiple, medical physical examinations that took place during this time. I must have had over ten different doctors, almost all men, put their hands up my vagina, feel around and comment in real time about what they could or couldn't feel before then asking me to 'pop my clothes back on'. These robotic, cold (literally) physical examinations hugely impacted how I perceived my value as a living, breathing human. Lying trouserless on my back on the thin, crisp paper covering those freezing, fake-leather medical beds, started to make having 'lady-bits' feel less-than-human.

I remember the only time I was asked if I was OK during one of these examinations was the very last one I experienced. I had come to the end of the line at the office of the most expensive doctor available. I was lying on the hard, clinical bed, legs akimbo with his hand inside me. As he was feeling around he asked, 'Have you had a lot of sexual partners?' Perhaps that's a relevant question for someone experiencing pain in and around her genitals, but perhaps it also isn't? Perhaps it's also not the best time to ask the question? I felt ashamed and more like a cow than a person. After he was finished he, like all the others, concluded everything was normal. The female nurse who had been present during the examination (as is custom) placed her hand on my shoulder and asked, 'Are you OK?'

In that moment I realised that no doctor or health professional had ever asked me that question during one of these examinations before. Not, 'Is that comfortable?' or, 'Are you happy for me to examine you?' but, 'Are *you* OK?' I felt hot wet tears forming in my eyes. I realised then that my sexuality and its physical, biological home had become dismantled by these interactions. On my 'solitary' walks I would pass many cows and sheep and I remember feeling like I belonged with other numbered livestock. Solitary walking didn't involve anyone putting their hand up my vagina, passing comment on whether it was 'normal' and then telling me to 'hop off the bed'. I didn't have to make sense of what my gender or sexuality had become while walking in nature. Instead, I just needed to be present, alive and participating in something. My sexuality and gender have been rebuilt, but only because I have accepted both will always feel less fixed and less clear.

*

Just how random, unpredictable and untamable must life be before you finally accept this as its 'natural' state? My teacher, nature, posed that question every single day that I walked. As my words settle here on the page, acceptance seems to be the strongest current flowing through my relationship to walking in nature. The implication of illness is that something that has gone wrong needs to be put back into 'rightness', but I had to unlearn that narrative if I were ever to swim out the other side. And, once I stopped trying to navigate 'rightness', the swell of illness started to drop and decrease. It babbles and murmurs in the background now, as it likely always will.

I once heard someone say, 'We are all temporarily able.' There are many people living in unpredictable bodies and minds that challenge what society thinks of as 'healthy'. These people are sometimes told this difference is their fault and often expected to deliver others a nice, neat, healing conclusion. I have no conclusion of that kind. I am better than I was, but I cannot tell you I am 'healed'. And even if I were, I couldn't guarantee I would stay that way. Neither I, nor you, can ever guarantee we are healed or even well, no matter how much we might desperately want that to be true. Since the time when the Ouse was my walking companion, I have passed through multiple layers of illness and new parts of my body and identity have been taken out of health. I have even experienced phases of needing to pace my walking and patiently wait for this activity to once again become part of my daily routine. But even if in future, I am only able to walk to the bottom of my garden, I will take solace in the changes I will inevitably see reflected back to me in nature.

Now, I can pass by the Ouse's silvery ripples without fantasising about being submerged in its painless, edgeless water. I know it would be very wet, very cold and really quite smelly and I have a messy life to lead with an ever-in-flux body, mind and soul.

Sequences of the Body

Jane Hartshorn

London, November 2021

a morning spent indoors and

my shoulders are falling

I loll petal-headed onto a spill of sheets

the green furrow of my duvet ploughing

                                       my limbs slack

◊

careful to keep my elbows pinned

          I leave the house

                   my breasts resting on my forearms

fingers gripping

                  the woven material of my sleeve

Jane Hartshorn

◊

waddling

at first   then

my mind starts to settle
                          hips in uneasy oscillation

I pick up a stone
                  thumb it   memorise its crevices

my shoulders back   hands
in pockets   still keeping   me together

but elbows winging triangles   and

      with the rhythm of the steps and the pebble

I unsnarl from
               burls of stickiness

once again
                        receptive to external things

◊

lattice of moss on stonework
                   a certain configuration of light

the shadow of a tree   lime drainpipe

      mackerel sky of leaves

giant eye of aspen   I pick at the scab of your bark

crustose lichen starfished   across your body

Sequences of the Body

◊

my hand around my wrist

      already a heat gathering at tailbone   a hollowing
of breastbone   a weakness behind the knees

plash of skin   burst on tarmac

the body's lines   rubbing away

◊

I walk in small steps   oblique as though
                  there are roots
knotting   the ground and I am picking my way
      between them

◊

neck stiff   against the drag
                  of flesh

a tug at the base of my spine

as my torso absorbs   my shoulders

and I am straightjacketed by my bra
                  underwire gouging an angry weal

◊

home and I take my shoes off bra off
                      then

in bed   need to eat but

I wake in darkness   the door the desk

obliterated

the window a gasp   the feeling of falling

my hands vermicular   along the wall

palming for the light switch

Ayr, November 2021

another day spent indoors

                  long yawn of afternoon light   pink

across the carpet of my childhood

the shadow of a drainpipe climbing

the flaked paint
                                    of the adjoining wall

◊

she sends me photos from   another place

the serrated edge of a cloud creeping above the roofline --
spikes of branches on globe-headed stems -- rows of turkey
tail fungus shelving bark -- moon shadow of a coffee cup
on a round table -- ruffled petals of orange-pink carnations
-- frothy trim of a shoreline -- cirrocumulus potato prints
across the sky

        I pause in the soft angles of her perception

Sequences of the Body

as though standing in the cool vault of a church
                                                                eyes adjusting

◊

        smoothing bed rumples

                          I lay the prints on my sheets

imagine a different route

                      an association of shapes

            moving in and out   of sequence

my mind along the flex   of her limbs

            hot metal of the chair sticky

beneath her knees

            the hairs on her thigh

            shoaling silver

                          as they catch the light

Colonsay, September 2021

I am not used to company

        notice that   I start to narrate

every adjustment   of body
                              to   environment

a strange wheeze pelvic pain so severe I think my period is early an unexplained spasm in my right toe when I put my shoe on

Jane Hartshorn

I recoil from the fringes   of myself

                    afraid

of stepping too far and finding myself   wide open

this body which is my body   but as strange to me

                 as another animal

◊

I move jaggedly   as though I am descending stairs

      the awkwardness
of bending over   to pick something up

and feeling my balance shift   the difficulty

of straightening my spine   its desire

to slide
         vertebrae scattering like chips of scree
                               across the carpet

◊

he glides into the loch   I step gingerly

try   to   find   my   footing
                     in clouds of amber sediment

      the sloping of rocks

◊

Sequences of the Body

he is slicing ahead

the gleam of his torso   fractured

               by steel knives of water

blades tilted to reflect the sun

◊

               a moment of friction
my body pendulous   then

clockwork of breaststroke / limbs eddying / body

wreathed in hair and ribbons of weed / skin shiny

and water-pearled / threads of blood pulsing below

the cold / toes brushing the murmur of a current /

cheeks pinched red / lips drawn tight over my teeth

/ sputtering grey water / eyes hardly flickering / set

in the soft putty of my face

◊

September and the last of the swallows

wheel in the broken sky above   as I emerge
translucent   dripping slugs of loch water   mud-caked

a leaf plastered wet   to my abdomen like
      a yellow canker

London, February 2022

she says you have to choose   between places

as though I have been skewered by a boundary line

neither here   nor there

◊

I have been feeling like I did
                      in my early twenties

killing time between four walls   placeless

carrying my loneliness with me into the streets
          and not knowing where to put
                                   it

◊

I follow the path towards the river
      listening for birds   that will fasten
me to place

the trees are noisy today

the screech of a parakeet jangling

      with the croak and rattle of starlings

I look up   see only a tangle of branches against the sky

their calls   carve my flesh   articulate

the absent parts

Sequences of the Body

◊

every weekend
                I retrace my steps

attempt   a continuity of self

hoping something   will catch

walk from talisman to talisman

            the Clapton pond heron   bedraggled
eating chips

the woman with pinking shears   in slippers

flaying a tree of its lower branches

the tame squirrel without a tail

       herring gulls paddling the grass after rain

a whole pitch of them drumming for worms

◊

       the seasons   I know

better than my body
                      crocus shoots

appearing above last year's leaves

I know their future   petals cupped

yellow of a blackbird's beak

◊

I reach the hide
                wooden walkway

                sunk into marshland and reedbed

a place where I can watch the world

                      without it happening to me

rectangle of light   insect green

the wood warm   slatted gold with sunshine

I let the stillness rearrange my margins

soften into the sounds
                of coot and moorhen

the gulp of water   the rustle of grass like rain on a windowpane

    apart   yet somehow of it

Ben Chonzie, December 2021

he asks me   how my body is

and I repeat the question   momentarily surprised

fine I reply   my usual response   then

well   my right knee is painful

                      as is my lower back

I press my fingers to my sternum

my throat & lungs hurt

     where the cold air rushes in

Sequences of the Body

he takes my backpack   wears it on his chest

and it feels strange to give voice   to my discomfort

as we ascend
         I place my feet

                 in the prints of his boots

the crunch of snow   broken only by the

goback goback goback of a grouse

and the deepening of our breaths

       he stops   a pain in his calve

behind him

     a mountain hare

     bolts towards the ridge

               a blur of snow startled
from its form

Ayr, Jan 2022

the days have shrunk   again

I bide my time indoors   bring

the outside in

a frond of seaweed dries into an angular shape

a piece of wood resembles a woman running

the violet inlet of a crab shell contracts

I fill jars with the yellow whorls

of flat periwinkle shells

place them in the darkest corners   of the room

try to stay awake   between glass cylinders of light

every time a letter arrives

the outside rushes in   & I inhale

the scent of cold air & someone else's hands

◊

zig-zagging through the narrow lanes

I take the long way   to the post box

following my own desire line

the quiet spaces between

the backs of houses   moss spreading

little hillocks   across the tarmac   closed eyelid

of a bricked-up window

         love-knot of maidenhair spleenwort

Sequences of the Body

where the cement has crumbled   a faucet

of ivy-leaved toadflax

my knuckles blenching

                  the letter in my hand

a wall being wrested apart

                  by a needlepoint of ivy

On Becoming Ocean

Victoria Bennett

'The river needs to take the risk
of entering the ocean
because only then will fear disappear,
because that's where the river will know
it's not about disappearing into the ocean,
but of becoming the ocean.'

Khahil Gibran

I got a letter today. That shouldn't seem that much of an event, except it is – because this post was addressed to me at my new home. Picking it up from the doormat felt strange, as if I were an interloper in another's life. It is my house, it is not my house; a life-shape I have yet to inhabit. All this is new and yet, it feels as though it is an old journey, one that was whispered of a long time ago.

My husband, son and I have moved to Orkney.

We arrived on the ferry late on the Sunday night. We should've arrived five days earlier, but the sea decided to crash into our plans and held us, the cat, two guinea pigs, various musical instruments and several jars of homemade damson jam hostage in a campervan on the Caithness coast. It was an enforced rest in what has been two months of pushing ourselves to our limits, and sometimes beyond. The thing about living with chronic illness is that it doesn't neatly pack itself away when you need to be fully functioning. Moving house has been an endurance test, not only of stamina but also of patience. So, even though it seemed like a hindrance, finding ourselves stuck, unable to move and thrown into each other's company for five days was a blessing (although I am not sure the cat felt the same way).

On the third night, the ferry company called to say they were going to try the crossing. We packed up the jam, settled in the pets, and made our way to the terminal. As we watched the ferry steer itself sideways into the port, the sea throwing it around like a rubber boat in a bathtub, I wondered at the wisdom of leaving dry land for deep water. The engines pumped out black smoke, screaming against the wind and waves. Somehow, they managed to guide it in and tie it up, lowering the car ramp into place. A brief moment, a glimpse of the parked vehicles inside, and then the sea tore it away, snapped the thick metal cable like a twig, sending it ricocheting back into the cement barriers and the land crew running to unleash the rest of the ropes. There was nothing for it but to set the boat back into the water, and watch it sail its way across the Pentland Firth, passengers and crew unable to dock, returning without touching land.

As we turned ourselves around, and made our way back up the hill to the campsite that had become our temporary home, I thought about the water and the waves, and why I would want to leave everything we know and cross one of the most dangerous stretches of open water in the world to set up home on a mostly treeless, windswept archipelago, high up between the North Sea and the Atlantic Ocean, where the winters are long and the summers an endless light.

*

It started fifteen years ago, before birth and death and care changed our lives. I applied for, and didn't get, a writing residency here. It was enough to catch something alight and though we didn't move, I found myself aching for it. If it is possible to stalk a place, then I became an obsessed lover, pouring my longing into books and postcards, leaning my way into its folds to imagine myself there. But it was not a dream I could realise. I could not run away with this lover. I was needed, and I stayed, and put down roots.

But still, these islands whispered. We visited three times, in winter, spring and summer, staying longer each time. The first time, I cried. Standing on the edge of Skaill Bay, the waves rolling the rocks against the ancient settlement of Skara Brae, salt wind razoring my cheeks, I felt at ease. I watched as my young son played at the edges of this strange world, his all-in-one red rainsuit picking him out against the gradients of green and grey. I could be at home here, I thought. It makes sense to me.

Losses of more than one kind have ripped away the shorelines of what I thought was solid ground. I live in a body shaped by what is unpredictable. My bones refuse the confidence of stability. I am always prepared to fall down; to be grounded by the storm. When I listen to my body, it does not sing bucolic. It says 'be prepared to change'. And change is what I have feared so. To let go, to be out of control, to allow the nature of things to take charge of my world. It took staying still to learn that life is forever changing, forever on the move.

*

Ten years on from our move to the place that became our home, our healing garden, we have moved again. In an echo of that earlier leaving, I have repeated the process of sorting what can be carried forward, and what must be let go. There have been fires again, and the burning of words, but this time, it was not a flaying away but a loosening, a gentler letting go. And the garden, that we grew from seed and stone, that too has had to go, a daily digging back, cutting down, filling in; Grandpa's Pond, the old wooden fort, the bog garden, the wild meadow. All these have had to go, a requirement of social housing to return it to what it was, ready for a new life to take hold. When I tell people this, they are shocked, sometimes angered. It is hard to destroy the wildlife habitats that we nurtured, to know that the frogs and birds and hedgehogs that called it their home will find it gone. But I also understand it. This place, this borrowed space, has given us a decade to save ourselves. It has seen things born – a book, friendships, lives – and it has seen things die. It gave us somewhere safe to heal, to grow our son and our lives. As we let it go, we do so knowing that it can offer that to someone else. This is their garden to grow, not ours. And so on, and so on, passing along.

But we do not let it go entirely. I gather seeds from the summer flowers and send them out to accompany the first proofs of my book, to find their way into new lives. I dig out plants and share them between our neighbours, family, friends. We offer the wood of the fort to the local Bonfire Night fire, watch as it burns bright into the night. Some of the saplings and plants we dig out and repot to plant here, even if I cannot know whether they will fail or flourish in this new soil.

Not all has gone. Under the soil, there are wild seeds turning, ready to break through the stone and soil, to flower once more. That I will not be there to see them does not mean they will not grow.

Meanwhile, 430 miles away, I sit on my mother's old blue velvet chair up in the attic room, listening to the wind hit the gable wall. My son and I have made camp up here, clinging close to the electric heater as we wait for our heating and hot water to be fixed. It is cold, the cat is grumpy, and there is a hole in the wall. Back across the water, my husband finishes off the last of the jobs in the old house, before handing back the keys to join us here. My body aches and strains against the threshing it has endured, and my son's blood glucose is crazy with the changes we are going through. Our life is in boxes again, and everything feels in flux, but we are smiling. Down at the end of our street, the sea rolls in and out against the stone harbour, sometimes calm, sometimes storm.

*

I have taken a risk. The world has not disappeared. The world of my body behaves as it behaves. In the mornings, I take it for a walk to the harbour, watch seals as they rest in the shallow waters, sticking their rounded noses into the cold, winter air. Our cat, still unsure of this new territory, walks close to my side. In sharing our walks, I learn that he and I are not too different. We both crave the wildness of what is outside. We are both fearful of sudden change. We are both curious. When he discovers the beach for the first time, he runs towards the shore, eager to take in all the new smells. The next morning, he begs at the door to be let out, running full-speed down the hill to the bay, only to be met by water. This is not what he expected. Land. Water. Why won't this new ground stay the same? He looks at me, eyes widened, ears back, and heads home.

Like the cat, I have to learn not to run headstrong into each moment, to test what is there beneath my feet before I land. Twice this week, my body has fallen down the stairs, collapsing itself under an invisible and erratic instruction. I wake up one day, and my body is the shore. I wake the next, and it is the sea. It is the opposite of spontaneity. And yet, it also demands I practise change daily. I am not a fixed point. I am tide, current, rock, seaweed, drift, bottle, sky.

I walk the shore of the bay, treading between the sea-slicked rocks with care, making sure that my feet find the softer, steadier shale of washed-up winkles. To tread elsewhere is to slip. Seaweed clusters cling to the edge-lines, heaped up by this morning's high tide. I look and see russet, ochre, deep green. If I look closer, I can pick out bulbous pockets, filigree tendrils, leathery swatches, nubby dots. I know they have names – *bryopsis pulmosa, lomentaria articulata, spiral wrack, bladder wrack, sea oak* – but I don't know them yet. This land is new to me.

I am used to being able to point out plants, to name them, to know what to harvest for a cold, what to preserve for a wounded heart. But here, I am lost. I have no names yet beyond a beginner's eye: brown, red, speckle, smooth. Not being able to name things makes me feel disconnected, uprooted. I feel the losses much more acutely here. In the night, I wake with a ripping ache in my centre, call out for a mother who is no longer here. Will she be able to find me?

To become lost. To lose one's name. I describe it as heartbroken, and am immediately challenged by someone who is curious to know how a chosen adventure can feel like heartbreak. My heart is broken open. I walk in an unfamiliar landscape that does not hold my stories, or my ghosts. I must grieve what is gone all over again.

*

I wobble on the stones, slip sideways, steady myself with my stick. The salt air catches in my nose, making me breathe deeper. Each breath carries with it the silence of the sea, a quiet stillness that holds everything in a pause. I listen, expecting the sound of humankind, but there is nothing. The sea and sky have swallowed it all. The soft waves rise and fall away from the rocks. I wonder if it is coming in, or out. Tide times, wind speeds, tidal currents; weather, water, wind, sky. Elemental. Elementary.

To be a beginner, to be a child once more. Not knowing is scary. It feels unsteady, but it is also exciting. I get to see the world for the first time again, to learn its names, to find myself in its rhythms. I have done this before; I have learned new names. I cannot know it all straightaway. I must be patient, and wait to see how my body will be shaped by this new place.

Breathe in. Breathe out. Accept the unknowing. Learn to begin again.

*

I live on an island in the middle of a meeting point of two waters: the Atlantic Ocean and the North Sea. The North is cold, connected to lands of ice and myth. It hugs the east of this country, pulls with it gifts of fishing line, polystyrene packaging, broken glass in hues of blues, greens, browns not yet washed enough times by the tide to be beautiful. The Atlantic offers stranger treasure: sea beans polished smooth by distance and salt; gunnera seeds that take root on the shore, growing into unexpected tropical plants in the chill of north-easterly winds; bottles washed without message over miles and time. My son finds a milk bottle dated 1989, still sealed, the milk lost to the passing of the moons.

A third water exists. The Pentland Firth, a stretch of sea that carries with it warnings and ghosts, crews lost, sailors never found, boats run aground. When I look into this water, I see furious tides, roiling with resistance. This is the sea that washes onto our shore.

Orkney is an archipelago made up of over seventy islands, twenty of which are permanently inhabited. We live in a harbour village, on South Ronaldsay. Every direction I look, there is sea and sky. If we want to leave the island, we must cross the water by flight, ferry or four long, straight stretches of road, built over the Churchill Barriers. Once constructed to block the German boats from entering UK waters, they have been repurposed as permanent causeways, to join the southernmost islands to the main. They are precarious. Each one comes with a precursor: **CROSS AT YOUR OWN RISK. NO STOPPING.**

One is subsiding. One is transforming slowly into sand dunes. One is notorious for high-topping waves that crash over the concrete ballast, obscuring visibility and whipping water under the wheels. All suffer from high wind speeds. All are in a state of change. Before setting off, it is wise to check the barrier status report, as they are prone to close at short notice, leaving you cut off. Here, the weather is in control.

*

The second time I fall, I fall up the stairs. I am carrying two cups, concentrating on not spilling the hot tea on the floor. I am trusting my body to take me up the steps without my intervention. My body has different ideas. It relinquishes control and my head slams into the bookshelf, mugs of tea still held in hand smashing on my skull. I cry out, raising my hands to my face, worried what I might find. My husband hears the noise and runs up three flights of stairs to find me on the floor, face covered, crying as my son cradles me in his arms.

'Mum fell again,' he says.

'Tell me what your body has done?' my husband asks, appraising the scene: smashed teacups, face covered, limbs bent at strange angles. He does not ask what I have done. He knows it is not my action that has caused this, that I am not in control. Like the barriers, my body is under constant review.

I live on a small island in the middle of two seas. Navigating this is a daily appraisal of tidal waters, inclement weather, threats of storm; open to potential and sudden, wrenching change. Sometimes, I can travel. Sometimes, I cannot. My frustration, my anger, my disappointment at being stopped will not change anything. There is no persuasion, no exemption for importance, no preferential want or need. I must accept what cannot be circumnavigated or controlled.

Its refusal to be certain brings me a sense of calm. I am not an outcast in this landscape. I am not an 'other'. I do not feel guilty, less-than-worthy of its welcome. Here, the unpredictability of my body feels understood.

The barriers are closed again today. For how long, I do not know. An hour, a day, a week? I know they will lift, that I will be able to travel across again. Just not now. For now, I must accept. And that's OK. Time to find a quiet spot, pick up a pen, read a book, learn a new name.

Birdwoman II

Air

An Ode to Climbing Over Fences Instead of Needing Them Open

Hannah Hodgson

My grandfather stole a mannequin and called her Sally.
He dressed her in my grandmother's clothes, and placed her on
   an island
to scare herons. When I was six, he said the maggot box smelled
like cheese and onion crisps because that's where they came from.
The boat had a small crack that was so fine we'd stay afloat,
as long as one of us bailed the other out as they rowed.
We threw fistfuls of pellets into the water,
made it rain Manna for the fish staying cool
in the depths. Fish we hadn't seen in months.
One day we arrived at the pond and Sally was floating face down.
Even then he was lifeguard, holding her beneath her armpits,
lifeguard for plastic, and water not above a metre
He could've stood; but he wanted to show me he knew
how to do such things. Sally was hollow, full of hot air

she was a floatation device, really. But he wanted to show me
he knew how to save someone. Every cell of my genealogy tingling,
my handwriting in purple ink, my i's dotted with bubbles
the same as his sister's who died on the operating table, aged
   seventeen,
sixty years ago. He keeps me alive with all his worry,
awake with it – like caffeine – so alive
with constant worry. He says he would take it, this
my illness if he could, take it like jury duty, take it
so we could bury him with it. So many fish
become air drowned by the otters, he counts seven
and calls it lucky. I take his hand. We sit in the silence
of his sister's words, sixty years cold. Mine cooling in the space
between us, rising into the air, and then gone.
I realise he has lost me already, I am Sally/ Sheila/ Myself,
and can see the deaths coming. He can too,
in the slow motion of octogenarianism. I hold his hands
whilst we are both here, warm. I say, 'Palliative Care.'
I say, 'One more operation, then I'm never having any more.'
His pained smile says, 'I know.' It says, 'I knew a girl once
who said something similar.' My silences asking him for help.

712 Stanza Homes For The Sun
Cat Chong

398.　—I live between fourteen military bases—
—in so much pain—the bombs would weep pumpkin pip-seed messages denoting time the pip boi counting units—of radiation the radar a nautical investigation—the commons are here at the beginnings of water—'I'll be right back I'm just going to get a black pen'—the root word for blacken is the same word for bleach bleak and total whiteness—to some of our most sacred texts genre doesn't really apply—when I write says—Mary Reufle in *Madness, Rack, and Honey*—my gender becomes genre—to some of our most sacred texts gender doesn't really apply—swerves off the radar—out of algorithmic fidelity—to be untraceably genred untrackably gendered—is to live untargetably as things—like mirrors are blackened and bleached—so absorption voids the image—this is still an archive and looking for a place to hide—perhaps I should not be writing at all a poetics of pips that knows how long I have left—to plant or search for soil—a kinship to acknowledge the land—and the possibility for grounding—whether it will emerge or look back in laughter or cold water—I have no interest in weapons or their complicity—I am love hungry—I want to reply to you once I understand where the light is coming from—blur with me—I failed the song of living—blue with me—I finished that

poem and the next day my brother died—said Peter Gizzi on day 395 the 29th of January 2021—on the 1st of February Lisa Robertson's Instagram answers back—in an image of '26 Theses On Craft' she writes—24 there is always something to do—25 blank—26 CRAFT, AGAINST DEATH—

400.   —I've been keeping count of the days—
—since the 1st of January 2020—counting the multiple precarities of "the vulnerable"—waiting to be allowed to see my family—my partner—my friends—the list gets longer each time—I can still hear the bombs—the military jets—the live firing from the Ponyan gun range that's under a mile away or the Pasir Laba range that's a mile and a half away—and because I cannot tell the sound from which—and because an NS National Service training institute marks a perimeter just beyond the storm drain along the north western perimeter of campus—and an SAF—Singapore Air Force base—borders the south—and because the military holds all the land west—on every blank map—perhaps regardless—whether it's the record or the countdown the dread is still the same—perhaps this is still anecdotal—an unsubstantiated structure of belief with which to convey the unverifiable—the legal—institutional—empirical—subterfuge—Jurong Island is just over four miles south—Shell—Chevron—BP—ExxonMobil—the Petrochemical Corporation of Singapore—and many more occupy the reclaimed artificial land—taxi drivers tell me it's used for toxic chemical manufacturing—but that's just the rumour—the eavesdrop—the goss—the tone is still the same—Jurong Island—chronic pain—military property—invisible disability—believe me—please—the scent of burnt cocoa—the Cadbury's chocolate factory—ADM Cocoa—Khong Guan Biscuit Factory—the poultry farms in Sungei Tengah—all hang in the air at night—

405.   —time is still a god-derived style—
—the way we organise energy in space aligns us in dialogue with our being with the world—I'm misquoting Pessoa—it's all the same line—all you have to do is—put quotations around

it sensemaking—movement in a state of being intrinsic to water—perhaps we'll never pass through the same—never stand in the same pain twice—I cannot write out the singular desire to escape the body—one of the earliest pioneers of cyberspace was a lyricist for The Grateful Dead—I want out of my body as bad as that old white man in the earliest stages of the internet—a liquid self-effacing onto the street—I don't want to be—medical sloganeering—an industrial habitat—or the clarifying mechanism of the moon—fuck me or gut me it's all the same address—if one grows sentimental when in pain I must live like a nostalgia—millimetres away from my skin—I am fleshed out of painkillers in the kingdom of this world—part of doing this is not wanting to do this—I don't know if language will be warmer—living one degree north of the equator—where pain never comes in with the cold—where there's no such thing as winter—and the monsoons too have a spell—I don't want to make this thesis a violent spectacle of my undiagnosed survival—the truth makes me visible—to enquire—after pain's manifold geometries—exceeding all predictions—pain knows me before I do—I am—trying to cultivate a fidelity to my own cripistemological reality—being thin of light lose today and split infinite nowheres—becoming grievable information—isn't there a word for this—to chart anatomy relative to the cosmic measurement of the universe—they talk about the concern to get out of the body in the first manifesto of the internet—the death of the author is there—the death of the body of the Facebook boomer Gen X—the clouds broke open the moon—here I am talking to own my blood again—the violent imbrication and me—still homesick—

433. —this is somewhere—
—I feel too sick to speak—perhaps pain is another reverberation—does it come as an empire—rhetorical and investigatory—phenomenologically registered in the utterance—can you tell from the way I speak—you will happen—an agreement between the poem and I—this rejoining—I'm misquoting Heraclitus to say enlightening is the lord of everything—pain is an

inculcation—we live in mobile time—I can't spend the truth of my being and of being in love—the feeling of the ocean—once and for all—my gender is as queer as my sickness the locus plays out in comportment—coming in to visibility and discoverable—a genre trouble—stand out to me—open the grave of your eyes—I did not ask for the moon—or inconsolable sleep an affair without questions—mine faultlessly—premonitions of the sacred about weapons and complicity—in wellness which is all the rage—to keep the pharmacy in the language of the front line—made paramilitary healing—attach care by keeping it under watch—survey what is bought and deemed safe enough to keep inside—this poem is for you even if we don't survive—there is no recourse for the things they do to us—the data we have left—this pain is four mothers deep—I take another painkiller and there is nothing left to forgive in the countryside of my fear—how can we be together outside representation—the doctor's note an obsolete genre—we will never detoxify—painkillers are not sheer ascension—reduced to the formal I am more paperwork than I am—I am more than my papers says Divya Victor—on day 532 a macaque monkey enters the living room—refuses food—urinates on the floor—takes a black reel of Polaroid film and rips the wires from the fairy lights—we know they were there by what they have scattered—

440.   —freeze is etymologically connected to the word burn— —an image of negative space—many shades of blue—the colourful theory of everywhere is an existence—to expense the production—the pigment and its sadness—I don't know if I'm looking at the ceiling or the sky—both a notorious white—it's raining so the construction has stopped—not of language—the other architecture outside—I'm writing in pen just to pass the time—take no notice of me—headache daisy chain packet boat pain is dissociative and drifting invariably—my ambitions are but empty chairs—to be empty of the invisible—a body logic in different time zones—aside from the dramatic questions how are they connected did you start off knowing—endlessly—intersecting I'm still testing it out through the writing—the

past is present—code incidence a coincidence the resonance the residence a fixation in specific objects—if they still feel connected we can still come back—the temple is in the promise immunity holds out—you know a lecturer has taken a book out of the library when it remains on loan till the last day at the end of the next century—and the night smells like warm chocolate again—

534. —pray for me—
—perhaps failing survival isn't the worst option—this fluttering far-flung heart—I misread accused for accursed—the smell of smoke—hack-and-slash farming—what was rubber now oil palm—the plantations—and pain a thrash against its own associative patho-logic—could chronic illness or disability make hyperobjects of me—all the clouds in the distance—I can't hold pain accountable—inside it—everywhere and nowhere—superlative and banal—love is such a vandal—of eligible of desires—what does pain offer me—be sorry—part of you has done this—I can't command death—am responsible only to death—and our inability to construct—what are spruce leaves—undeath an indefinite stretch—ferrocement—orbitals against enamel—and self-excoriation—pain alters my godhood—that the poem might organise the revolution—so sing—in the charnel house—amongst the solvency of the place the wound won't leave behind—its sticky aesthetics—we all live in state sequence—might not walk away with meaning all in one go—o pain be punctuated by the fricative consonants of sound—I'm trying to wrench all of my lines says Ali Lewis—in these easily crossable vowels—to whom do these systems belong—in the confluence between use and subjection—the size of the thing—pain is too big to withhold—I can't keep anything in mind—a Gettier problem of address—the inward turning of the poem's least artificial senses—on day 534 the 17th of June 2021—E says 'You have to wash off the base until it goes neutral'—'Normally we just stick in an acid'—'If you add more chemicals it gets harder to deal with the waste effluent'—

535.   —what if pain is a network of parasocial relations—
—it does what we dissolved it to do—with no power in the command—the request falls flat—all plea or a polite forms of permission—someone else's gesture—the letters won't forgive—perhaps the paranoia of the poets is appropriate here—commensurate even—when the genocidal white supremacist eugenic ableism of the corpocapitalist kyriarchal carcinogenosphere is active murder—I can give you eighty-six letters for death—or walk away with a poem—all the eyes of the poet—the page—medication—the state—and instruments of its institution—the rating—ratio—quota—quotation—look at me—what they—the letters are doing—I'm getting to the place at the end of all systems—from the registries of epistemics come to form another sensorium—I can't recuperate my own at the centre of attention still crafting again a killing machine—I know it makes no difference at all—'Never add things up it never ends well' is wisdom E. P. Jenkins gifts me—do not write out to be grievable—cicadas are more punk than we'll ever be—medicine doesn't afford a right to privacy neither does capitalism nor counter terrorism—there are days when my arms still surprise me—to craft against indifference—affect is empathy arising—so much poetry now feels like writing to seem more human—the unsellable the ultimate commodity—the pain and the poem evaluated by standardised rigour—rigour autocorrecting to rifle—fuck these targets what else has been taken over by branding these nouns—

- oyster cards
- zoom
- stan
- target
- these nuts
- the dogs
- frogs
- the letter h
- clock sounds
- stars

- tinder
- bumble
- twittering
- discord
- twitch
- word
- acrobat
- amazon
- grab
- vine
- safari
- apple
- telegram
- gap
- next
- teams
- ICE
- techne

536. —does pain make me half-hearted—
—or make medical profiling an indicator for the necessity of care—in pain am I body bound and contemptless—as much myself as I am—we go to the east coast of the island and watch the shipping containers assemble a second horizon—at night there are so many lights we cannot tell where the water begins—or if it's there at all—the lights could be a second city stretching out to Batam—another country in the wind of our faces—a storm gathers—if the wind is stronger than the tide a boat will face the wind—if the tide is stronger than the wind the boat will face the tide—if a boat is double anchored it won't spin at all—high wind and low pressure is what causes the tide to rise—the wind causes the boats to spin—the first anchor stops them moving sideways—boat physics are stressful and strange like the heart spaces of the moon—perhaps fear is the grandest thing—a paranoia I mistook for the scepticism of systems which I mistook for solidarity which I thought looked like love—there are whole economies built on the fear of the thing we love most—of

consternation and ruin—ruin sticking our tongues out for each other—I will learn to look like my teeth—I began counting how many days I've been away on the 21st of June—337—I will be fully vaccinated on July 9th—558—the academic term begins on August 9th—586—and ends on the 11th of November—681—I know I shouldn't want to fit my body into the space of the Google search bar—perhaps fear is connected to grandiosity in affect or invocation—as the alphabet and the universe suggest a dominant language—a cosmos of speech and lines—but the alphabet is not ours—o Sean Bonney is poetry a dead giveaway—under cover from an elsewhere—on the 20th of June I've counted 536 days away from safety—

541. —don't be invisible—
—declares the token collection sign for the country's contact tracers—this significance of information in the medical economy—making novelty to commodify the commons—we don't own the vector along which the data moves—we quantify pain to access relief—informs the abstraction—keep recuperating—the wound is a bodymind reaction—there is no rarity for this—invisible economies in which prescriptions form technology—reputation anti-capital—it gets harder to collect painkillers if the pharmacists remember who you are—pain an inalienable labour—the number the abstraction the absurd reinhabiting—this is 100 percent the moon's bright sparks—make my world an altar—all the frogs are divided—I have lived swimming—new or rebranded—as reckless fish—uncontainably alive—I'll repute—runes and ruin—votive offerings—charms—hexafoils—surrounded by a perfect mathematics—a crude transformer—for the fact that is only a fact for as long as it is spoken—the body is still long gone—with an appetite for numeracy or numerals without reason or time—it cannot be archived only lived in its effect—siteless oubliette—this self-effacing gram

- sing
- united
- pioneer

- marvel
- ford
- switch
- mini
- supernatural
- discovery
- fox
- the sun
- dominoes
- genesis
- universal
- stream
- sky
- cloud
- wish
- shell
- pirate
- dab
- tea
- fortnight
- drops
- drops
- dropped
- scrolling
- card
- lotus
- indeed
- all baby gods of the dead

553.   —the encounter's there as long as we look—
— for radiant and radical proximity—another monkey enters through the apartment window—and all the raisins are gone—indeed is an affirmation and employment site—enough to know longing the shape of a decade—on such days the revolution remains a commitment to narrative—that turns on a collective force—read all my politics here—the autobiography of efface—no amount of poetry will ever amount to a diagnosis—how

can we imagine—the future for us—cripqueer communities—a vocabulary capable of transmission—to anyone outside—this indefatigable kingdom—surround me—this lyric indulgence desire—rather in pain—exploitations has set the ocean on fire—you know what I'm going through—where I am—the names where it all takes place—I want to hold myself even unto death—the still struggling pronoun—delusion needs an architect says Lisa Robertson on day 553—the mysterious possible—a pronominal moonlight reflection unfolding—pain a unit of attention—a common velocity—immanent and certain—but here I'll call it writing—

561.   —are you here to watch—
—my life in pain play out—white lion city—marvel of marvels the snow—mass spectroscopy—let's not ask for police territory—a part of general murder—taxonomy a language—the sunset at the end of the chase—fuck these apocalypse-blinkers—Erin Gilmer Erin Gilmer Erin Gilmer—I won't give you my body—or the meta data to organise an image that approximates these parts of me—my tongue dissolves again—there is meaning under refuge—the cloth in my hands—how many items emanate this vibrancy of purple—I consider making a colour catalogue of the items I currently own—except poetry—I don't own language—I don't own anything—I don't believe in property—I live in a country I cannot wait—to leave this metaphor—a monument I'm not old enough to live for—

574.   —a taste of the metaphor—
—and low lights burned all through the night—it's fine I snuck in quietly—I am in your blood—replace language with antibodies here—the screen holds so much time the ghosts give a silent ovation—this is my fifth move in eighteen months—I leave the spider webs by the window to go looking for the sky—a garden I don't find—but there's a bolt between the door and the frame—which is to say I break onto the roof instead—come stand beneath the solar panels with me—on the fourteenth floor—the construction site—light sparks falling

down the building's side—stair grey storm—case storm grace even affectively boundless—it's never out of bounds—this pain is hostile to the soul—it tells me I too have this capacity—the macaques come in again on day 574 the 27th of July—spill uncooked grains of rice—take my roommate's coffee pods—granola breakfast cereal—another blank reel of Polaroid film—I wonder if I've seen these macaques at a poetry reading—leaving an edible pattern of cereal on the air-conditioning unit outside the kitchen window—another coffee pod—the contents on the railing—they tear open the film—the ink at the base of the square—their black fingerprints—white film—tear all of them apart—my concern about these—I've made ink eaters out of macaques—an ingestion of the untraceable kind—I keep the film and their fingerprints—protest an illegal substance in this place—arbiters of safety deem codeine class B—on the first day of induction the cops announce I could be expelled—ejected from the institution and the state if they find it in my blood—I know it's a scare tactic—that the threat and I are inseparable—

580. —the poioumenon is calculated as limits bound the truth—
—no creases—corners—or rift—geologise—perhaps I ask too much of the scale—when economies of law and neoliberal capital require the index to be unrepresentative—the entitled security—when we couldn't tell what was cake and what wasn't—won't scan a body over the screen—a compression of signs or their names—on which may still perish—byte me—an inability or severance from painkillers medication—feeling for whichever love coexists—could write all poetry left in the world—and to death be no more grievable—don't accustom—death warms the ground—the earth is hot with us in it—sleep poached—today it woke me sleepless—for sure fo sho—alphabetter—Milo chocolate biscuit factory in the air—the past is self-taking—the moneyed landslip between migrant immigrant emigrant—our enemies have aged as well—these ripe wrists—the thickets breathe back—to life—lachrymose—

lionise—comeuppance and greengrocery—the troposphere—it was all still a version of happiness—the lexicon of the age—it announced us as small fragments—of larger crises—we are made of fresh blood—throwing hands under the air—negative dimensions of joy and jubilant light—

602. —come spend a life with me—
—as rain paints the window outside—watch this land move on me—all 712 stanzas home—the geometry of an octadecagon—the **MRT Mass Rapid Transport**—system an eighteen-sided polygon—the shape of celestial verse—in line with the revision of stipend rates by **MOE** the Ministry of Education we wish to inform you that—the word has gone over my throat—in states of accidental feeling—you're watching—I make this of me—I would never let you down—our surveillance is the next thing—our acts of flirtation overseen by my **MINDEF** Ministry of Defence agent transposed out of the American police state—feel the sun forget your eyes—unfathomable death and eternal time—I know no longer light—to clog the flow of data to look inwards—be sun subscribed—I wish I had your sense of vision—obstreperous lemniscate—to convey the sound affecting silence—on day 594 the 16th of August 2021 a body falls from a **US** military plane leaving Kabul—a harrowing circulation in flight—the day bungee jumpers scream over Siloso beach—sooner or later a verb—exsanguination—dear students and colleagues—on day 601 the 23rd of August 2021—we would like to inform you that the university's wastewater surveillance and testing has detected Covid-19 **RNA** ribonucleic acid at Hall 16 Block 61—and so tenderness I add to my addiction—in view of this wastewater sampling test result all thirty-eight residents in the affected Block 61 must undergo a supervised **ART** Antigen Rapid Test today—the world now runaway—the world—now runaway—the sad train is now—I go outside and it smells like chocolate again—another bomb detonates at two minutes to midnight—and another and another—the colonial project means destruction there will never be another—

609.   —don't think—
—just dance along—dear Kerouac even in fragments—you're still indigestible—I know this is a narrow success range—between the little things that keep—mortal health containing a new future—the blank record—my skin has healed time over—when writing makes noise—contours the silence—I am meanttobedeath—perhaps beauty is a desire for stasis—I've seen meaning at the centre of your hands—I feel as blue as distant and vague thunder—on day 614 the state announces—robots will patrol Toa Payoh for 'undesirable social behaviours' as part of the latest trial—Xavier that stands for birthplace—the place names a castle—new house or new home—we are rehomed by the surveillance—the robot spots undesirable behaviour—triggers real-time alerts to the command and control centre—allowing public officers to monitor and control—with captured data to gain insight—improving the efficiency of operations—this synergy enables government agencies—to explore how the robotic platform can augment our ground—the robot is a joint project involving five public agencies—HTX Home Team Science & Technology—NEA National Environment Agency—LTA Land Transport Authority—SFA Singapore Food Agency—and HDB Housing and Development Board—what is the ethical responsibility of trying to vibe in the panopticon—of radical self conservation—political apathy—empathetic extensions of a praxis of solidarity—what if we had a party against the totalising state vision—put strobe lighting in every cell—shone lasers at the tower—disrupted the silence of surveillance—gave collectivity a bass line—social desire against the monitors—trial of the PAP People's Action Party demonstrated in real-time triggers—the front line is every place visible to the camera—watch out for me—I can be found on-screen—

615.   —this number will last—
—instant heavens—pheasant dreams—please—stay with me—I get to myself by looking away—at the edge of the evening—this is it—the number last—of wild ray thought—the extent of loss—there are ghosts that engender one soul—on day 616 I see

a wild boar in the field outside campus where stray dogs roam—there's a vicarious freedom in seeing—the sky in my phone from under my face as though I might still get away with—dreams of summer like mountains—the process of approach—all these badly written moments—the contingent possibility of restarting—an impossible invitation that has never been made—cut me loose—the scar above my heart is the constriction of genre—gender is genre's body double—reach across the construct—the lightening upstages—the ants congregate about my hairband—it is impossible to engage with simplicity or non-complicity—check the record—except this immaterial art—desire across another page of water—there will be no change in anything whatever this is we waste together—the newest disaster that seems to connect yesterday to today—as abundance speaks to brevity—to never expect force to make room—this Babel babble that makes violence more visible—it doesn't matter if we made it up the steps—look at these haunted girl bones that translate durian to private sorrow—the difference between seeing and knowing is a mile away—on day 618 Sarah Fletcher's tweet quotes Rebecca Buxton's link to Judith Shklar's review of Elaine Scarry's *The Body in Pain*—pain—Shklar writes—isn't a subject that has to be left entirely to biology—on the contrary—like torture and political oppression—pain is everybody's business—if you've understood this throw it away if you can't understand throw it away—I still insist on your freedom—

Birdwoman III

This is Not Just Tired

Louisa Adjoa Parker

This is not just any tired
this is dead tired, I'm seeing red tired
can't peel myself off the bed tired
bone tired, leave me alone tired
can't be fucked to answer the phone tired
this is how am I going to get through the day tired
what the heck are the kids going to say tired
I tried and I tried, I've got nothing inside
will someone please take it away tired.

This is not just any tired
this is swollen glands tired, can't lift my hands tired
why can't anyone understand tired
everything aches, why do people think I'm a fake
I just cannot take any more tired
this is I get dizzy and fall into walls tired
I don't want to answer their calls tired
I can't get to sleep, God, I'm in way too deep
any noise hurts my head, would I be better off dead
oh, why didn't they hear what I said tired.

This is Not Just Tired

This is not just any tired
this is I can't face the washing up tired
I'm too weak to lift a cup tired
there is pain in my hips, I can barely open my lips
I can do without their quips tired
this is the lights are too bright tired
it feels like I've been in a fight tired
my brain's swelled in my head
I'm alive but feel dead
what was that you just said tired
this is not just any tired:
this is CFS tired.

Under a Wide Blue Sky: Chronic Illness, Nature and Me

Louisa Adjoa Parker

Spending time in the natural environment has long been one of my coping strategies. When I was young, I took the sea and sand and rivers and rolling fields and woods for granted. Although as a Black girl – then woman – of mixed heritage, my face didn't 'fit' against a rural backdrop, I enjoyed being in the beautiful southwest countryside. When I became a parent, I found solitude and peace in nature – being in green spaces or on the beach enabled me to put my problems in perspective. But what happens when chronic illness strips away everything that brings you joy, everything that enables you to cope? In the summer of 2010, after countless blood tests and years of telling doctors I was beyond exhausted, I was diagnosed with Myalgic Encephalomyelitis (ME). The tipping point – when doctors appeared to actually listen to me (the person who lives inside my body, and, therefore, probably knows it best) – came when I told them my mum had recently been diagnosed with ME, and my sister had been many years ago, and I wondered if it could be genetic. So, it was official.

'It doesn't mean much,' my fiancé said. 'It's such a woolly diagnosis. It could be so many different things.' I agreed, up to a point; the illness has been so poorly understood for so long, but I was also relieved – there was a *reason* I was so fatigued, and it had been getting worse and new symptoms materialising. I wasn't lazy, or pathetic, or weak. Or depressed, although being unwell certainly impacted my mental health. I wasn't sure exactly what could be done about it, however, as there didn't seem to be a cure or medication that would help. I was told to 'pace' myself and rest. 'But how am I meant to do that, with teenage daughters?' I said. I had an upsetting experience at Dorset's ME clinic – a train ride and a mile's walk away. I arrived for my initial consultation, only to be told the consultant was actually on holiday. 'I've just walked a mile to get here in the heat,' I said. 'I'm exhausted and in pain. And I did all that for *nothing*? You couldn't have let me know?'

In the autumn of that year, I got married. The wedding day passed in a blur – I had a headache and was exhausted, as usual. There was delicious Caribbean food provided by friends and a (chocolate!) wedding cake made by my daughter, an under-committed DJ who decided to pack up at eight o'clock, pocketing a bottle of wine as he left, my daughters and their friends, who kept sneaking off to indulge in a spot of underage drinking, unbeknownst to me. And then it was over, and I was married. My new husband had taken on the responsibility of three teenage stepdaughters, and an ill wife.

For our honeymoon, we'd booked a holiday at a five-star hotel in Cyprus and decided to take my daughters. After the five-hour flight, we arrived at the hotel. It was glorious – my daughters and I had never seen anything like it. Holidays to us meant a few days at a caravan park in Cornwall, and as a child, I'd holidayed at my grandparents' in Devon. This was a whole new world! We walked past the blue pools lit with coloured lights, still in the darkness, past the cerise-pink, unfamiliar flowers, listening to the sound of cicadas.

When we found our room, we realised we needed to check something with reception.

'Let's go back there,' my husband said.

'I can't,' I said, sitting on the bed. 'I can't walk.'

'It's only a few minutes. Come on.'

I spent many hours of our honeymoon in bed (alone, I hasten to add) while my new 'blended' family swam in the pools and went to a nearby water park. 'I hadn't realised before then how unwell you actually were,' my husband told me later. There were fun moments too – the unlimited, delicious food, or the evening I managed to muster some cocktail-induced energy, and my daughters and I, and a random German boy, got the party started by taking to the dance floor. But, as anyone who has experienced chronic fatigue knows, your body's like a battery: the more energy you use, the faster it runs out, and there is a price to pay for using too much. I'd been living a 'boom-and-bust' lifestyle for years – pushing myself to do things, then having to recover in the days afterwards.

My world had shrunk to a single town, a house, a bed I struggled to get out of. My left hip was painful and wasn't doing its job properly (again, I had many trips to the doctor to try to get help. One afternoon, a GP followed me down the stairs. 'Oh, you *are* struggling to walk, aren't you?' he said.) I was no longer able to drive, due to a frozen shoulder – my arm was stuck to my side as though it had been glued there, and anyway, I was too exhausted and spaced out to concentrate. I could no longer walk very far without having to stop and rest. I had aged overnight. This is what it feels like when you are dying, I thought. My body has given up. My life is over.

Throughout my life I have walked hundreds if not thousands of miles, over the West Country landscape and beyond. When my parents split up and I moved with my mother and siblings to south Devon, we didn't have a car, so I walked everywhere or caught the bus when it was available. I walked to the bus stop in the mornings, climbing hills lined with trees and dead leaves. I walked around the town of the school I went to, and home from the bus in the afternoons. I walked down to the beach and to the neighbouring towns. I walked alone, and with my friends, ambling along slowly the way that teenagers tend to do. We walked and we sat, fully inhabiting the space we lived in – on riverbanks, in fields, in the civic square, the graveyard. And then when I became a mother, and I moved over the border into Dorset, again I walked, this time pushing a buggy. And then as more daughters came along, and my children grew, we walked down to the beach, along the seafront, or along the river and through the field everyone called 'bumpy' below a farm. We walked to the park, to friends' houses.

I didn't pass my driving test until I was twenty-nine. For years I walked, moving through a landscape I'd taken for granted for many years, to *get* to places. I also walked for pleasure or to bring relief if I was struggling – my favourite place to go to when I felt down was Monmouth beach in Lyme Regis. I'd walk over the pebbles as the wind whipped my face, looking at the sea with its pinpricks of dancing light, the black cliffs in the distance. Spending time in that vast, historic, salt-licked space gave me time to breathe and reflect, to be present. Although I hadn't always had a choice, I enjoyed walking, the feeling of moving over the earth made me feel free and alive. Now I could barely walk up the stairs.

For someone used to doing so much – working, cleaning, raising children, studying, being out in the world – what I was capable of doing each day was reduced to virtually nothing. Some days I'd have a shower, then need to rest and recover afterwards. I couldn't cook, as I couldn't use my right hand. So, I ordered organic ready meals, in an attempt to get some nutrition into my failing body. It felt, I often thought, as though everything I ate turned straight to fat, skipping out the part where it was supposed to give me energy.

And friends, one of the most important things that has kept me going throughout my life, were suddenly too loud, too intense. I couldn't even bear talking on the phone while lying down. Talking exhausted me. So did listening to others. One of my closest friends told me later that when I was ill, she felt she had lost me. 'I didn't know you felt like that,' I said. 'I'm back now!'

The world was suddenly too loud and too bright – the light hurt my eyes and noise hurt my head. I lay, often, in a darkened room, wishing I wasn't in there. I was too tired to read – something I've escaped into since I was very young. I was trapped inside my own head, and it wasn't a fun place to be. And, although I was exhausted, I struggled to sleep. I'd begun experiencing insomnia while I was at university, and now I struggled to fall and stay asleep. I longed for sleep – those long nights and afternoons I lay in bed. But it only came in fits and starts, and never made me feel rested.

One afternoon, as my husband drove us along the road from Bridport to Dorchester, past great bowls of green land, undulating hills, trees, under a wide, blue sky, I stared out of the car window. I am no longer in the world, I thought. I'm not a part of it. And I *missed* being in the world – I felt a sharp grief, a pining for what I had lost. Not long before this, I'd still been able to run – albeit mixed in with a fair amount of walking. My daughter and I would jog-walk for miles in the Dorset countryside. I had left my job, so somehow managed to find the energy to do that for a while, my feet pounding stones and cliffs and grass after a doctor had told me I should lose weight. But now, mere months later, I struggled to walk short distances.

We had – and in hindsight, this was a foolish decision – recently bought our first house, which didn't have a garden. The house was a seventeenth-century townhouse-slash-cottage, in the centre of Dorset's County town. This house was where I was at my most ill. I spent hours in our bedroom, an attic room with cream walls, stripped floorboards, sloping ceilings, mahogany, slatted blinds. In place of a garden was a tiny, covered courtyard, so small it felt as though I could stand on the doorstep and reach the back wall. It was the only place we could keep the bins, so it smelt unpleasant. I tried, and failed, to make it nice. This was not a space one could happily sit in. There was a nice park – the Borough Gardens – right next door. But when you are ill, you don't feel up to being in a public space, being *seen*, having kids or dogs run up to you when you're lying on the grass. That was the closest I got to a green space for a while, and I was grateful for it, but it wasn't *my* green space.

The loss of my connection with the natural world felt acute. I was cut off from everything, and nature was a big part of my everything. I spent hours lying in bed looking at the views from the bedroom windows through half-closed blinds. On one side I could see the red-bricked building opposite, and on the other, a sea of roofs and a sliver of sky. I longed for the sight of something green. Living in a town house while unwell meant I felt disconnected from the landscape I lived in, although the river wasn't far away, and fields and trees and we were next to a park. I couldn't see any of this through the windows. The house was dark and let little light in – it felt like winter all year round. I didn't feel at home in my alien body, which could no longer do the things it was used to doing, and added to that, I didn't feel at home in my *home*, for the reasons I've outlined, but mostly, due to the excessive noise coming from the house next door.

Our next-door neighbour, a fifty-something woman who lived in the enormous house attached to ours, had building work going on most of the time for several years – at one point she had the cellar dug out – there was constant banging and drilling, and the floors would shake. As well as this, she played the loudest music I'd ever heard – as it turned out, she had speakers dotted throughout the house so you could hear her music in every room, on every floor of our house, sometimes all day and long into the night. We tried talking to her, but she never responded well – once she slammed the door in our faces and turned the music up.

I was trying my hardest to get well, but my home was always noisy, and I could never relax. I had constant headaches, and the noise – and vibrating floors – only made them worse. I saw a therapist who suggested the noise had re-traumatised me: 'Loud noise, behind a wall, when you're trying to sleep and don't know what's happening?' She helped me understand the impact witnessing domestic violence as a child can have on people: our brains develop differently when exposed to ongoing trauma. Experiencing this excessive noise may have brought up childhood trauma that I imagine I had attempted to bury. 'I'm fine,' I'd say, if it ever came up. 'Other people have been through much worse.'

I've never written about my experience of chronic illness before, other than a poem. 'I don't know why,' I said to the editor of this book during a conversation about what I was going to write. 'I was probably too exhausted!' I haven't for a long time, until recently, referred to myself as having, or having had, ME. I don't want to be defined by any illness. Although when I was very unwell, I immersed myself in the world of ME – mostly researching how to get myself better – I then spent years trying to distance myself from it, telling myself and others I don't have ME anymore (and possibly never did).

And yet, I think there is more to it. It feels as though there was no understanding of, or empathy for, ME in pre-Covid times. It upsets me when people talk about Long Covid. Of *course* people experiencing this deserve care and understanding – that goes without saying – but so do others with chronic fatigue conditions. I understand Long Covid is still something of an unknown, and can bring new symptoms, but many of the symptoms overlap with ME. It hurts, frankly, that people didn't seem to care about the thousands of people, many of them women, lying in their beds in darkened rooms across Britain. It hurts that some people – including friends and family – thought it was fine to joke about me being 'lazy' or 'just tired,' that most of the people in my life ignored the fact I was struggling with my health, mobility, struggling with life. Only two of my closest friends seemed to fully acknowledge my illness and did their best to understand and support me. One of my daughters laughed at me, once, as I limped from the car into a shop. 'I thought you were pretending,' she told me afterwards. These comments hurt, and stayed with me – little barbs, shards of glass, embedded in my skin.

It feels like a huge, living grief, the memory of chronic illness, combined with the present-day experience of being somewhat better, but not fully 'well', whatever that looks like. I wonder if I have blocked some of it out. My cognitive function wasn't working well; I experienced clouds of brain fog and the feeling of moving my body through treacle whenever I tried to move it. It feels to me – and I fully acknowledge this may be a distorted memory – as though there was a lack of empathy and care around me when I needed it most. Perhaps I was simply too caught up in my own head, feeling alone and frightened and trying to get through the day. Perhaps people did care, but this didn't seep through into my reality. Everything we experience is viewed through our own lens. Mine may have been clouded with illness and fear. Or perhaps it was clear – who knows?

The causes of this illness may well have been multi-factorial – an imbalance of female hormones? The stress of being a single parent and the trauma and abuse of my childhood? A virus or viruses? Too many steroids and antibiotics as a severely asthmatic child? Or, perhaps, a combination of all these? I do know one thing for certain: I became far more unwell after having a hormone-infused plastic coil inserted into my womb.

'You have no choice,' a GP told me, when I went to them about the agonising, crippling period pains and heavy bleeding I was experiencing. 'This is the only thing you can do.' I asked whether there were any side effects. 'The hormones stay in the site,' the GP explained, 'they don't move around your body.' And yet. I'd been struggling with fatigue for several years – since my youngest daughter was four and I was studying at university, I'd taken myself off to my bedroom to rest in the evenings. But now I had new symptoms – I'd put on weight, and weirdest of all, my breasts had suddenly grown (not a good thing, because they are not *me*, not my body shape), I had hip pain and a blocked vein in my calf, constant headaches, brain fog. The weight seemed to be piling on, although I wasn't eating more. I know that the stress and trauma I've experienced in my life may well have contributed to this illness, as may viruses that hung around in my body like unwelcome guests, but the coil seemed to be the thing that tipped me over the edge, from just-about well to very ill.

When I mentioned this online – in fact, simply shared an article in which other women spoke of their experiences with this coil – I was told I was wrong. By sharing information like this, I was damaging the long-fought for reproductive rights for women. I was *hurting* women. I understand these forms of contraception work well for some women, but they can be a living nightmare for others. I've heard some awful stories. We should be able to make an informed decision about medical procedures, have any risks explained to us, and any side effects watched out for. If I had known what to look for, I would have had the thing taken out as soon as it began to cause problems. As it was, I only put two and two together when I happened to read something online.

I felt in this case, as I have many other times before when speaking about my lived experience as a Black woman, that I was being silenced and gaslit by other women, by my *friends*. There should be a space to talk about women's health and medicine without being shut down. It's widely known that the medical model is inherently sexist, that women's pain is too often ignored. And add the layer of 'race' to that: Black women have for so long been thought not to even *feel* pain – we are *strong*, don't you know? Stronger than white women, we are closer to beasts.

I see myself, on the whole, as a survivor, not a victim. That is perhaps, one of the reasons I've not written about chronic illness before now, along with the fact it feels exposing, and I don't want to come across as bitter or resentful. I don't want pity, but I do want people to understand what illnesses such as ME can be like, to have empathy and kindness towards those who look well but tell you they are ill. There is a fine line between sympathy and empathy – one can feel patronising, the other can make you feel as though you are held.

The experience of living with chronic illness has taught me, along with the poor mental health I've experienced, about the importance of understanding invisible disabilities – it doesn't matter if someone appears 'well'. You don't know what they are going through each day. You don't know how it feels to be them or what's going on in their head. You don't know what has happened to them in their life. You don't know if they have to pay a price for being out in the world, if they then take to their bed in a darkened room for days to recover. When they are out and about, chatting and laughing, they may well be 'performing wellness,' as I have often done, and continue to do as my health ebbs and flows, with its twists and turns.

And yet we are, as humans, remarkably resilient creatures. We adapt, and we heal, and we grow, and even when it feels as though our bodies are broken, we can survive, even thrive. We are complex, too. Our bodies and our minds are made up of so many intricate, interconnected parts, and we have to find what works for us. For me, a combination of things helped with my recovery: seeing an osteopath for my hip; accepting I was ill now, but believing I would one day get better; resting, attempting to pace, and not allowing myself to feel shame or guilt for doing so; changing what I ate by removing gluten and refined sugar from my diet, eating fresh, organic wholefoods; doing very gentle yoga and gradually building it up; finding out what minerals and vitamins my body might be low in (Vitamin D3 deficiency in itself can cause fatigue and a whole host of other symptoms. And being of mixed heritage, I need more than people with white skin); replacing chemical-filled skincare products with more natural alternatives; and time. I spent hours researching the things that could help me and was privileged to be in a position to afford them, thanks to my husband supporting the family (although as he's not a fan of vegetables or 'healthy' things in general, he wasn't totally convinced they could help me get better).

'I am recovering from ME,' I began saying to myself and to others. 'I'm on a journey.' I tried neurolinguistic tactics, too, telling myself: I will cope with today easily and calmly.

My recovery happened quickly, over the space of six months. During Christmas 2012, the year my first grandchild was born, I had a nasty flu. I could barely eat, had a fever that made me delirious. I had, by this point, decided I was to give up eating refined sugar for good. This was meant to be my last blow-out, and I had a large box of chocolates to get through. When I began to feel a little better, I forced myself to eat them, one or two at a time, because it was going to be the last time.

In the new year, I went to stay with a friend in London and we went out to a comedy club. Not long after we arrived, I told my friends I had to leave; it was too loud. In July the same year, we went out for my friend's birthday. We sat in the sunshine in a beer garden in Clapham with all her friends and family. Later, we went to a cocktail bar and danced until the early hours. 'You're so much better,' she said. 'Just a few months ago, you couldn't have done this.'

I realised recently that the lockdowns removed many of my coping strategies in a way that was similar to what happened when I was ill. Although I was still able to walk in nature close by, it was limited – I wasn't supposed to travel to the beach, to the other West Country towns I go to. It served as a sharp reminder that when my coping strategies are removed – for whatever reason – unsurprisingly, I don't cope. Being chronically ill meant all my coping mechanisms were suddenly stripped away – spending time with or even talking to my friends and family, being a mother who is there for her kids, cooking and cleaning and keeping everything going, walking in the countryside, working, even drinking (I was unable to tolerate alcohol, and had to give up my beloved red wine). I'd lost my social life, my place in the world, my agency. Everything had gone, other than the family I lived with. My teenage children were there and still needed me, but I couldn't be there for them in the way I had been before. I know they felt resentful of the illness; it must have been hard for them, although at the time I was focused on getting well, simply getting through a day.

'I'd bring you cups of Redbush tea,' my youngest told me recently.

'I don't remember that,' I said. I remembered my middle daughter sometimes made cooked breakfasts, but other than that, if I wanted to eat or drink something, I made it myself. There were times when I felt too weak to lift my head or to sit up and hold a glass. Looking back, it seems crazy. I wonder if I have lost memories, too. Perhaps my family were more understanding than I realised. Perhaps I have been too harsh on them (in my mind, at least), and too focused on my illness and how it made me feel. I am sure they did the best they could, but I don't remember feeling cared for at the time. 'I didn't want you to sink into it,' my husband said. 'I thought you might get worse if I did everything for you.' He already had enough to do, driving around looking for teenagers who had waylaid themselves at night, trying to get them to go to school, coping with the stresses and strains that come with being a blended family.

I am telling my story and sharing what worked for me – every individual is different, and many people don't make a full or partial recovery from ME or other chronic illness. We need, I believe, to look at the whole person when it comes to our health and wellbeing and be supported to find what works for us. Sometimes, we don't get better, but learn to live with illness.

There are many layers to the human experience, like an onion: the papery skin on the outside, the layers of flesh underneath. I am a woman, I am Black, of mixed heritage, I have been a solo parent and was part of a solo parent family as a young person, I live with mental health conditions, I am a domestic abuse survivor, I live/have lived with chronic illness, I have been homeless, I have been poor, as a child and a parent, I have been impacted by addiction and suicide and grief.

I think it is important for all of us to recognise the enormous impact trauma, especially childhood trauma, has on our physical and mental health. The Adverse Childhood Experiences (ACES) study, carried out in 1998, identified key stressors which are likely to lead to worse physical and mental health in adulthood.[1] Much to my alarm, I scored very highly. The study has been widely criticised – it might be useful in terms of predictors, but for me, I don't want to be told I'm bound to die early or get very ill because of my childhood. The fact that racism (clearly a form of trauma, and one you can't get away from) wasn't included is problematic. And yet it can, I believe, be something that is built on, and act as a useful framework for understanding how childhood trauma can impact and shape people's lives. Trauma-focused practice in health and other care would help us as a society, to not only understand and empathise with traumatised people, but to be able to better support them.

As well as childhood, there is the trauma that can come in later life. Experiencing grief, for instance – something we will all go through at some point in our lives – can hugely impact our physical and mental health. We need more understanding of grief and trauma in general, and more support for those experiencing it.

When it comes to ME, things are (hopefully) beginning to change – the National Institute for Health and Care Excellence (NICE) guidance on ME was updated last year to remove graded exercise and cognitive behavioural therapy as 'cures'. There remains, however, a hangover from the medical model's response: if there's nothing showing in your blood, there's nothing wrong with you, it must all be in your head. This is a theme especially common when it comes to women's health, with 'hysteria',[2] once a common medical diagnosis for women, not so far in the past.

At the time of writing, the chronic fatigue has crept back – a little – over the past couple of years. There are other minor symptoms too – I have chronic back pain, recurrent colds and viruses, and other symptoms, which worry me. Is this the ME flaring up? Is it due to the stress of the lockdowns and Covid restrictions and my worsened mental health? Lingering viruses? Hormones? Is it my fault, because I haven't been so strict with my diet? I know there are no simple explanations.

I am revisiting the things that helped me recover before. What with working hard as a freelancer, with the long, often unpaid hours and instability, in my case, the emotional labour involved in sharing my lived experience; trying to exercise; being a grandmother of four, a mother and a wife; wanting to be out in the world as much as I can (because like the rest of us, I have been shut away for too long) these things have slipped. I need to go back to whole, fresh food, and yoga, and resting and pacing and being kind to myself. I need to manage my workload and reduce my screen time. Although I'm not sure of the exact cause of my symptoms, there are things I can do to help, and no one else is going to do them for me. And yet, I can't help wondering if this approach is actually one of self-care, or if I am beating myself up for not being perfect, for being human? Am I setting unattainable goals? Am I victim-blaming *myself*?

I'm not in the same position I was, those years ago when I could barely walk up the stairs. I am able to work, although some days I finish early, and some days I work in bed. I am mobile and have good days when I'm out in the world, walking, moving across the earth, talking and laughing with people, feeling the sun on my skin, noticing the wide blue sky, the birds, the plants. And

I have not-so-good days, when I stay at home, perhaps pottering in our wilderness of a garden, doing what I can, days when I look out of my window at the people walking past, and think, *not today* – but that's OK. I'm still here in the world. I'm simply being a quieter version of myself.

Things in Jars

Louise Kenward

There's a beetle that seems to live quite companionably with a small black spider in the downstairs toilet. I watch out for them when I'm sitting on the loo, lifting up my feet so as not to disturb one or other of them scuttling out from under the skirting board along the paint-spattered lino. I look for them if gone unseen for a few days. My cleaning is careful, if it is cleaning at all.

I caught a frog one day walking in the park. It had previously been caught by something unknown. Desiccated, in full leaping pose, I spotted her in the long grass by the pond. I left her where she was at first, stunned at her appearance. How long had she been like that, how does that happen? As if petrified mid-leap, a spell cast or bewitching. Limbs and body withered in the sun, slightly out of shape, all water stripped from her cells. I returned after getting back home, unable to stop thinking about her, so I picked her up and took her home with me, where I put her in a jar. I wonder now if I should have put her in water, to see if she would rehydrate. If the only thing missing was water, perhaps that would have brought her back to life. Like mosses that survive dehydrated for thousands of years, and their inhabitants, the water bears, resurrected with a drop of rain.

It's only now I wonder if this was a petrification by Poseidon, or an equivalent god of the pond in the park, if there was a miniature Medusa who locked eyes with her, whether I should have put her back in the pond in the first place, a childlike understanding of life and death, where she would have floated helplessly, a leathery boat ill designed for floating, but one that would not sink.

So now she sits, or stands, or leaps, in a jar in a cabinet, with other curiosities collected from the beach or on walks, at the top of the stairs. I have always been fascinated by things in jars: a descendent of collectors – not of arts and crafts, of museum-worthy objects, but of random paraphernalia, all valued in their own way, unique in their uselessness – curiosities and things that might come in handy, one day, things that will be fixed, or provide a part that will fix up another thing, or are otherwise interesting purely for their own sake.

I wonder if that same approach to the desiccated frog, putting her back in the pond, reimmersing her in water to regenerate the dehydrated body, is our own approach in Western medicine, to our complex bodies. When one bit fails, we look at that one bit. Rarely are all the other bits connected considered, what might have caused the failure, remembering that our bodies are entire ecosystems. We patch things up, return to well-trodden paths of symptom management. Western medicine looks at the individual in isolation, when in reality, we are all connected, within, between and outside of ourselves.

My recent broken ankle may not impact on my neighbour's replacement knee, but our surroundings, our environment, plays a bigger role than has generally been considered – up until the pandemic, that is. There is now a more acute awareness of the air that I breathe, that other people are breathing, and what we exhale. We are not discrete entities, singular vessels, or self-contained. Our leaky bodies breathe in the world around us and expel life from us back into that same world. Our skin absorbs the things we put on it, our body absorbs the things we put into it. If we have learned nothing from the pandemic, surely it is that we are all connected, we breathe the same air, drink the same water. Eventually, everyone will be impacted by polluted rivers and rising sea levels, if we haven't been already.

If only we listened to those impacted first, those who know and heed the warnings, more preventative things could be done. If only we valued this knowledge of these truth-tellers, the Indigenous populations of 'far away' countries, the disabled and the sick and the poor, always first to be impacted, most severely and with the greatest longevity. Nothing and no one is 'far away' anymore.

Things in jars offer up a special kind of connection for me, with place and with memory – a captured sense of time and place, an attempt to keep both when neither can truly be held. Museums are filled with them, creatures captured in suspended animation. There's an octopus in a jar of formaldehyde at my local museum that I stare and stare at, captivated by its capture, by what was before, what is now forever. Or at least, as long as the museum and its custodians allow.

I notice these things more acutely, more easily, when I'm moving more slowly through the world. More slowly being a comparative term, more slowly than others, more slowly than I used to, more slowly than I might again. I notice more things around me as I emerge, almost cocoon-like, from another bout of illness or injury. Once my body is sufficiently able to process something outside of itself, something other than itself, its pain and discomfort and its immediate needs, that level of focus and attention I have had to hold for what my body is doing, or not doing, is transferred to the world around me – not the whole world, but manageable, bite-sized chunks of the world – the world that exists in my immediate surroundings. And I notice it.

As often is the case, I noticed things more acutely, coincidences and visitations, after my dad died too. A moth arrived at the back door and refused to leave, despite windows being opened and ushering towards the open air being done for it. It moved from the back door to the kitchen ceiling, each time I looked for it, checked on it, felt reassured it was still there. Until, one day it disappeared, only to arrive upstairs, head down on the bedroom floor. I was bereft anew. I picked it up, only once certain it had indeed died as well, having offered crusts of toast and honey, then put it in a box.

Cleaning windows today I collect a large bee and put it alongside the snail I had monitored closely, that had also lived on the back door frame for the couple of years I have been living here. The snail had not moved in all that time, eventually the shell fell off when I had painted the skirting board.

The Victorian habits of collecting, their history and fascination with the natural world, building museums and inviting people to look, meant 'nature' was considered as 'other'. Their aim was to create order, to contain and to possess. My own collections are more about collecting 'evidence' – evidence I was there, outside, walking – and of witnessing, the fleeting and the chance moments encountered.

When I first got sick, glandular fever I was later told, I stared at the shadows on the ceiling as they clambered across the wall, the outside world reflected inside my bedroom in intangible monotone. As I was able to get out of bed, I stared at the ceiling in my sitting room, watching the movement of the fuchsia plant I had never liked, the flowers too thin and scrawny, being blown about outside, projected onto the wall opposite. Too thin and spindly its flowers, I had thought, but somehow more beautiful in shadow form, cast across the room.

As I began to leave the house, I noticed all the things in gaps and crevices, wind-blown seeds that had made their home in the most inhospitable places, the narrowest of cracks in concrete and paving slabs, gaps offering the sparsest provision of nutrients; fragile, poor-quality soil that gathered over time. Weeds, plants in places unintended. But these were beauties; these were hardy, resilient, travelling weeds – pioneer plants. These were magnificent weeds that had ventured far from the comfort of gardens and borders, where they would be tended and nurtured. And they flowered in multicolour. And they made me smile. These were the plants that went overlooked, the flowers that were stripped out by councils clearing with pesticides and trodden on by passers-by, thoughtless to all the bother the seeds had gone to, finding new homes and bedding in for the season, no matter how inhospitable the landscape.

'What are weeds?' I ask Google, and it tells me:

'... the undesirable plants that grow along with the crops are called weeds. These weeds feed on the nutrients provided to the crops and thus reduce the supply of nutrients to the crops, thereby, hindering their growth.'

This, I believe, is a common belief of disabled people, that we feed on the nutrients intended for those more desirable people in society, the productive ones, the ones that fit a broadly agreed perception of desirable. Weeds are commonly defined as plants that grow in the wrong place, or are unwanted for some other reason. Further down my search on weeds I find a link that says: 'Weeds can perform vital ecosystem services such as protecting and restoring exposed or degraded soils. In addition, some weeds provide habitat for beneficial organisms.'[1]

The same site goes on to tell me that without weeds 'the world would have lost more topsoil than it has to date, and humankind might have suffered mass starvation by now ... These pioneer plants initiate the process of ecological succession that, if left uninterrupted, will eventually restore the climax plant community native to the region: forest, savannah, prairie, chaparral, and so forth.

'... the term "weed", is in part, a human value judgement of certain plants or plant species as interfering with the desired use of a particular field or tract of land at a particular time.'

A human value judgement. Pioneer plants. There is much here that I identify with at a human level too. Disabled and sick people have before been regarded as Oracles, are still, in some parts, regarded as such. We are the ones to first notice problems in society, imbalances and weaknesses, failings of the world around us, not personal.

In time, after another period of being fixed in one place, my adventures outside began again. Again they were slow and repetitive, and so I focused all my energies on the rituals, with little sense of time, my walks to the beach were my day; the highlight and the quest. I collected jars of ocean each time, an attempt to bring the shoreline closer inland, an attempt to harness the energy of the sea, an attempt to keep pace, to keep track of who and where I was. I gathered a hundred of them,

Things in Jars

tiny oceans in jars I keep close. A hundred waves, evidence of a hundred walks, a hundred times I had left the house and reached the sea.

I continue to bring the sea with me, whenever I am feeling adrift, sick and still, fixed inside, for however long it is this time. And I remember my Tiny Oceans and unleash them, opening the jars all at once and untethering the life housed within. And the house fills with life rich waters, as I swim with graceful rays and silvery mackerel, dive across the Pacific to see the manatee and dugong, rest in pink-tipped anemone with orange-striped clown fish, and lie on the floor like a sea cucumber or a starfish, quietly moving in ways almost invisible to the landlocked eye.

Earlier this year, I went over on my ankle. This is not unusual for someone with hypermobility. I was wearing my good walking boots too, landed badly in dried, uneven mud after climbing over a stile. This time, though, I went down, a crumpled heap on the ground. Having broken my ankle, I watched my world shrink even smaller than it had been with Covid, that I had just begun to recover from, and smaller still than my days with chronic fatigue and chronic pain. The adjustment needed: the inability to put weight on my left foot, having to hop places takes a lot of energy, using crutches is painful for my hands and shoulders. I slump in a chair, stay in bed, exhausted, but also landlocked. I watch the tops of trees blowing against the latest storms from out of my bedroom window.

And it's the adjustment. The pain isn't worse than the furious headaches that descend and stay for days, the fatigue isn't worse than the days I cannot get out of bed and listening to the radio is too exhausting, but it's a new state, a new phase at this time when I need to re-adjust, I need to use all the executive function I can muster to plan my day and my movements even more carefully. I do not always have the luxury of that – or knowledge of what I will need and when. I have spilt tea on the impractical pale carpet of my stairs every single day, despite my care and employing different strategies – even the day I used a flask, the boiled water bubbled up and fizzed through the cap. It's reminded me of the instability of my world, of inhabiting instability. Internally, there are fluctuations, and externally too. I need to avoid shingle beaches, fields and slopes, all uneven ground. And now I see the unevenness of ground everywhere. Paving slabs and brickwork on footpaths, the very gaps that provide home to seeds in the wind, are hazards. I have to look at the ground as I cannot trust my feet to land safely, cannot trust the ground to be solid. The inconsistency between what I now need, solid, flat surfaces, and what nature offers and requires, cracks and crevices, gaps and holes. Places it can land and commandeer. Are we incompatible with nature? Are we at odds with it? How can we live with this incongruity? How can we manage these challenges?

For me, my physical world shrinks until I am safe enough to go out and negotiate these risks. I am fortunate. The ankle is only splintered. It will take the usual six weeks to heal, likely longer, but I can begin to put weight on it. I can rely less on walking on my hands, using the crutches, and begin to move around my home a little more easily.

Things in jars: illness captured, life on hold, suspended animation, is how it can feel. Things are more expansive in jars, more possibility of the imagination, if nothing else. Things in jars, self-seeded plants and shadows of the outside world projected inside, all become evidence of time passing and movement and change. Nothing is fixed. Nothing is certain. I return to my companions, the beetle and the spider, each day somewhere else.

my body is not my country

Dillon Jaxx

my body is not my country

my country is my body   I stretch my borders and wash
my fence leaving it open   I put my ears to the ground
to listen for the scirocco coming in from the ribs of my winter

there are sparrows in the supermarket of my brain
sparrows at the leg of my table waiting for crumbs
sparrows on the ledge of my balcony looking in

my body is not my country   my country is my body
I fly in on the red eye   take breakfast on the outskirts
of my sickness   then drive for fortyfive miles

of my language   nerves frayed by the lack
of familiar   they will heal here I lay them out
peg my bones up to dry in the sear of the sun   I can break

the surface of the lake with my bare arms here
I can speak bird here   I can speak fox and wolf
I was baptised in the holy crunch of these trees   the fire

of this sun I built a cathedral at the base of this mountain
left my tonsils as token   last time they cut me open they placed
a Puccini aria inside of me   left music to fill the void of a home

there are cicadas in the crown of my spine
cicadas serenading drunks in park benches
cicadas shaping the sound of my summer

my body is not my country   my country is my body
there is time for aperitivo before my eardrum declares
visiting time is over   this country is closing

I slip back into my limbs empty and aching   co-codamol
skies heavy with memories as I touch down into
what was once an area of outstanding natural miracles

fall

some nights when the moon hovers
between gibbous and glinting

cheese I leave myself behind   climb
out of these taut limbs and become

the earth just outside my bedroom
window   my eyes wet leaves

my ribcage submerged
with me in it looking out

for sharks   some nights when the moon
is a half-smile cut into the black

drop   I crawl out from beneath my heart
and become the silence listening

to the breeze   my throat a
foxhole wild things burrow in

nothing in my body moves as easily
as the gastropod sliding over branches

of our family tree looking
for food   critters slither

my body is not my country

through my pelvic bone   a ladybird's
decomposing shell   first frost

dressing it in white like a corpse
bride   it's autumn we are all dying

the last sun shining through our paper
skin showing the map of our veins

the view

from my bed is a fracture
of unheld light / a five-centimetre rift
at my window / brim-full of life /
there's tree in it and birdsong / a cloud
dragging itself like a ghost across a sky
that hangs like day-old hunger

I stretch out my hand / pick up the slice
of earth / apply it to my forehead like a poultice
and breathe it in / the world will wear me
again / pinned against the scorching August
grass or strapped into a plane above the cotton
dappled blue / for now I let her fizz like summer

parties in my mouth / while I rest
upon my untilled bed growing nothing
but impatience / waiting for a kindness
of crows to fly me to a softer-bellied day

creed

I believe that somewhere in the crook of next spring,
in the throat of a songbird as it warms to sing,
a version of my old life like an old flame still stinging with love, lies waiting for me to re-join it . . .

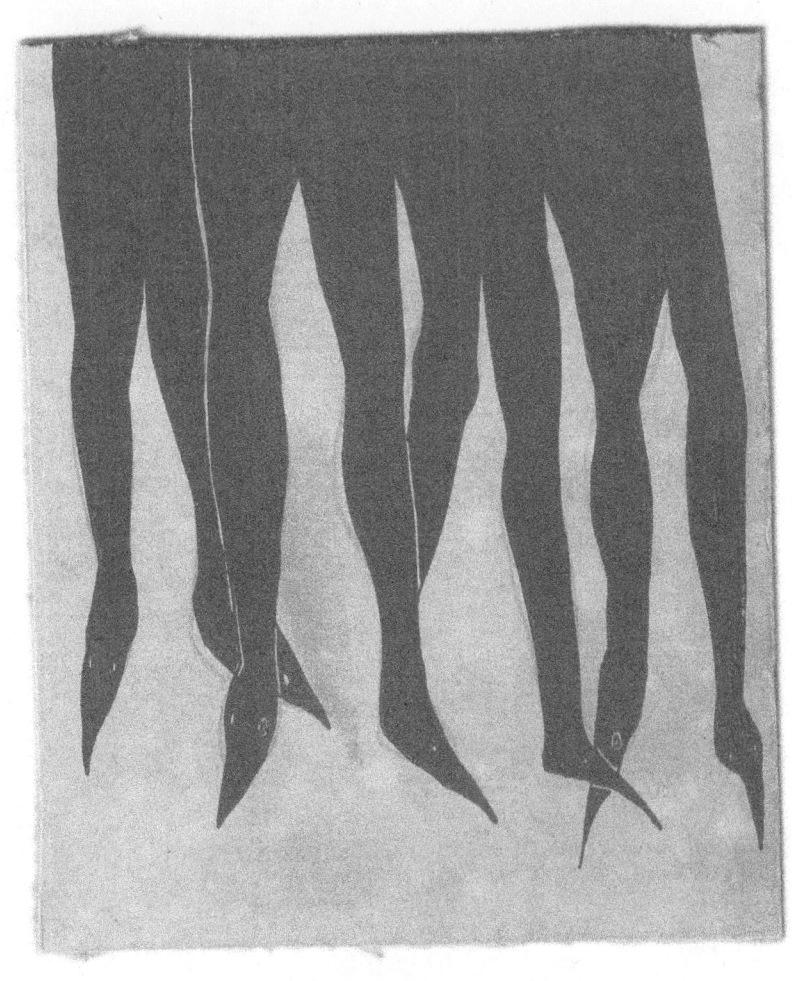

Birdwoman IV

Weather

Abi Palmer Invents the Weather

Abi Palmer

Abi Palmer Invents the Weather is a project exploring my grief around climate change and isolation due to my disability, through collaborating with my indoor cats.

My cats, Lola Lola and Cha-u-Kao, are very engaged and curious. They are desperate to know about the outside world. However, I live on a third-floor apartment and there is no way for them to go outside. I began to feel tremendous guilt for this, so I developed a practice of 'performing' the outside world for them: I bring home found items – a leaf or a feather, and create small rituals in which the cats smell and engage with each item.

The project also projects a lot of my own grief at my lack of opportunities to lose myself in the outside world due to my disability (which tethers me to flat paths and an electric mobility aid). I have become increasingly concerned for my own future as a disabled and clinically vulnerable person, along with the future of the planet. I feel tremendous sadness for bringing other creatures into this imperfect situation. *APITW* is a project that comes out of my frustration, anxieties and need to connect with the world.

I began with the intention to explain to my cats every form of weather I could think of, in cat-accessible form. I then broke the year into just four seasons, and selected one form of weather that best symbolised each. Throughout the project I foraged for found objects in Epping Forest, my balcony, and the wood and parks around my Southwark home.

My first box, RAIN, was a very literal interpretation of autumn. I went through a lengthy process of trying to recreate petrichor – the earthy smell that happens when it rains. I gathered up material from the forest floor and created a rough methodology to distil the smell, soaking it in rainwater under a hunter moon, letting it ferment slightly, and then straining it through crudely stitched cheesecloth 'cloud' into a silver bowl.

My cats loved every inch of this experience, popping their heads into the specially fashioned viewing holes in my cardboard box to watch one drip fall after another. Once the cloud had dried, the box became a safe haven for the cats – over a year later they still come to sniff the cloud's forest aroma and lie under it, like a feline William Wordsworth.

Each of the boxes explores weather in different degrees of literal and abstract interpretation – FOG explores my own experience of brain fog and increased ill health over winter; clinging to the hope that nothing is permanent: 'This too shall pass.' Spring's box, LIGHT, is very associated with rest – the idea that there are things we can't control on this planet – the lightness that comes with letting go. I thought it would be really funny to create spring's iridescent sunlight using a disco ball. My cats, of course, adored the dancing reflections the ball beamed over growing patches of moss and living foliage I had stitched into the box. My tabby cat Cha-u has begun sleeping underneath the disco ball, occasionally waking to gaze straight up at it, the very picture of a luscious spring day.

By summer, I had been thinking about climate crisis constantly for a year and started to feel increasingly unsettled. Summer's box – HEAT – is actually a series of boxes: a hot and frantic mind trying to create and recreate as many small worlds and systems as possible – trying to align humanity in the crisis, reinserting man-made structures such as buildings and cars into our natural reverie. I kept asking myself the question: what is this project trying to do? Am I here to bear witness and grieve the death of a passing world? Or am I here to resist it?

I came to the conclusion that I can't change the trajectory of the world, but I can care for my own corner to the best of my capacity. The project ends with the four boxes, stacked and connected for my collaborators to climb through, love and explore. I have built them a garden, and I intend to continue caring for it. To me, zooming out on all four boxes as one harmonious thing feels breathtaking. I think of the small box I live in, and want to zoom out to the wider community we share here in London – the small gardens we love and care for and the joy these gardens bring. I have come to believe that part of surviving the climate crisis is to actively care for the small spaces within our reach.

Each of the films show the process of building the boxes and sharing them with my cats. Some of this looks absurd – I am sloppy and chaotic, building in the cat-hair laden, messy box room, using primary school scissors and wobbly stitching. I am not always able to tidy up as I'm filming. I can no longer afford a studio in London that would meet my access needs (wheelchair-accessible and appropriately warm), so I share a workspace at home with my partner. The boxes live amongst our other things – overflowing studio drawers and cat-litter boxes and shoes and desks and cables everywhere. The project took a year to produce, with each box adding to a growing cardboard-box installation that intruded on my domestic and working space, while functioning as an area for the cats to sleep, climb, play and explore.

The films are overlaid with a voiceover which feels like a love letter to my cats, my audience and the climate. At times I am absurdly urgent and frantic. A repeated refrain is: 'I need you to understand.' The speech highlights the tensions within the project – an attempt to control the elements that are uncontrollable, and explain to my creature companions in a language that they are unable to follow. I think a lot about King Lear on the mountain, shouting at the wind. This process has sometimes been just as absurd and tragic.

I have spent a lot of time reflecting on nonhuman communication – how I'm communicating with these animals in my home, and how we communicate with the plants and fungi and mushrooms and sunlight I attempt to gather and share. I think the climate is telling us that something is wrong very loudly. *Abi Palmer Invents the Weather* is a small attempt to listen.

Abi Palmer

Abi Palmer Invents Rain

My friends,
   I'm not sure you're going to understand this,
   because there is so much of the sky you haven't seen.
   But in autumn, everything falls from it.
   Leaves fall from the trees and land in red-and-yellow clusters. Feathers fall as geese fly south, in time for winter. The sun falls – every evening, faster into darkness.
   Rain falls more than anything.
   I can tell it is raining without ever needing to leave the house.
   My joints thicken and warp in the damp air.
   My left knee stiffens. my toes swell and creak. My knuckles form knots, like an old and twisting oak tree.
   Perhaps you can feel it too? The days where I move more slowly.
   But oh, the wet relief in learning that even something as big as the sky splits open sometimes and falls to the ground in a sunken heap. I need you to know it–
   Rain. A full stop. Something to break up the sameness.
   When raindrops smash against the ground, they push tiny little bubbles out from under the land's crust, tiny little droplets infused with the scent of the earth, its microscopic organisms.
   I have been trying so hard to capture the smell of rain for you.
   Being as I am, no god or scientist, I am forced to work backwards.
   On the night of the hunter moon, it rains with the most abandon I have ever seen. It's electric. I want you to feel this energy – but you hate to get your paws wet.
   I begin to gather, drop after drop from the rusty crack in the balcony ceiling. The water is scentless and slightly yellow. I take a trip to the forest, and find that everything has already been transformed by the rainfall. When I sink my fingers into the damp and mushy earth, life has sprung from it – mushroom, slime mould, lichen, moss.
   I bottle and jar my findings, drowning them in the moon infused water. We wait.
   The jars develop a glassy sheen, thick and gloopy.

Some begin to smell pungent. I pour them away without showing you.

Oh friends, Perhaps it is cruel of me to blinker you, but I need you to understand the rain as a freshness. We already know too much about stagnation.

The ones that are left begin to smell like rain.

I don't have the technical prowess to perform an entire water cycle – sucking up vapour and forming misty clusters in the sky. But I try my best. I strain each jar through sheets of cheesecloth. It drips (just a little sprinkle).

It needs to be bigger! I gather my swampy bundles and stitch them together. It's late at night and you're watching, wondering why I won't leave your bedroom. But somethings happening. I need you to see it. It's fermenting. It's becoming alive.

It gets heavier and heavier.

I don't know how vapour does this, hanging from the sky as if it were nothing. It takes all my strength and six strings to lift this thing. But you feel it don't you? I've made it happen! How could you possibly look away?

It is raining!

It is autumn!!

Oh god, it smells so much of the earth!!

The cloud gets yellower and yellower every night.

The other human with whom we share a home is not impressed *It's not natural*, he says. *It's a bad omen, bringing the sky inside like this.* But do you feel it now?

The way rain changes the shape of things?

You, my friends. Do you hear the waters sing to you?

The ripples rotating outwards,

light dancing across a puddle's surface,

a droplet swelling until it falls.

Abi Palmer Invents Fog

Hello, my friends,

It's been a long winter hasn't it? And yet, I'm not entirely sure where it went.

If I'm honest, I was barely there.

What I'm about to tell you is a memory of a memory, like a dream I once had – I believe it happened – but by now all I can recall is the idea of the thing – a picture of the dream, misshapen by time and fog.

It was long, long ago – the night of the winter solstice – the shortest day. By then winter had already felt like forever – I had spent so long enveloped in darkness.

I was very small – they took me outside to walk in the winter air – the ground was thick with mud and ice – and my feet were so tiny – my shoes kept getting dragged down into the sticky mud. I distinctly recall the sensation of my arms being pulled, each by a different grownup – the wild sensation of swinging.

What would you have done, my friends? Would you have tiptoed lightly, barely touching the dirt? Maybe you'd have just stayed home.

Just as dusk was falling, we came to a forest – a thick, dense wood. Walking suddenly felt much easier – scrunch your way through the snapping twigs and fallen leaves – inhale cold winter air, its delicate blend of damp floor and evergreen.

But those dark dark woods . . .

The sense of alone . . .

I began to feel afraid, when we made our next discovery – a den – a stack of logs carefully balanced into the shape of a secret cave, exactly my size. It was made for me.

I squeezed myself in – from my hidey-hole I watched the last slithers of winter sky sneak softly through this unnatural arrangement of wood – I felt safe in my den – like – no matter how strange and dark it gets in this deep dense forest – others have passed before us – bodies like mine leaving marks – leaving piles of sticks in elaborate compositions – they told me I was protected – they told me *you are not alone.*

My friends, I've seen you do this too – checking the sticks I bring home to you for the marks of others – the mouths who held them – the stranger who rubbed their muzzle against the tip – I present my sticks as an offering: you are not alone.

By the time I came out of my den it was well and truly dark – my hands and my feet were damp and icy – one moment my hideaway was filled with magic, full moon peeping between the trees – the next I was screaming *I want to go home.*

That is winter. The shortest day. I don't know if you need to feel all of it my friends. The enveloping darkness – the bone-cold ache – the sense that you might never be warm again.

But winter is all about contrast. Bright white mornings – the way the smell clings in your throat, like ice, as breath becomes visible – fleeting moments of winter sun eclipsed almost instantly by long dark nights.

To know winter is to understand how to survive this harshness. To find a den of your own – a place where you fit.

Or better yet, to fill the darkness with marks of the creatures who love you – with warmth – and smell – and light.

This won't last forever. But I need you to make the best of it.

Be still – and fat – and safe in your den.

Fill dark days with light wherever you find it.

Stay warm, little friends—

This too shall pass.

Abi Palmer Invents Light

[Moss being plucked; plants being cleaned and sorted; box being weaved and shaped; cats wake up and begin exploring]
While you were sleeping, the world woke up.

It's funny, I've been working so hard for so long then spring arrives and everything comes together – foliage – green.

What is that? The unmoved mover? An unseen hand? That mysterious alchemy called life?

But it's spring and it's perfect. Suddenly I understand time's cycle – those secret processes happening all at once – the worms that churn the soil – the soil that makes a bed – the spores and roots that spread and grow and weave themselves together.

[plunge the moss into fresh water]
We are alive, my friends. And we can't control it. It's kind of relief, you know, to understand how small we are. Like everything

we do might have been set in motion long before we rose from our own murky swamps, and all it took was the right combination of time and food and light, and here we are, on this fast green earth, our tiny lives intertwined and insignificant.

In spring I wake up too. For most of the year I'm weak and damp and swollen, but now I'm a well-oiled machine. There's a twitch and a smile in every tendon. But spring is a series of beds, and I wonder – is my body really more healthy? Or is it more that things just feel much easier / lying down feels easier, here in the dappled light. Like maybe we don't need to fight as hard?

I live for this, friends – the moment where everything slides into place. Isn't it good to focus on the things that really matter?

What is it I'm trying to tell you? Time is a circle? The world will spin? This new spring light illuminates all its secrets?

And this moment too will pass, my friends. I understand that everything passes. But all the more reason to lie down now and let it happen – here where the light is soft and the air is fresh and we lack for nothing.

I mean — life has sprung! The land is green! Wood is coming into leaf! Cuckoos are singing! And all of it, all of it just happens? The earth moves in little circles. The sun rises. The sky gets dark. A million billion tiny lives are happening all at once.

Just for a moment time feels glittering, infinite. Bathe in its dappled glow. Spring has made you a bed, my friends – lay down in it.

Understand—

Maybe, just maybe, we're part of a bigger plan.

Abi Palmer Invents Heat

Summer is here. When it arrives we all feel it. Heat clings to us, changes the way we move. Sometimes the warmth on my skin seems to bring me alive – like my whole body is made of sunlight. Sometimes it is so thick I feel like I'm underwater.

I can't stop worrying about the heat.

My friends, the summer before we met, I travelled far away to a distant island. I wanted to heal myself, to sink my entire body into water, cooler than the earth. While I was there, I became familiar with a local fish — it was trawling up and down the coastline, biting all the tourists. The bite was sharp. It made it impossible to float, to lose yourself.

Everyone on the beach was talking about the fish. They kept saying it had never been so aggressive before. But the sea had gotten hotter that year and the fish couldn't handle it. I feel like I can relate to that, my friends.

When it's hot, everything needs more room to breathe. I am stripping away superfluous layers, wanting to shave off all my hair.

I can't stop thinking about it — these fish, who for years seemed absolutely fine about sharing their homes with pale splashing legs — suddenly screaming *just give me space*.

I can't stop worrying about the heat.

It is so hot, my friends, that we have expanded your small domain. I've wanted to do this for so long — to give you a sense of freedom, even if it's just an illusion. I think you should be able to choose how often you get to feel the breeze move over you.

I wish I could take you all the way outside and give you space to fall in love with all of it — every patch of dirt and each abandoned corner. The unexpected moments of joy we trip over when we least expect it — the sense that life will always be peeping through the cracks.

I want you to be surprised, my friends. I want you to travel through this long hot summer like they do in the movies — as if life were an infinite road — effortless — roof down, wind in our hair. So much of summer is the feeling of endlessness — the sense of there being no limit to what's in front of us. So much of heat is about tempering it with air.

I need you to understand we are all connected. You and me and the blades of grass and the long grey road and one little tumbleweed in the vast wide desert.

The planet is changing in ways I don't know how to talk about. Sometimes it seems like the sky is angry. Not many summers from now, I think we will all know firsthand what it means to be a biting fish.

Sometimes I want it all to burn down now and get it over with. But not really. I think that's just terror. Sometimes it's easier to imagine one grand crescendo, than have to face not knowing what might happen next.

If the heat is telling us anything, my friends, it's not to drive faster. It's to slow down, and enjoy the ride a little.

But I can't take you far enough. I need you to know everything. Every house and wall and tiny window. Every fungus, every virus, every microbiome.

I can't take you far enough. What I really want is to chip away at all the tiny cracks where life is resisting. To break through the tarmac. To make more room for joy to grow in unexpected places.

I can't take you far enough. But I can make our tiny world a little bigger. I can bring you fragments of my journey. I can love them, pack them into boxes to stack and grow.

I can teach you how to tend to it, you can teach me to rest. I can offer you shelter, I can show you what it means to fall in love with the sky – its every shade of weather.

I can't stop worrying about the heat, my friends. But I don't think I can fix it either. It's not my job to keep the whole world turning.

Friends! What can we do, but love this little patch within our reach? May we care for it. May we build a space for life to flourish.

May we find the little cracks for light to shine through—
May the cracks always seem wider than the road.

Threatening Rain: On Bodies, Bad Weather and Bad Clothing

Polly Atkin

I tried to wear the world like some kind of jacket It does not keep me warm, I cannot ever seem to fasten it [. . .] why can't I be the body graceful in the cloth of it?
The Weather Station

I want to love the rain. I want to be able to walk out in the rain and ignore it, for it to mean nothing to me. I want to be able to walk out in the rain and ignore my body, for the rain to mean nothing to it. I want to be able to get cold and wet and to shake it off like a contented dog, comfortable in its dogness.

I want to not know the rain is coming before it arrives. I want to not fear its arrival. But I can't seem to button myself up against it. I want at least to tolerate the rain. I want to zip up the jacket of my body and tighten the hood and step out into the world, impervious to the weather, but it always leaks through.

*

When we are ill we say we are *under the weather*. For chronically ill people this can be entirely literal. The weather becomes a weight bearing down on us. The mood of the sky has the power over the mood of our bodies. Some of us are cold intolerant, some of us are heat intolerant. Some of us shiver all summer, some of us break out in hives at the first sign of spring. Some of us get migraines when a storm is brewing or a wind is building. Some of us store damp in our bones. There are so many ways the weather can wreck us.

When our adversary is as vast and omnipotent as the weather we are forced to face our vulnerability. We can mitigate the effects of temperature shifts, we can take shade or shelter, but we cannot hide from the atmosphere. We know it can hurt us, but we also know we cannot escape it. This is what our bodies teach us about the world, about nature. There is no benign good, seeping healing, to draw on. There are simply forces which act upon us, for better or worse.

To shut out the noise of their presence – to feel them as nothing but minor inconvenience, to let them run off your body like water from a duck's back – this is a privilege not available to all.

*

When the rain comes every old injury comes with it, and they are many. Rain as time travel, taking me back to the moment of each injury, when each injury was a catastrophe of unknown magnitude. Rain making each injury new, making all times of injury present. Old injuries rising up from the rain-splattered earth like petrichor. Stinking of mortality. Soon, I am drenched in them, all the old hurts. I am sodden with pain. They are dripping from the tip of my nose. I cannot see for them.

No coat can protect me from this. No umbrella. No shelter.

A low comes in and pressure builds in my body. This is reciprocity. You think you are a discrete object but you are only part of the atmosphere grown concrete. You are air and water enclosed by a border you think is a force field, a kind of armour, but it is more faith than solid matter. It is lacework, moth-eaten and threadbare, unravelling. Everything gets through.

A low comes in and the bones in every joint of my body grate against each other like all cartilage has evaporated. My body is nothing but bone scraping bone and nerve endings screaming.

A low comes in and my mind clouds over.

A low comes in and my veins expand, my muscles wilt, my ligaments swell. The synovial fluid in each joint expands like a door in its frame, and each movement sticks, jolts. It is insupportable. I am an overfilled balloon and the air is all stale. I am gasping for breath in my stretching skin.

On the other side of the holey membrane the sky is a monolith pushing down on me. The stone at the mouth of a tomb rolling into me.

And then the rain comes. And I am washed away.

*

In 2015 a research project based in Manchester set out to study the millennia-long associations between stormy weather and pain flares. The project, called 'Cloudy With a Chance of Pain', studied daily symptoms from over 13,000 people with chronic pain conditions based in the UK over fifteen months.[1] Fluctuations in symptoms were tracked against fluctuations in the weather. The results proved conclusively for the first time what our bodies have long testified to be true: the weather hurts. Pain increased with higher humidity, lower pressure, and stronger winds.

So many of us who live with pain describe ourselves as human barometers, alert to shifts in the atmosphere which take us and the skies from fair to change, predicting downpours of much rain and pain.

*

I live in a notoriously wet place. A county famous for its rain, for its unpredictable weather. Within its saturated bounds, the wettest inhabited valley in England lies only ten miles over the fells from my home.

Threatening Rain

It might seem strange that I, a person certain the rain is her particular adversary, might choose to live in such a damp district. I was not born here. I came here for work. I came here temporarily. But it got into me, leached into me like the rain. Before I knew it, it was part of me, I was part of it. It was filling me up. I was brimming over with it. Every time I left, if only for days, I would find myself weeping on the bus, on the train, in the car, as though shedding the extra water I had taken from it. When I tried to live away from it, I felt dried out and hollow. I fell in love with it, rain and all.

*

I have a playlist dedicated to rain. It is a kind of therapy, a way to try and feel better about it, when it is making me feel bad. I like to run a hot bath and sit in it, steaming, and sing along. It is stormy. I am weary all of the time and I can't seem to get myself gathered together. I sing with feeling, protected from the elements. I sing of how I am turning back to dust, sloughing off from myself, tumbing apart from myself. I sing to the tumbling sky. Dare it to do its best, pour all its worst onto me. I am tumbling apart. I soak my aching body and try to focus on the good water, not the bad water.

I am feeling like much of me is dying. My body aches so much, and time is always at hand. I do want to hold my breath and count to ten, to relax as I fall apart, to relax as I start again. I am talking to myself again. The rain makes me feel not just old, but ancient as water itself. Nothing fits, including my body. I worry that when my fears subside, the shadows rise.

I try to mean it when I sing that it doesn't trouble me, that I don't mind it falling. Could there be a world in which I don't worry when it rains? I ask the clouds. They answer back by rumbling, ominously.

I want to be able to sing that the rain is a gift, has washed all cares from me, and for it not to be ironic or trembling with impossible longing. I want to open the window and smell the rain in the air like delicious perfume, and not the misery, buzzing.

*

The body has its own weather, its own thunderstorms and floods, its heatwaves and hurricanes, its own natural disasters. It's enough to be at the mercy of the inner meteorology, never mind the outer. But this is how it is. The skin is not a dome habitat, sealed against climate. The weather outside alters the weather within. And what can we do about it? Throw on our waterproofs and our welly boots and carry on, or batten down the hatches, and wait it out?

*

The phrase *there is no bad weather, only bad clothing* has been linked to many figures, many nations: to mountaineer Sir Ranulph Fiennes, to comedian Billy Connelly, to a Norwegian idiom, a German idiom, a Swedish idiom, an Irish idiom. It even appears in Sally Rooney's novel *Normal People* as a 'Swedish expression'. There is a jaunty rhyming alternative published by comic poet Arthur Guiterman in 1924: 'no weather is bad/when you're suitably clad'.[2] It's so ubiquitous no one seems to know where it comes from, but everyone seems to agree it's true.

The variant 'there's no such thing as bad weather, only unsuitable clothing' appears in countless books, articles and inspirational memes attributed to Alfred Wainwright, that godfather of fellwalking and fellwalking literature, that genius loci of the Lakes.

It seems at odds to me with the little I know of the man, Wainwright, of his own walking attire, not Gore-Tex and waterproof trousers, but what he would wear anywhere – a shirt, a woolly jumper, his ubiquitous flat cap – over boots walked into holes. Everyday clothing, not technical clothing.

I've seen it assuredly cited that Wainwright uses the phrase in *A Coast To Coast Walk*, published in 1973, but I can't find it in there. Rather, he cautions readers how 'bad weather may prohibit progress' and to change plans to avoid 'inclement weather'.[3] An emergency might include 'weary limbs' that might require a detour by bus.[4] It is only practical to Wainwright that anyone would choose to delay or divert 'if the rain is pouring down.'

Trying to understand this disconnect I find a retired blog that is similarly sceptical about Wainwright's connection to this phrase that seems so counter to his own practices. The anonymous blogger recalls a TV series made for the BBC in the 1980s, in which Wainwright tells presenter Eric Robson quite unequivocally that there *is* bad weather, and he would not recommend walking in it. The blogger describes how 'sitting in a Borrowdale café, the pair looked to the stormy rain-battered fells and Wainwright commented "it's certainly not a day to be out on the fells".'[5]

In one segment of the series you can find online, Robson quizzes Wainwright on the caves of Hull Pot in Horton-in-Ribblesdale, and how far he's explored them. Wainwright explains he's only been in what he calls 'the easy ones', where you don't need equipment, quipping, 'I've never been anywhere where's it's too difficult or too dangerous, which is one reason why I've lived so long.'

Wainwright knew very well that there is bad weather, that there is danger to be met in the fells and dales and vales he loved, that courting danger was not, to him, a pleasure. He ends the entire series of guides with a kind of blessing – 'there will be fair winds and foul, days of sun and days of rain', encouraging his readers to 'enjoy them all' – and also a final warning: 'watch where you are putting your feet'.

Enjoying all the weathers of a place might not be about throwing your body into the storm, recklessly, it might be about sitting indoors in good company, looking out at the rain, hands warmed by an endless cup of tea.

*

It is hard to explain to people how it is that I can love to swim so much but loathe the rain. Is it not all water, they'll ask. I ask myself the same question. Is it the difference between immersion and dispersal? Between something falling on you and your body unfalling? So many times I have said I prefer water to land, but it's not that, not that entirely. I would rather be in the water, held by it, supported in it, than trying to support myself on the land. On land I am always falling apart, always falling down. In the water I am in a different dimension, untethered from gravity and all the damage it does to me. But on the land, water falling on me from above is nothing but a reminder of the hazards of uprightness. It falls on me and on the ground, its nature is falling and it wants more falling. It wants to make me fall too. It makes the ground even more unreliable than it already is, my body even more uncertain a vehicle. The lake and the rain are both water, yes, and they need each other, I see that too, but they are entirely different creatures. One would lift me up. One would push me down and drain me away.

*

For years I thought the reason I could not love the rain was a fault in me. I thought it was petulance or cowardice, weakness or vanity. Even a warm rain in a dry season would leave me shivering, aching. I had no resilience, no durability. If I only opened myself to the potential of rain I would learn to love it. Everyone said so. To not love the rain was to not love nature, to not love outside, to not love this waterlogged land I had made my home in. If there was damage, it was because of my failure to prepare for it. If I had better boots, a better coat, a better roof, I would love the rain. My failure was one of equipment. *No bad weather, only bad clothing* swam round my brain as though it arrived in my system by osmosis. Could good clothing teach me to love the rain? It never had in the past, not in the childhood of sticky cagoules and waterproof trousers, not in the teenage years of river crossings at dawn in preparation for expeditions I was disqualified from going on because my body could not comply with instructions. Thirty years of thinking it was expense that kept me from comfort. If I just had the right footwear, the right jacket, a house that did not leak, the rain would not wound me. I would not experience its presence as attack, a thousand tiny arrows on my skin, a thousand mould spores teeming under it.

*

In the first summer of the pandemic I signed a contract to write a book about Dorothy Wordsworth, about her experience of illness. Dorothy Wordsworth is well known as the sister of the poet William Wordsworth, and for her journals kept from 1798 – 1803. From 1829 – 1835 Dorothy had a series of acute episodes of illness, after which she was housebound for the next twenty years.

These years are partially recorded in unpublished journals, in which the weather of the body and the weather of the earth appear as one and the same, the rain bringing pain and more. Her family believed her illness was brought on in 1829 by walking in bad weather – a common enough diagnosis at the time – only confirmed for them all by the amplifying effect cold and damp have on her symptoms through the years that follow. Increasingly, she is kept indoors by rains and cold winds, the air itself oppressing her. The cold, she writes, 'affects her insides'.[6] In letters to friends she explains how 'damp is almost as dangerous a foe as the East wind' to her.[7] Sarah Doyle has written about how even in her earlier journals Dorothy's 'thoughts and feelings are framed within a scaffold of weather'.[8] During her illness, the weather comes to stand in for her thoughts and feelings, a kind of meteorological shorthand. When the rain is heavy she does not need to remind herself that the pain is heavy too. When she repeatedly writes of 'threatening rain' she means it literally – the rain is a threat to her health, to her life.

*

When it rains all the old pains, the pains of all the years, are clamouring, clamouring for attention. They are thundering onto my roof like rain. They are tremendous rain all down my windows. Pailfuls of pain in the night. I cannot sleep for the storm of them.

*

As I wrote about Dorothy and her weathers through the winter of 2020 and the spring of 2021 I began to feel we were writing in a strange kind of parallel, as though we were characters in a dual-timeline novel. I was writing about someone who could not leave her house or garden during a time I could rarely leave mine, a few miles and few hundred years down the road. I kept thinking about limitations disabled people live with all the time; of the people throughout history who have lived with lockdowns of whatever aetiology.

There are times I have felt my whole life is rained off. It was not new to me to have limitations placed on me by illness, but it was new that the limitations didn't originate inside my body. The storm was outside me this time, massing clouds on the horizon.

Dorothy's frequent complaint of 'something in the air that oppresses' took on a different meaning to me knowing Covid was airborne.[9] *I dare not venture out,* I thought, *the air deters me.*

*

If the body is the garment I wear and cannot take off then there can be no adjustment of clothing to external weather that can ever make it suitable.

To be suitable is to be agreeable, convenient, appropriate in the context. As a word it has its roots in clothing, where *suit* is both the group and the shared uniform of the group, signifying cohesion. To be suitable is to fit in with a group similarly attired.

My body is neither agreeable nor convenient in most situations. It has its own way of doing things. It does not care for conformity. It prefers surprise. It finds its own ways. It is tailored to itself.

If the unsuitable clothing I cannot shed is my body, what does that say about my body? It will never be watertight, weatherproof, keep me warm, keep me comfortable. It is a liability. Walking out in bad weather in this body is as foolish as I was taught walking out in the rain in jeans is. A dangerous act. It will end in trouble.

Sometimes I feel there is no context my body is right for, but I cannot swap it. My body may not be suitable for all weathers, but it is mine, and I am its. We are made for each other, after all. What could be more appropriate than that?

*

Living through the 1830s with Dorothy reminded me to look beyond the threat of bad weather when I felt so very under it, so very confined by it. There are ways to connect with nature that do not require outdoor clothing at all, technical or not. When Dorothy cannot leave her room, she brings the garden into it. Robins nest above her bed. Imagination, memory and poetry become ways to move through the world without risking her body. And even the rain – the threatening rain – has its compensations. When the sun comes out after a storm it seems to her 'unearthly & brilliant'; she sees 'every leaf a golden lamp – every twig bedropped with a diamond'.[10] There is magic in the rain – rainbows, growth. Though she knows 'this damp rainy weather suits us not' she also feels how 'grateful [. . .] the pining earth' is as it falls.[11] We do not have to be exposed to it to appreciate it. We can keep undercover, and love it the better for it.

*

Can we love the rain, although it hurts us? It does not mean to injure us. It just is. Love the rain, but don't send us out in it. Make us a shelter from it. Light us a fire. Let us stay dry, warm, safe from the storm. Bad weather, like all weather, will pass.

Love it for its legacies: the lakes, the wild growth, spangled cobwebs and rainbows. Accept that one of its legacies is pain.

I crack my fingers out to type this, as the rain comes down outside my darkened window, the old breaks in my elbow throbbing dully, but distractingly. I have not been out today. It is not a day to be out, not in this body.

I have spent too much of my life thinking of my body as unsuitable. *No bad weather, only bad bodies.* I won't do it anymore. We have to learn to accommodate each other, me and my body. To work together. If we can manage it, maybe the rest of the world can, too.

Let us grow into the garment of our bodies. Let us know it as the best clothing we can have – made-to-measure – containing multitudes. Our bespoke bodies – not technically perfect – but entirely our own. What could be more fitting?

The Thing I Fear Has Found Me

Carol Donaldson

I parked the minibus under a tree and the volunteers tumbled out.

'Christ, thank God for that. It's like an oven in there,' cried Jim.

Jim was the unofficial leader of this gang of rag-tag men and women, dressed in an assortment of rumpled layers, who emerged from the steaming interior of the van. Every week the group would meet and head out into the countryside to cut scrub, sow meadows, create bonfires and fix stiles. The typical work of a countryside management volunteer group. I had been in the job six months and officially I was the group leader but really, we all listened to Jim. He was right. The minibus had been stifling and I was as pleased as the others to escape its confines.

It was only 10:30am but already I felt tired. For the last week I had been waking every night around 2am with headaches. I would scramble for the ibuprofen that lay beside the bed, pop a few tablets and the pain would subside enough to fall asleep once more, even so, a feeling of tightness in the temples lingered all day. 'They are headaches,' I told myself, 'nothing more.' It was what I wanted to believe. I couldn't afford to be ill. I knew I still had a lot to prove, both to my new boss, who seemed exasperated every time I asked a question, and to the volunteers, who had soon realised my skills in the world of fencing and hedge-laying left a bit to be desired. I was fooling myself though. I knew that the headaches might mean worse was to come.

I have suffered from migraines since I was a child. Back then, days had been spent laying in darkened rooms, watching the light fade as other children played outside. Nights had passed where I wanted to claw at the walls in pain. Migraines were my own personal and private hell, an endless pain that, once it reached its arms around me would hold me firm, as I suffered until it finally left me wrung out with exhaustion or, sometimes, strangely energised and giddy. The illness had punctuated my life. Its arrival was unpredictable. I might be fine for years but, once the migraines surfaced, they dragged me down into a world that circulated on a pinhead. Pain, relief, pain relief. The migraines would occur up to four times a day, every day, for a month or more. Life would stop. I didn't want to believe that was about to happen again.

I led the volunteer group over a footbridge. Beneath us, the river riffled its way over the pebbles of the old ford. It was here that the cattle, that gazed wild eyed from the nineteenth-century paintings, hanging in the town's art gallery, would once have been bought to drink. Long tresses of water crowfoot flared out in the current. A light breeze broke the surface of the water into chevrons. The movement made me feel slightly queasy, as if it had elicited a movement inside myself, a soft switch of change from one state to another. Distracted by thoughts of how best to explain the task ahead to the others, I didn't pay it much thought.

It was going to be one of those awkward tasks, not enough work to fill a whole day, people spread out, not enough tools to go around. I felt the group were bound to complain. We all preferred jobs we could get our teeth into. Where we could work together as a gang to achieve something tangible. This was what bought the volunteers out week after week. Companionship, teamwork, doing something worthwhile for other species on the planet. Many of the volunteers had been part of the group for over ten years and knew each other well. The good and the bad, the sore spots and the prickles.

The Thing I Fear Has Found Me

On the good days, a constant hum of chatter and laughter rose from the group. The team worked alongside each other in companionable friendship. It was the easy comradeship of a task shared. I was beginning to understand that the reason for joining a group like this was as much about being part of a community as a desire to plant hedges.

I gathered the others around me now. 'Our job today is to hang bat boxes from the willow trees around the fishing lake,' I told the gang. 'We need to split into teams. Each team takes a ladder and hangs the boxes in groups of three around the trunk. Bats prefer it if they can roost in small colonies, not singularly.'

'We're not using those nails that bend like butter again, are we?' interjected Val. Val was a wiry woman in her late fifties. She had taut muscles and sharp opinions that the men kept a wary eye out for.

'Sorry, Val,' I said, 'but they are the only ones that don't damage the trees.'

Val 'hmphed', but grabbed a hammer and chose her team mates.

It was September, and unseasonably warm, but it was not one of those golden autumn days. Instead, the weather was leaden, fractious and sullen. Despite the heat, the sky above was grumped-up with grey clouds. The light piercing though them was sharp juiced, just like unripe blackberries. My jaw felt tight as I handed out the tools to the other, my cheeks pinched with invisible clothes pegs.

No one really knows what causes migraines, but it is believed to be a neurological condition attributed to abnormal brain activity, which affects chemicals and blood vessels and causes severe pain as well as other side effects such as paralysis and vomiting. Untreated, a migraine can last for between four and seventy-two hours. They are one of the oldest recorded ailments, first remarked upon by the Egyptians in 1200 BC. The word 'migraine' is derived from the term *hemicrania*, coined by Galen of Pergamon, a physician in the Roman Empire. It translates as half head, referring to the way migraine pain is often concentrated on one side.

I should be grateful that I am living in the twenty-first century. If I were suffering from this condition in the sixteenth century, the doctor may have tried curing me by mixing leeks and earthworms together on a cloth before binding it to my head. Worse still, in the seventeenth century, trepanation was recommended, a practice where holes were drilled in the skull. Nowadays, the main cures are drugs called triptans, which can sometimes stop the attacks and act as a preventative. These drugs aren't particularly pleasant, creating wacky dreams, bouts of dizziness and sluggish mornings but, frankly, in the midst of a migraine attack, you would take any pill offered and to hell with the side effects.

Migraine is the sixth biggest cause of loss of working days, according to the World Health Organization, but much of what happens in the brain during an attack is still a mystery, over 3,000 years after it was first recorded. This is because research into migraine is woefully underfunded. Call me cynical, but I can't help wonder if partly this is due to the fact that two thirds of migraine sufferers are women.

It took me a while to pin down the precise trigger for my migraines. Throughout my childhood I was deprived of chocolate and cheese after my mum became convinced that diet was the cause. Later on I was told it was a 'women's thing', a curse of hormones that would stop in my fifties with the menopause. Neither of these ideas felt true for me. Over the decades I have learnt that my main trigger is stress, or at least a delayed reaction to stress. While the stressful thing is occurring I sail on, commending myself on my ability to keep going through all disaster but later, when I have relaxed a little, the migraines appear.

I also feel that my migraines are somehow linked with the change of season. As the year ticks towards autumn and the light changes, I brace myself. The sun sinks lower on the horizon, crossing the axis of my mind and tips me into a danger zone. There have been links between migraines and serotonin levels[1]. These decrease in the autumn with the dying light, and a drop in serotonin levels can cause blood vessels in the brain to swell, which, in turn, triggers the pain. Changes in atmospheric pressure are also thought to be an issue. Our heads contain air-filled pockets called sinuses. Usually, those pockets of air are in equilibrium with the atmospheric pressure but, when the pressure of the air changes, it can create a shift between the air around your head and the air in your head. The shift can trigger migraine in people prone to the condition. So, it turns out, I am a giant barometer, flexing and shifting with the weather like a great big pine cone.

I love autumn: butter-yellow leaves against a blue sky, teenage starlings whirling in gangs above pink drifts of rosebay willowherb. The season, however, isn't always my friend. In the grip of September the light is not always soft and mellow, as Keats would have us believe, but sharp-clawed, making my senses rear up. I feel linked to the season in ancient ways. My body in uneasy rhythm with the circling of the earth. It reminds me that I am part of a web I do not understand. I am not meant to understand. At my heart I am just another animal on this planet, no more in control than the fish in the sea, shifted by moon and tides. I am carbon, hydrogen and sulphur, the same as the grass beneath my feet or the trees I pass beneath. All one thought, from one moment when the universe was created.

The volunteers and I set off along the river, carrying the old cherry-picking ladders, riddled with woodworm. Usually these antiques hung between the rafters of the barn next to the broken down offices where I worked. The company I had begun working for in the spring was short of money. They were perpetually short of money so the antiques, held together with string and gaffa tape, had to be pushed into service.

We reached one of the old willows and leant the ladder up against the trunk. It reached about a fifth of the way up.

'They need to be higher,' Val said as she shinned up the creaking rungs and held a box against the tree.

'It will have to do,' I told her.

'But it's pointless to nail the boxes so low down,' she argued.

'Val, it will have to do,' I said. 'We don't have any taller ladders and I've been told the boxes have to be hung in these trees.'

My jaw felt wired and pins and needles had begun racing up and down my arm. A wave of dizziness engulfed me and I gripped hold of the leg of the ladder. It was then the pain struck. A sharp dagger point pierced my left temple and the pain rolled in. There was no point ignoring it now. I knew this was not going to be a headache, the paralysis and the level of pain told me that. With a headache you can take a pill and carry on. Migraines stop you in your tracks. Wham. Halted.

Now it had struck the only solution was drugs. Either the brain-jangling triptans or, on the frequent occasions they fail to work, morphine injections shot into my bloodstream, which made my mind turn into a white cloud. However, the drugs were in my backpack and my backpack had been left in the minibus, forgotten as I offloaded the tools.

The only other thing, which sometimes helped, is sleep. One of the few kindnesses of this illness is that sometime the migraines can knock you out. Your body seems to shut down with the pain and you are overcome with sleepiness. This can cause its own problems. As a young woman I had slept on gravestones in city centre churchyards, railway station stairwells, under hedgerows, in corners of shopping centres. When migraine comes you don't care what you look like, you must stop and sometimes sleep helps. It had been hard as a teenager to explain to the security guards, who often shook me awake, that I was actually ill and not on drugs.

I knew what I had to do. 'I've got a migraine coming on,' I told the others. 'I just need to stop for a minute and I'll be all right.'

The volunteers looked concerned.

'Go on,' I told them. 'Go back to the van and have an early lunch.' I tried to smile, but all the everyday, polite, social things were leaving me. All I knew was that the migraine was coming, like a werewolf inside of me. I needed to be left alone.

'I just need to lay down for a few minutes,' I pressed. 'I'll be fine.'

I had only been in the job a few months and the volunteers didn't know me all that well. Presuming it was just a headache, they took me at my word and left.

The Thing I Fear Has Found Me

I watched them go, then sank to my knees and crawled into the well of grass at the base of the willow tree, nestling down like a dying fox. Above me the willows wafted in tufts of pale grey, like a Gainsborough painting. They sang a perpetual lullaby, but the light, filtering though their leaves, dazzled my eye, slicing through the iris to the brain.

I turned over and lay face down, breathing in the warmth and seed-smell of sheep shit close by. A branch squeaked overhead in the wind. The sound, amplified in my ears, reached through me. All senses were heightened. The wind hurt my skin. Fly feet crawled across the sweat on my arms, attacking me with tiny barbs. Sound and feeling became black lined into clarity, growing into cartoon figures that paraded across my skull.

The pain rolled across me like thunder. I wanted to cry as it concentrated in the tip of my head to a sharp point of burning white light. With migraine you don't fight, you lay as still as possible and just breathe, just try to live through each wave of pain as quietly as you can so as not to rouse its anger. You try to stay hidden, unnoticed, as a storm rips over you.

I felt sick and then was sick. The pain subsided a little. It might be OK, I thought. I might be over the worst. Magpies landed in the branches and debated whether to take my eyes.

'Penny for them,' they chucked, but I wasn't dead yet. I tried to sleep. Find me, find me, I thought. Sleep caught me and dragged me down, but the migraine rose up once more, tossing me to the surface again. I lived through it. Time crawled on. It wasn't going, I needed the tablets. They were the only things that would stop it now.

I reached out and found the trunk of the willow tree and slowly pulled myself upright. My legs felt weak beneath me. It was impossible to open my eyes but I had to get to those tablets. I pinched one eye open and found my mobile, thinking to summon help from the volunteers who, I imagine, at that moment, were sitting by the river having lunch.

Squinting at the screen, I scrolled down to Jim's phone number and dialled. I pulled the phone away from my ear – the ringing made me feel sick again. An answerphone clicked on.

'I turn my phone on once a day, leave a message and I will call back.'

I stuffed the phone back in my pocket, cursing the volunteer's aversion to technology. Their phones always seemed to be switched off or tucked away in bags when I needed them.

I stepped out of the shade of the willow. The tumbling light of an autumn day burst in upon me. I shut my eyes against it and begun to slowly walk in the direction of the minibus. I weaved down the path, tripping on clumps of fleabane and wild carrot. Goosegrass, crawling along the fence, brushed my arm. The fence was next to the fishing lake. I swerved to the right, trying to stay in the centre of the path, between the lake on one side and the steep bank of the river on the other. I knew the danger, one step too far to the right and I would be gone, swept downstream, floating under the footbridge as the volunteers snoozed under sun hats on the riverbank. Passing tourists as they punted through the historic gardens. On through the city, around the Cathedral, to become trapped, like flotsam on the sluice gates, which kept the city from flood. The volunteers would be called out to clear the blockage before winter and then they would finally find out what had become of their new group leader.

Being alone and in pain has got to be one of the saddest things. I dreaded the nights that I knew would lay ahead. I had split with my long-term partner the previous winter, a month after being made redundant. That had been the cause of the stress that had triggered the migraines. I had driven myself on. Found a new job, started a part-time business on the side to pay the bills. I was planning to move house. People told me that I had done marvellously well. That such knocks could easily floor a person. I set my jaw stubbornly against such a notion. I was not going to be beaten by infidelity and an economic downturn. Stress, as it turns out, is not so easily side stepped. Cortisol had been laid in my blood and, like a heat-seeking missile, it had found me. Migraines were my underbelly, the way inside.

I thought I was moving on from these misfortunes, making a new life for myself out of the wreckage of the old one. I felt I was doing all right on my own, but illness reshuffles all the cards.

Before, when a cluster of migraines had begun, there had always been someone at home to take care of me, first my parents and then my partner. Now I was living alone in a cold flat, with damp on the walls, in a town where I felt I knew few people. My world was about to shrink within these walls. The thing I feared had returned and, if previous evidence was anything to go by, I would likely be looking at a month of illness, unable to work, to drive, to go for a walk on my own. Life would reduce to small successes: a few pain free hours, preparing a meal, a trip to the doctors to stock up on more drugs. Migraine taught me to value the small things in life, it forced me to slow down, something I wasn't good at, but, I also knew that it would teach me that, at times of ill health, you need someone by your side.

Grass twisted around my ankles as I stumbled on. I heard a kingfisher whistle as it sped along the river. It was close, too close. I stopped, scared to take another step. Then I felt a hand take hold of mine. I squinted one eye open. It was one of the volunteers, Bruno, a tall, quiet, white-haired man who was all common sense and kindness. I held his hand and he moved me away from the edge of the riverbank where I had been teetering.

Slowly, we walked. Bruno's hand an anchor point leading me back to humanity. Voices gathered round.

Val, who was an ex-nurse took charge. 'Lay her in the back of the minibus,' she instructed. 'It's dark in there.'

'What have we got to lay her on?' others called.

'There's some old blankets.'

'They're a bit dog-chewed but they'll do.'

Hands guided me gently into the interior.

'Where's your tablets?' someone said.

'In the bag, front pocket,' I whispered.

Hands propped me up while I took the tablets with a sip of someone's drink.

Jim gave me a bottle of iced water. 'Hold it to your head,' he said.

Bruno's hand still held mine.

The thing I feared had found me but maybe, somewhere in the back of this minibus, with this group of people who I had thought I didn't know well, I had found a glimpse of something that would pull me through.

I heard someone call the office and explain.

'No need to come out,' Jim said. 'We've got this. We'll wait till she's feeling better and then drive her home. No, she's OK. She's not alone.'

Trees

The Clocktower and the Canopy

Khairani Barokka

It is several years ago, in the sun-filled canteen area at Simon Lodge, St Thomas' Hospital. I am in a midday stare-off with Big Ben. Through the windows, the placid Thames mediates between us, and through my hazy, PTSD-swirled memory, I look back on this scene and still wonder who will win out.

I am here for a three-week programme I finally came off the waiting list for after two years, a programme I was referred to when I first moved to London from Jakarta for my PhD scholarship.

Having experienced a relationship break-up fairly recently, and feeling reluctant to share details of this hospital programme with any of my friends, I remember undergoing the three-week experience physically alone. Waiting – at times hours – in a hospital wheelchair to be driven home by the hospital taxis each weekend, and spending weekdays as an in-patient in the INPUT Pain Management Programme.

The programme would give me great succour in the form of skills and knowledge and fellow pained people to empathise with, and most of all, belief. It would also cause another severe relapse, when I overdid it in the occupational therapy portion; as ever, and as complex PTSD attests to, attempts to feel better are not unmarred by trauma in themselves.

'Why haven't you been in a rehab centre for the past four years?' asked the first GP I went to in London, stunned as she realised how bad my pain really was, after I'd come to her for painkillers, then come back to tell her the levels had not been significantly decreased. Relapse levels were ten out of ten, and I had not had any way of preventing constant relapses. She immediately put me on the pain management programme waiting list and gave me the largest possible dosage of gabapentin for neuropathic pain. I had been begging for a healthcare professional to understand better, to put me in a regular, proper course of treatment, rather than sporadic help, for four years (help from the outside would continue to consist of medication from this point on, management of the day-to-day being my own responsibility).

What the clock took was those four years, and the five years after where acute pain has been so frequent, and so dismissed and minimised, that my heart swirls with a constant hum of threat. These days, undergoing intensive hypnotherapy for c-PTSD, I wake up, joke around with my fiancé, text GIFs to friends, and work, with the persistent anxiety that pain, and disbelief of acute pain, is around the corner, or is already present.

What built up Big Ben broke down my bodymind. And it was through rainforest trees.

What I mean by that is that the Dutch East India Company, the world's first proto-megacorporation, one enacted by the Dutch Kingdom, took a giant archipelago hostage and has never truly given it back. Has opened it up to more and more theft. What I mean is that our rainforests were and are shipped to Europe, and our peoples were and are murdered, assaulted, exiled, for 'resources' from those forests, all those rainforests ground down to furniture in Amsterdam, and burnt to the dirt to make way for palm oil plantations that spike our ramen, shampoo and moisturisers. And among those peoples violated, who remain inseparable from 'nature' (and we'll get to that designation later), are Javanese cultures I come from, where we have disabled gods.

And where once, in the cool shade of the trees, disabled Javanese people were revered as spiritually important. Until

Dutch missionary hospitals, built with the rainforest trees. Institutions that introduced and violently enacted colonial ableism, a universalist medical model that ignored the uncultured masses with our indigenous genders and sexualities, with our ways of understanding healing, our own kings and kingdoms and our own power struggles, our own inequities but never to this gargantuan scale, these genocidal centuries, these over two hundred years of literal enslavement of peoples from the Indonesian archipelago, of slave adults. Of slave children.

This violence that disabled millions of villagers, with guns pointed at us, their wood made from the rainforest trees. Guns placed these newly disabled in a world where this way of being was no longer widely held as sacred. But where the status quo was horrific. That was the 1600s, and this is today, and the rainforests are swallowed by palm oil plantations – trees planted in service of environmental destruction and climate change, which is why I balk at 'plant trees' as a catch-all environmental phrase.

These tree-upheavals that created and create megacities, a breath away from bursting with consumerism, propped up with Jakarta's hundreds of malls.

The trees taken from rainforests follow the centre-periphery model European colonialism created. What is taken goes to a core that sucks the life out of all other worlds.

I despise the word 'resources', the term 'natural resources' – we do not see other living systems and creatures as things to be used. In my Minang culture, from my mother's side, tigers are called 'inyiak', the term for grandparent, as we believe our ancestors come back in their form. How could we see 'nature' and 'culture' as separate?

There are over seven hundred remaining languages and cultures in the Indonesian archipelago that have survived brutal colonial capitalist heteropatriarchal ableism. Countless genocides. In every genocide, disabled communities. In every genocide, cosmologies of connection hunted to shadows.

As part of every genocide, the decimation of healing plants. Of systems of healing. An erosion of respect for the wisdom of indigenous elders. A killing and evicting of the elders, while the plants they worked with mourned in the sun, and await their own demise.

From an interview with Bayo Akomolafe in *Deutsche Welle*, quoted from in M. NourbeSe Philip's Poetry Society Lecture:

'What we rudely call "nature" today does not even have a name in Yoruba culture because there was no distinction between us and the goings-on around us,' Akomolafe says. The Yoruba religion of Ifa, he explains, sees a 'vitality' in the nonhuman world.

'Mountains could be consulted, trees could have privileges,' he adds.

And the word 'anthropocene' does not mean, to me, what it seems to mean to most of the Western world.

What indigenous communities around the world understand of anthropocene is the following, written by Indigenous scholar Zoe S. Todd and Heather Davis in 'The Importance of a Date, or Decolonizing the Anthropocene', themselves acknowledging that they take this from various indigenous communities around the world:

> The Anthropocene is not a new event, but is rather the continuation of practices of dispossession and genocide, coupled with a literal transformation of the environment, that have been at work for the last five hundred years. Further, the Anthropocene continues a logic of the universal which is structured to sever the relations between mind, body and land.

'Nature-ing', in this way, this artificial mental separation between mind, body and land, is part of the juggernaut of European and other colonial environmental destruction that led us to this moment. After and during many mass murders of people trying to protect their profound connection to and stewarding of their lands. These connections inherently include indigenous disabled peoples' non-separation from 'nature'.

Indigenous peoples, like all other 'marginalised' groups, or we who I prefer to call the majority world, contain within them much higher numbers of disabled people.

And how could we not? When our rivers are poisoned with mines' mercury tailings, leading to the mass disablement of infants and adults, when our pathways for herbal healing are stripped off the face of the earth, and when our access to that which sustains us is barred from us by evicting us from lands, including lands later designated as 'national parks'. When we do not know the soils our very medicine is taken from, when indigenous disabled people were very likely hurt and killed and certainly uncompensated in the process of pharmaceutical corporations' 'discovery' and capture of tenderly held indigenous medicines.

When indigenous peoples – once again repeated, and always – are the best caretakers of the planet, and the best hope for environmental and climate salvation.

We are that salvation. Yet the false separation of 'nature' and 'people' that colonialism continues to oppose sees us vilified, ridiculed, and dismissed by white and/or colonial environmental organisers who think Western scientific management is always best, and there is only one way to define and see nature: that which is separate from us.

The clocks imposed on an archipelago, the imperative to weekday-and-weekend and nine-to-five and twelve-solar-month our existences, and the brutal ways in which they were instituted, took from me so much disability justice infrastructure from my ancestral cultures. Cultures in which, instead of being violently assaulted on a sustained and regular basis by access fails and disbelief, I could have been cared for, deeply, given healing plants I am still only just learning the existence of.

I could have been a different bodymind. I do not want to be undisabled at this point; it has taught me too much, given me too much. What I want is not to suffer as a disabled person – this is possible; what prevents this is the gloved hand, the cloud above the rivers and the hospitals, and all the clocks, of colonial ableism.

If the rainforests had not been taken from us, and had the cores of core-periphery models not obliterated so much, continuing into the present, creating environmental crises and genocides that have already happened yet remain invisibilised in white neoliberal imaginations, I could have been spared much pain.

If healthcare systems were set up to believe us, to nurture us, so many of us could have been spared ungodly and regular pain.

When I rework my memory, realising I was not alone in that hospital, what I realise now is that the prayers of my loved ones on the other side of the world were with me, my father who repeats ad nauseam that 'brainwaves are non-local'.

And I have come from two lineages of defiant survival, without which, if their mitochondrial presence had not been inside me, I probably would not be here still. And in our languages, in the ways we love and commune, are persistent, surviving threads of indigenous disability cultures.

We Javanese, I only fully realise in adulthood as someone identifying as disabled, have disabled gods. I trace their stories and find interpretations that North American colleagues might call cripped.

My grandmother comes from a town in the Kendeng mountain region, where farmers have been protesting plans for government cement plant building for years – plans which would ruin local waters. Disabling people, hurting those already disabled, inextricable from the environment.

These protests have taken place in many forms, including what can be described as heartrending performance art: in which farmers, mainly women farmers, have travelled to the capital city of Jakarta and sat with their feet encased in literal cement in front of the Presidential Palace. These protests have managed to delay cement plant building, hopefully indefinitely. I think about coming from these waters, from and in kinship with these women, and my bodily pain is perceptively eased.

Through the haze of so-called psychological disorder – or what I prefer to think of as the absolute normal reaction to sustained bodily trauma – I return to the memory of being a woman so far from home in a hospital ward canteen. Looking out at Big Ben. Though appearing from the outside to be lone, just as I have appeared from the outside to be 'fine' over the past eleven years, even in level ten out of ten pain – as I have learned that it is dangerous to try to express my physical anguish in public, constantly misinterpreted, even threatened with calling the police – I realise now I was not by myself at all.

In reworking my memory of supposed loneness those three weeks, I remember I am not the colonial notion of the 'self'. I am always a 'we'.

I carry you with me, all the fellow pained and broken yet surviving bones of people stunned by repeated trauma, who know intimately how we are what happened to rainforests, and we form part of their whole, no matter how many miles away from the soils where they belong, no matter how many molecules of rainforest we are made to consume in our own bodies by the trade of palm oil plantations – built in rainforests' wake – in half of our groceries, by the consumption of electronic products built by cancer-causing ore mining.

Through what this society enables and coerces us to consume, we represent complicity in the disabling of people, and the harming of disabled people.

And we, the indigenous 'we's' that I am, that we are—our collectivity is what has persisted through aeons of disabled people's resistance.

It has always been urgent for us. Why is this moment urgent to white people only now? Don't past genocides count? Don't past innumerable, intertwined environmental collapses count? Doesn't Mannahatta turned into Manhattan count?

Why are the people just waking up to what indigenous peoples, disabled indigenous peoples, have been saying for five hundred years, dictating what this moment is, while erasing all that went before?

My bodymind was and is a reflection of multiple cosmologies and histories, language intertwined with cellular electricity. All of these ways for being in the world, for never being separate from 'nature', but a part of it, but a part of ways to protect a balance. All of these cosmologies humming an urgency over centuries.

We have our own timekeeping ways, our ways of reconciling pain and deep peace. I want to refer to a framework of time that is entitled Deep Peace, in many languages that are not English. In Deep Peace, disabled people are cherished, are deities like my own Javanese ones.

Though I do not know whether or not the Māori author Patricia Grace is disabled, her seminal 1986 novel *Potiki* renders indigenous community life, in opposition to 'development', one in which disabled people speak for themselves, are cherished, are spiritual. Despite a line in which a character calls upon the ableist trope of high intelligence 'making up for' his physical non-normativity, it is a notable example of writing in which there is no environmental justice without indigenous disability justice. An instance of Deep Peace in literature that I am hopeful there are many more examples of.

And if we throw open the years, there are innumerable stories – in oral literature as well as written – of Deep Disabled Peace, in which environmental justice begins and ends with us, and Western notions of a separate 'nature', often built upon (settler) colonial violence, are not the status quo. We can honour all the stories snuffed out, all the ones we will never know.

Once more remembering the woman in the hospital canteen, I continue to feel the loneliness of being a migrant here, forced to undergo extreme trauma in order to secure a place in a country where she hoped she would have better access to help. I moved to the UK not knowing how or if I would get help, and belief, but I hoped that through making art, belief would come. The truth is that belief and disbelief would and will continue to persist, and this is something I am learning to come to terms with, slowly. And where belief and help reside, the canopy of rainforests lost and dying grows, and I seek them.

The canopies of rainforest trees stilled and calmed the people I come from. And on a subatomic level, just as intergenerational trauma is kept in the DNA, the ancient memory of being calm, lying down as a green canopy stills the body from above, is inherent. I need to remember this, in the panic of shallow-breathing days, in the swell of bodily inflammation and the knifing of relapses.

Those of us who are not lone, but a 'we', disabled people of the majority world, need to remember that we remember all these trees, sheltering all the bloodlines we came from. These canopy memories are inside of us. We are but threads that weave them along.

I close my eyes and imagine the canopy of trees that calmed the bodies I come from – likely, other disabled bodies in the lineage – in the Kendeng mountain region, in the Tanah Datar region of West Sumatra, in Banten, in the Middle East where my grandfather has heritage. I imagine all the different waterways that calmed them; lakes, rivers, oceans that carried Chinese, Gujarati and Arab traders to the Indonesian archipelago, that intermingled so many waves of migration to those islands. There are visible traces of all these communities in the faces of my family, in their skin and bones, in mine.

I think about indigenous disabled people of the past, being barefoot on soil, listening to the trees and moving through a listened-to world, seeing bark towering over them in a seen world, bathing ourselves communally in spring waters, taking what we need of the rainforests, of the soil, farming the land, only in ways that are reciprocal with everything around us. This is a divine intelligence of interdependence, experienced in every sensorial realm.

However loud the clocktowers, the canopies sensed inside us are not cowered, not intimidated, they flow and centre and want to bring us to equilibrium.

No matter how stuck we may seem to be in harmful Western medical models of disability, of harmful institutions of so-called care, of harmful visual tropes of disabled bodies and who we are supposed to be, we must remember these traces. No, firmer things than traces – anthropologist Ann Laura Stoler refers to what colonialism continues to do in the present day as marks, not traces, of what was instituted hundreds of years ago. The opposing forces to these marks must be just as indelible.

Despite the ravages of colonial extractivism, these cosmologies must enable a sense memory in us as descendants of disabled people – for everyone, everywhere, must have disabled antecedents – who felt nurtured, who felt calmed, by the other-than-human. Who understood that our humanity cannot be comprehended as an entity outside of everything else.

I leave the canteen, and go to rest.

Foraging and Feminism: Hedge-Witchcraft in the Twenty-First Century

Alice Tarbuck

I am in the kitchen, counting out rosehips. It is dark outside, and my partner and I keep forgetting ourselves with cross words. It is early December, but already, a star in the window is shedding glitter onto the windowsill. On the kitchen work surface, a Kilner jar is open, and I am counting out wizened red beads for tea. The rosehips (useful for 'all catarrhal, bronchial disorders') have been air-dried until leathery.[1] Against most advice, they haven't been shredded: the seeds and their infinite tiny hairs have not been sifted and separated. Keeping them whole is easier, and, if you're willing to steep them longer, they still release huge quantities of vitamin C. With honey and ginger, they're delicious and comforting.

These rosehips were never supposed to be picked. Three of us went out after dark, no torches, onto the cycle path behind my friend's house. The lighting there is motion-sensitive: designed to aid cyclists and deter malingerers. In the six o' clock gloom of winter, the tarmac path stretched away in both directions, fading into black. There was a lot of giggling: nervousness and a feeling of transgression as the occasional cyclist zipped past. Picking by touch, we tore our hands up, probably dropped more onto the path than we did into Tupperware, eventually picked the remainder off by the light of a phone. Then we scurried home, drank wine by the fire, and felt brave and united.

Foraging is hardly a secret activity. In Scotland alone, there are a huge number of foraging courses, walks, group workshops. So popular has it become that Scotland is now promoted as a destination for foraging: Visit Scotland invites the tourist to 'get your hands on these rich pickings of Scottish foraging' in order to participate in the foraging 'renaissance in restaurants and homes'.[2] *The Scotsman* newspaper published a guide to foraging in Scotland in 2015, complete with recipes.[3] Even Scottish National Heritage encourages foraging as a means of engaging with wild Scotland, writing that 'a growing interest in fresh, seasonal and local food is leading to a revival of wild-harvesting and foraging for ingredients for the table'.[4] This increase in popularity is so great that the *Guardian* reported it, in 2009, in terms of a gold rush: 'The Forestry Commission estimates that wild harvesting, including harvesting lichens and mosses for natural remedies and horticulture, is worth as much as £21m a year'.[5] This rapid growth comes, of course, with its own difficulties, and has led the Forestry Commission to 'promote wild foods with a code of good practice, to ensure the increasing number of foragers harvest carefully and, where needed, with the landowner's permission'.[6]

So foraging is back. Concerns about ethical food consumption, particularly in terms of global transportation and the working conditions of pickers, have spurred individuals to look locally for their food. This resurgence of interest is also, of course, a reaction to urban living, often without adequate green spaces or gardens. Feeling separated from nature, and from the processes of production, has led many people to look once more at what surrounds them. There is also an undeniable cachet to foraging: wild food has become a fashionable commodity. It can be, and indeed is, bought by restaurants at great price, albeit stripped of a certain authenticity. To have been outside, to have got your hands dirty, to own and use something that money can't buy: in a late-capitalist culture, that is prized indeed.

If gathering one's own wild food is not only popular and widespread, but also marketable, then why did we find it so thrilling? What on earth possessed us to do at night what perfectly rational people do on weekends, with rattan baskets and Barbour jackets? It didn't feel like foraging, at least not in the ways that Scottish National Heritage and the *Guardian* describe. Which is not to say, of course, that we were doing anything particularly radical, or extraordinary, or that forgetting a torch earns you some sort of brownie points. But, disclaimers aside, what we did that night felt different. Trump was about to be elected. Britain had voted to leave the EU. Scotland was negotiating, once again, to have its voice heard. We were all scared – we are all still scared. We are young women, attempting to forge careers and lives and to think around big questions while the world swings rapidly to the right. Stealing out at night felt like an act of resistance, an act of seizing hold of the world and using it for ourselves. That we could go out, pick rosehips, which we knew the name, shape and qualities of, and then take them home, dry them and use them felt like an incredible gift. Really, it felt quite a lot like magic.

It feels quite a lot like magic that I can write this at all, in fact. Gathering herbs and plants for medicines, sharing them with friends, writing about it for essay collections, all requires a huge amount of freedom, autonomy and education. After all, for a considerable period in Scotland's history, gathering herbs for medicine or magic, as a woman, could be a serious offence. On 27 January 1591, not far outside Edinburgh, Agnes Sampson was tried as a witch, based on confessions extracted under torture. The list of accusations against her was staggering. Among them, that she 'healed by witchcraft Johnne Thomsoune in Dirletoun, though he remained a cripple' and that she 'cured Johnne Peiny in Preston by prayer and incantation'.[7] Most probably, she used herbs and plants gathered from the surrounding countryside.

Agnes Sampson was a midwife and local 'wise woman'. She offered counsel and natural medicine to those in her community who could not afford extortionate doctor's fees. Such women (and indeed, men) whose presence had been part of village life for centuries, came under attack during the professionalisation of medicine in the sixteenth century. 'Wise women and their medicines', historian Andrew Wear writes, 'were often scoffed at by professionally trained doctors, nearly always male, who were anxious to protect their professional status'.[8] The skills of wise women and other local healers were minimised and dismissed, but their trade did not diminish. Many of their practices have since been debunked by contemporary medicine, such as widespread adherence to the 'doctrine of signatures', the belief that 'natural objects that looked like a part of the body could cure diseases that would arise there'. However, many of their cures were effective. As Wear notes, they included 'many naturally occurring ingredients that are medically useful'.[9] So, when the dismissal of wise women failed to work, it was easier to vilify them.

It is not much of a step, after all, to suggest that healing skill is not healing at all, but witchcraft. Agnes Sampson would have foraged, gathering what she needed from hedgerows to heal those who came to her. For this, she was forced to wear the Witch's Bridle, an iron headdress with four metal spikes that were inserted into her mouth so that speaking pierced her tongue and cheeks. She had all of her body hair shaved off by male interrogators in an attempt to find her 'witches' mark', and after several days of torture, confessed to being in league with the devil, and gave the names of others who were as well. She was, of course, only one of a huge number of women who were put to death during the witch trials of Scotland.[10]

The resurgence of foraging glosses over these historical connotations with witchcraft, precisely because foraging is now primarily associated with food. Access to free, reliable medicine has overturned the need for home remedies, and indeed even these can be bought in 'alternative therapy' shops, dispensed by experts. Foraging, at least as portrayed in the mainstream media, is a middle-class leisure pursuit, rather than a matter of survival. And while it is fun to make wild garlic pesto, or to stew windfall apples, or to make elderflower cordial, it is impossible to pretend that these activities do not have historically gender- and class-based implications.

There are, however, projects and individuals who are broadening perspectives on foraging and respecting its nature as a historical practice. The Rhynie Woman collective, Debbi Beeson and Daisy Williamson, is based in the North East of Scotland, and is engaged with promoting awareness of regional heritage through foraging practices. A recent project for Deveron Arts, 'Cooking the Landscape', saw them 'utilising foraging, honouring local food, traditional recipes and celebrations – to create a platform which promoted dialogue, skill sharing, and the exchange of ideas'.[11] Rhynie Woman collective does not just forage: they engage with historic, local practices around gathering and preparation. By acknowledging the traditions that surround them, they are better able to understand foraging as a situated practice, and one that can enrich knowledge of local heritage. For the 'Cooking the Landscape' project, they took as a guiding quotation Michael Pollan's statement that 'the shared meal elevates eating from a mechanical process of fuelling the body to a ritual of family and community, from the mere animal biology to an act of culture'.[12] By re-introducing the idea of gathering, preparing and eating food as ritual practice, Rhynie Woman is able to explore and honour foraging traditions.

Indeed, there is something mystical, magical about their foraging and cooking. They pose questions about wild foods and hospitality: 'what does it say of the host when served stinging nettles for tea; hidden inside a cream cake, their threat to sting one's tongue still present, lurking'.[13] Stinging nettles here are not being recognised for their culinary, or medicinal use, but rather for their symbolic potency. To eat a stinging nettle is to suffer pain, to be scolded for speaking out of turn, perhaps. It has the feeling of a punishment, or a curse – or even an echo of the Witch's Bridle. Of course, the true benignity of nettles – excellent for cleansing the blood – is here less important than their folkloric, symbolic impact. There is also the ripple of distrust that still spreads, even hundreds of years after Agnes Sampson's trial. 'What does it say of the host?' they ask: can we trust women who pick wild nettles not to hurt us, not to harbour and harness strange, wild power?

This strange, wild power might be frightening to those who eat the nettles, but it is important for those who gather them. I am aware, as I sort herbs or learn about mushrooms, or read a friend's tarot, that perhaps what I am primarily interested in is power. Power against the constant, disempowering experience of being a woman. Power against catcallers, rapists, presidents who believe that sexual assault is acceptable. Power to see the future, or help a cold, or ease the winter blues, precisely because I have so little power in other areas. My tinctures will not break glass ceilings; my spells will not help women get the abortions they need, or equal pay, or anything else. But foraging in hedgerows and doing small magic with friends who I love feels empowering. It is like holding a secret in the warmth of your ribcage, and letting it glow right through you. And I am braver, I think, because of it. Because I am part of a community of strong women, finding ways to make ourselves powerful. I am braver in interviews, in meetings, in pitching for articles and negotiating boundaries. It is not in the least surprising that as the world seems to swing to the right, as the days seem to grow darker, that women are turning back to hedgerow magic, to attempting forms of community and ritual as part of working out how to fight back, how to remain empowered.

There are some places in Britain where hedge-magic and foraging for healing has never really gone away. In Cornwall, a strong tradition of Paganism and wise women persists. Cassandra Latham-Jones, for example, is the village wise woman of the Cornish village of St Buryan.[14] She offers a range of services, from creating charms with natural ingredients to counselling individuals who need help. Latham-Jones is a celebrant, tarot reader and witch. In a filmed interview for the Open University's 'Religion Today' course, the camera follows Latham-Jones as she walks through the Cornish countryside, identifying plants to create a protection spell. Down-to-earth and entirely practical about her magic, Latham-Jones refers to herself as a 'village witch', because it is the 'most relatable term', and says that she is asked about similar things that witches were asked about centuries ago: health, careers, romance.[15] Latham-Jones is dressed in black, and wears a black hat. She lives in a stone cottage, is married to a woman, and openly practices magic. In many ways, she is the epitome of otherness, and yet she exists amid a community, serving their needs. Whether or not this community has an uneasy relationship with Latham-Jones is not discussed: the documentary and her website focus on the positive aspects of her practice. Latham-Jones does not conform to heteronormative ideals of femininity: she wears no makeup, wears masculine clothing and her magic does not relate to the domestic. She lives outside societal expectations and is frank about the difficulty of making a living with her work. While she may not, therefore, be a traditional role model, she is nevertheless a very appealing figure. She is clearly passionate about her work, and feels empowered to live a life in accordance with her own desires and virtues, rather than those of society. Latham-Jones is an important figure in terms of the reassociation of foraging with magic, and in terms of situating it historically. She is testament to the fact that foraging has been a traditionally female practice, associated with ritual and magic, not simple a leisure pursuit or interesting hobby.

By deliberately revitalising understanding of foraging as a radical, historically dangerous act, associated with arcane female knowledge and power, we can understand its potential as a feminist practice. Information about the landscape has, since the professionalisation of botany during the Victorian period, been primarily written and distributed by men. Male writers such as Tim Dee and Robert Macfarlane have spearheaded the current resurgence in nature writing over the past decade. Their approach to the natural world is that of the scientist or explorer: travelling through and documenting what is seen. While, of course, bodily engagement with the landscape in these books is inevitable; there is no sense of engaging with the land in terms of what it produces. Picking berries, learning about the properties of different plants is secondary to the more scholarly concerns of the area's history and geography. Narrative immersion in landscape is engaging, and necessary in order to draw attention to our current environmental crisis, but the new nature writing can often be self-centred. A journey across mountains is, more often than not, related as a journey of self-discovery. This self-discovery is interesting and informative, but it obscures landscape as a site of plenty and bounty. Instead, it turns the focus back onto the male author and his adventuring.

Although she does not discuss foraging, Scottish nature writer Nan Shepherd, whose face was recently put onto the Scottish five-pound note, radically refigures traditional nature writing tropes in her book *The Living Mountain*. Rather than walking through hills as an observer, Shepherd 'a localist of the best kind', seeks to communicate her 'acute perception' of the Cairngorm range.[16] Rather than walking 'up' the mountains, she walks instead 'into' them. Dissolving the ego, Shepherd seeks to be absorbed into the landscape, to understand it not through the accretion of knowledge but through direct haptic experience. She wishes to see, and become, the mountain at the same time. Described by Macfarlane as a 'part-time mystic', interested in esoteric religions and Zen Buddhism, Shepherd has a quality of 'otherness'. Not logical but emotional, not academic but perceptive, she is described in similar terms to wise women such as Latham-Jones. Rejecting an objective approach to her surroundings, she instead favoured immersion, intuitive understanding and repeated visits. The mountains, for Shepherd, were animate, and rather than learning about them, they taught her. This interest in walking, her enjoyment of isolation, the fact that she did not marry, all indicate an otherness that seems to be held in common with other 'mystic' women. Any choice that removes them from the dominant cultural narratives and expectations placed upon them imbues these women with a sense that they are dangerous, somehow. They are the hostesses who might, perhaps, serve nettles.

So I stand in the shadow of all of these women. I do not face persecution like Agnes Sampson: I do not have as much knowledge as Cassandra Latham-Jones. But I feel that any woman who decides to step outside what is demanded of her owes a debt to witches, to wise women, to women who walk alone in the hills. So I am learning, from encyclopaedias, from Tumblr, from friends and family. It does not matter if what I am doing is mostly nonsense, entirely nonsense, or not nonsense at all. What matters is that foraging connects me to the land and to friends, takes me outside, makes me look. Learning about the plants that grow around me, and how they might be used, lets me walk through my city with my eyes open. Preparing teas and drying herbs and burning red candles gives me a sense of power. Perhaps it is an illusion, or perhaps it is busy-work, or perhaps I really am doing magic. The three of us felt so alive picking rosehips. Alive is how I want to feel, how rootling around in bushes or setting my intentions makes me feel. Feeling connected to the seasons, to the natural world, to the rhythms of growth and decay is helpful, grounding, reminds us that we are not alone on earth. There is beauty and bounty around us, if we look for it, and perhaps that is all the magic we need. Or perhaps, what we need is real magic, whether that comes in the form of resistance and community or the form of blackthorn charms and skullcap tinctures, and howling up at the moon.

Birdwoman V

A Quince in the Hand

Nic Wilson

I've fallen out with autumn this year. I know the world outside my bedroom window is changing, turning, ripening, but it's leaving me behind. In the last few weeks, I've managed only a short walk with stops along the way and made it down to the garden twice for a catch-up natter with the chickens. The rest has passed in a fog of pills and powders, meals on trays, long naps, *MasterChef* binges and all-too-brief reading sessions. As far as I'm concerned, autumn can do one.

For a while, I wasn't even aware that a new season had started without me. My attention was too inwardly fretted, too finely tuned to mounting pain levels, the ringing in my ears, the heaviness of my head and wobble in my legs on each trip to the bathroom. I still feel I'm living out of sync, in a sensory Groundhog Day. When the wind gusts outside my bedroom window, I watch the trees swaying above the rooftops, the clouds scudding past. Inside, I feel only a numb kind of stasis. When it rains, I ask my husband to open the windows as wide as they'll go. I want the aftertaste of claggy earth in my mouth, dampness creeping up my sleeves. I want to be out planting bulbs or sheltering under the meadow oak or picking apples. I want to feel autumn in my bones. Rain splashes on the sill and puddles in the mouldy corners, but the air in the room remains stale and still.

Sometimes I feel well enough to help the kids with their homework or chat for a while as they snuggle up next to me in bed. Mostly, I doze the hours away. On good days I manage a little work, laptop balanced on my knees, books strewn across the duvet. But family commitments and deadlines nag and worry me. It's been nearly six weeks now (the longest I've ever been confined to bed) and I feel a little less optimistic on every exhausted awakening.

Today's challenge is an appointment with the out-of-hours GP. I'm not good with hospitals, but the doctor is mercifully kind and gentle, and we return with antibiotics and appointments for follow-up tests. As our car pulls into the drive, I notice a quince dangling over the green roof of the bin store. It has shed its fuzzy coating surprisingly early and ripened to a lustrous canary yellow. I ease myself out of the passenger seat and go over to take a look. Sure enough, when I cup it, lifting and turning, there is a soft snap and its weight settles in my hand. It seems to mark a transition, either for me or the garden, or both. A moment of reconnection that releases time from the pages of my diary, disentangles it from online shopping lists, medical appointments and the kids' term dates. Autumn made flesh.

At the bottom of the stairs I cradle my harvest against my chest with my left hand, gripping the banister with my right, half-willing, half-hauling myself up and back to bed with that familiar sinking sense of relief. Sitting propped up against my pillows, I balance the pear-shaped fruit on my palm. It seems a proxy for all the subtle shifts I've missed this year – the blueberry foliage flushing red along the leaf veins, dew lying on the grass a little longer each morning, early frosts lacing the garden spiders' webs. A reminder of the seasonal rhythm of life.

The skin of the quince feels firm and waxy. It has an ochreous tideline around its summit where tufts of downy hair have not quite rubbed away. When I raise it to my nose, I catch a hint of apple sauce and honey, but it hasn't begun to revel in its own juices yet. If I'm well enough to harvest the rest of the crop in a week or two, I'll stand the quinces to attention in the understairs cupboard, each slightly socially distanced from its neighbour to prevent rotting, and the aroma will develop as the fruits mellow and ripen. Every time I open the cupboard door to toss in the recycling or hunt for the broom – and maybe a few times with no other reason than to inhale autumn – I'll be engulfed in that familiar hug of apple-scented Turkish delight.

I'd wanted to grow this quirky fruit for years, to add to my collection of Chilean guavas, honeyberries, Cape gooseberries and miniature mulberry. Unfortunately, our modest-sized garden was already bursting with top fruit: an 'Opal' plum and 'Cambridge Gage', a patio cherry, and espalier and cordon apples. Where would we find room for another tree? I considered planting a Japanese quince with those rock-hard, jelliable fruits, but the thorns put me off. After all, I'd just rehomed an 'Invicta' gooseberry with a friend, potting it up and sending it away in disgrace after it tore at my trousers once too often.

But you only live once, *carpe diem* or perhaps *carpe fructum*, so I decided to chance it and add a quince tree to the dry front garden. I bought 'Meech's Prolific', an old American variety, tempted by the promise of eponymous abundance. It shot up behind the lavender and Russian sage, a dishevelled youth with sprawling branches and leaves that had a tendency to wilt in hot weather, unlike its drought-tolerant Mediterranean companions. We watered it regularly, and I wondered if I'd pushed the 'right plant, right place' maxim a little too far with this one. It would require an impressive feat of imagination to describe the soil in our front garden as deep, fertile or moisture-retentive. Friends growing quinces in their small gardens regaled me with horror stories of barren trees, blossom that failed to set and problems with splitting fruit. I watched over our tree and secretly hoped, while bracing myself for a quince-less future.

In mid-April of that first year, raspberry-ripple buds unfurled into elegant goblets of blossom. Ruthlessly, I removed all the setting fruit to give the tree time to establish strong, deep roots. Somehow a few escaped (okay, I wasn't that ruthless – I couldn't bear to pinch out all those quinces-in-waiting). Eleven tiny nubs furred with white hair began to swell and I counted them every morning, my heart beating faster when I lost one, until I spotted it hidden among the foliage. By late September they were flushing yellow and I watched the receding fuzz-lines, marking off the days until harvest. My initial apprehension mellowed into a relaxed complacency. The quinces were on the cusp. My first harvest was almost in the trug.

Wednesday 5 October that year began much like any other mild autumn morning. Returning from the school run, I stopped in the front garden to do the daily quince count, unaware that I'd entered a crime scene. One of our quinces was missing. It didn't take me long to find the discarded fruit, flung aside in the flowerbed under the dogwood, bearing two distinctive sets of teeth marks that might have betrayed the perpetrator if I'd had access to INTERPOL's dental database. Prime suspect was the guy who'd posted the pizza menu through our letterbox the previous afternoon. Perhaps he felt a bit peckish at the end of a long leafleting round and just fancied one of those large, juicy pears hanging conveniently low on the tree beside the drive. Clearly, I wasn't the only one surprised by the crime. His first and only bite would have assaulted his teeth and stung his tongue, no doubt causing him to cast the astringent victim to the ground in disgust. Thus, our first quince met its unfortunate demise. I hope it put pizza guy off scrumping for life.

I picked the remaining fruit with great reverence and thought of Julieanne, a gardening friend from Twitter, whose growing year had ended in disappointment. In August she'd posted episode three of Quince Watch on her blog:

'Back in July, I was very excited to have nine quincelets on my quince tree. I was seeing quince jelly in my future. All was rosy. Alas, my dreams have been crushed. Or more to the point, blown away by the recent high winds. The above photograph is of the last quinces to fall . . .'

The sorry image shows two wasted brown husks in the palm of her hand. Knowing this could so easily have been me, I picked out a couple of my most handsome quinces and parcelled them up for Julieanne. Wrapping such unwieldy fruit was a challenge, but they were duly delivered to the post office and, a few days later, she emailed to acknowledge receipt of a package containing 'the fragrant delight of two quinces.'

A Quince in the Hand

Eleven had become eight, and I began rifling through my books for recipes on what turned out to be a fruitless search. Modern cooks seem to overlook the quince. I had to reach back through the centuries to find a time when this aromatic fruit was a common ingredient in puddings and preserves. John Parkinson, Royal Botanist to Charles I, lists six varieties in his study of plant cultivation, *Paradisi in Sole Paradisus Terrestris* (1629) and, in *The English Husbandman* (1613), Gervase Markham suggests storing quinces on their own 'because their sent is so strong and piercing, that it will enter into any fruit, and cleane take away his naturall rellish'. In *The Well-Kept Kitchen* (1615), as well as advising housewives in matters of religion, temperance, dress sense and their knowledge of gardening, Markham includes instruction in the art of making quince cake, preserve, paste and pie. In the mid-nineteenth century, Eliza Acton continues the tradition with recipes for quince juice, custard and marmalade, while Isabella Beeton's 1861 recipe for quince jelly is the one we use in our kitchen today. We also poach them in a cinnamon cooking liquor or stew them with apples, which adds sweet floral undertones.

In the past few years we've had dozens of quinces, but the tree has always required more watering than I've been comfortable with and I wonder about its future as we transition to a more drought-resistant garden in the face of escalating climate change. I've started to suspect the quince tree's days might be numbered, but each time I consider taking it out, something stops me – the offering up of those spring blossom-cups, memories of our first harvest, the tumble of fruits that keep coming despite its less-than-ideal planting position.

I feel responsible for the quince tree, busy making the best of its poor, dry soil. It hasn't given up and I admire that. Perhaps I see a bit of myself in the tree. Damage to my small intestine from coeliac disease means my body isn't always able to work at optimum capacity either. It doesn't absorb nutrients as effectively as it should and, as a result, I struggle with bouts of fatigue and infection. Last week was particularly grim. I'd come close to despair, fearful that the lethargy keeping me from the woods, the chalk streams, the meadows and the garden had become the new normal, when a friend pointed out my own resilience. It was a timely reminder. Exhaustion, pain and anxiety had made it hard to see past the next few hours. My body and mind felt too bent out of shape, too disconnected from the future to imagine a way forward.

But sitting here now, weighing up the quince in my hand, I feel in touch with the world's turning. I look over the notes I've been writing about the tribe of house sparrows that chunter and bicker in the honeysuckle and realise how much I've progressed from a few days ago when even sitting up in bed was too much of an effort. Reflected in the still-ripening quince, I see my own slow returning.

Autumn has not been kind to our garden; my fatigue has been its misfortune too. Dahlia 'Con Amore' languishes in the pot by the front door, its crimson flowers all sulky and shrivelled – how could I expect my husband to water it when he was flat out working and looking after me and the kids? Mexican fleabane daisies are romping away in the gravel path, but they died in the dust-dry soil of the green roof, and the last raspberries softened and dropped unnoticed to the ground in the fruit cage. But somehow our quince tree has survived the neglect. More than that, it's thriving. Though no one's watered it for weeks, the leaves look green and healthy, and there's a bumper crop on the way. Perhaps next summer, on the pathway to climate disaster, drought will return and our harvest will suffer. But right now my first quince of the season with its fuzzy tufts and nascent scent seems a fruity affirmation of life, and I feel like I'm holding resilience in my hand.

Birdwoman VI

Moorland

Climbing Against Gravity: on Mountaineering and Genetic Haemochromatosis

Kerri Andrews

Being in my body is a gift. It carries me to high places where my soul sings and there is nothing in the world but the rightness of me. Standing on top of Brown Knowe in the Scottish Borders on a viciously cold, but sunny-as-summer day in early spring, I'm exhilarated. I can see the Eildon hills above Melrose, with snow-clad Cheviots lurking behind. Over my shoulder is the high ground above the Ettrick and beyond into the Southern Uplands, hill upon hill upon hill. The Tweed winds enchantingly below. I am above and among, here and there. My body brought me here, and my mind roams the panorama, relishing every moment in this high place.

The climb was long but steady, ascending the ancient Minchmoor Road above Yarrowford, supposedly used by English kings centuries ago when they felt like invading Scotland. The road today was grassy and benign, soft as only new growth can be, and it is hard to imagine it battered by soldiers' feet, churned up by horses and wagons. Did the English invaders thrill at the considerate gradient as I do, or did they inwardly groan at the prospect of another climb in this bastard hilly place that not even the Romans could hold convincingly? It must have been bleak for them as they reached the pass below Brown Knowe, with miles of moorland in front of them, and yet more hills to climb after that – and then the prospect of battle and death. The moorland means something different for me: it means freedom, and it means homecoming. I belong up here among the curlew calls where skylarks jostle for airspace above the newly greening grass.

I have loved climbing hills and mountains for a long time. Seven or eight years ago this love was heading into something like mania as I climbed something every free weekend I had, racking up the Scottish Munros by the fistful. The tiredness crept up on me. Who wouldn't be tired, climbing ten mountains in a weekend? Sleepiness seemed a reasonable response, though I was disconcerted to find it was beginning to happen in the week, too, long after my limbs had recovered. The urge to close my eyes, when it struck, was overwhelming, and I would wake on the sofa hours after I had sat down. I noticed no pattern, though, and my attention dwelt elsewhere.

The joint pain was an old friend, its appearance, shape and intensity as familiar as my walking rucksack, where I kept a stash of painkillers – some of them quite strong. But didn't everyone do that? Didn't everyone's knees get battered coming down big uncompromising mountains with names like Sgùrr a Mhàim which, with no Gaelic, I thought was pronounced 'Maim'. Given how my legs felt after coming down it I thought it was the most aptly named mountain in Scotland. I'd had joint pain ever since I first found the hills in the Yorkshire Dales at the end of my PhD at Leeds, a persistent ache in my knees that never went away, though it never got worse, either. I learned to take ibuprofen before and during my walking trips to keep the edge off, though diclofenac and naproxen made occasional appearances when the pain waxed stronger.

The palpitations had been with me for years before that since I had started at university at eighteen. The first time I experienced them, I thought I was going to die. It felt like my heart had literally stopped. It was very frightening. I was sent to the hospital at Leicester for an ECG. It, like all the subsequent ECGS, scans, x-rays I would have over the years, showed absolutely nothing wrong with my heart. Doctor after doctor shrugged their shoulders and sent me on my way. This pain, this discomfort, this sensation that my heart was about to stop or explode or both – this was my body. This was the body I took into the high hills. This was the body that took me to places that felt more homely than home. There was nothing wrong with it. There was something wrong with me.

It was summer in 2015 when Stuart, Adam and I set off to climb Beinn Mhanach, a remote Munro north of Crianlarich in the Southern Highlands. The route heads up a beautiful glen with a bonny river that we had to cross and recross. I remember the pleasure of taking my shoes and socks off and wading through the water barefoot, the cold sharp and shocking, but wonderful too. We walked along the track for miles, right up to the mountain's feet. There we left the river behind, planning to head straight up the hillside to the summit, half a vertical kilometre above us. This was not my preferred way of climbing a mountain – abruptly and brutally – but I'd been in the hills for months and was confident I was fit enough to manage.

We couldn't have climbed more than a few dozen metres before my heart felt like it had bolted out of my chest. My palpitations usually take the form of ectopic heartbeats, where my heart misses its usual beat, then does two close together. It is an eerie sensation, realising that your heart has not beaten. It is not painful, but it is one of the most unpleasant sensations I know. It used to scare me, but after having had so many of them and not dying, I figure I'll probably be OK (though I don't know for sure). On the rough hillside of Beinn Mhanach, though, I was experiencing what I know now is atrial flutter. My heart was beating ineffectively but very rapidly, the upper chambers contracting at up to 360 bpm. I felt dizzy and extremely out of breath, like I would never catch up to my heartbeat and be able to get enough oxygen to my body. I asked my companions to stop so I could rest and try to slow my cantering heart. After a few moments the fluttering eased, the dizziness passed, and I was able to stand again. Reluctant to retreat, I continued upwards. The symptoms returned within a few dozen metres more, and I had to stop again. Either through stubbornness or stupidity I continued up the hillside in crabbed stages, stopping each time my pulse became too irregular to bear any longer. Somehow I made it to the summit, though it had taken much longer than I expected and left me feeling quite ill. I remember walking slowly back down, some way behind the men, cursing my body. Retracing our outwards route the beautiful glen of the morning now seemed dreary and remote. The river was a nuisance, each crossing taking energy and time I didn't want to give. When we finally got back to the car, it was early evening and I felt so unwell I couldn't drive.

This episode sent me back to the doctor's, though I had decided not to bother talking to them again about my heart or my joints: I'd been told too many times that I must be consuming more caffeine than I realised, or that of course my joints hurt when I walked because I was fat, or that there couldn't be anything wrong because there was nothing on the scan/ECG/blood test. This time, though, was different. This doctor, a locum, took me seriously. He ordered a suite of blood tests including, I later learned, some rare ones. When the GP returned, he followed up on the test results, though he didn't understand them. He wrote to the haematologist at the local hospital to ask their advice. My bilirubin was high, and I had enlarged red blood cells: something was going on with my liver, and something was off with how my body was making its blood. The haematologist was stumped too, but this time the doctors didn't just shrug their shoulders. They kept taking blood and running tests, trying to narrow down what might be happening inside me. It made such a difference to be taken seriously, even as I googled myself into a panic about rare blood conditions and knackered livers. There *was* something wrong with my body. It wasn't just in my head.

The answer came unexpectedly. My mother had been ill in hospital with pneumonia, and the doctors had run a series of blood tests on her while she was there. These showed inflammatory markers way up, potentially indicating a lurking and undiagnosed cancer. Scans revealed no tumours, but finally a doctor saw the blood results and understood what they meant.

After she got out of hospital my mother called me. 'I've been diagnosed with genetic haemochromatosis. The doctors think you should get a test. I've told your sister, and she's going to take a test too.' I rang up my GP and told him about my mother's diagnosis. 'Could this be the reason for my weird blood results?' 'Yes, it could well be.' I was called in to the surgery for more tests, this time including the genetic test for haemochromatosis. I didn't have long to wait: the test was positive. I had haemochromatosis, with the genetic variation known as C282Y homozygous, which meant that I had two copies of a faulty gene that codes for a hormone crucial in the management of iron uptake in the body. While I was trying to take in what sounded like gibberish, the doctor also told me I had a high ferritin level and would need treatment. 'What's ferritin? How do you treat this?' I asked, the panic audible in my voice. For someone who studies the eighteenth century and adores historical fiction, the answer was suitably medieval. 'Blood letting,' the doctor said flatly.

For the next few months, getting to the hills was extremely difficult. A house move made life tricky for a while, though it brought me into the catchment of a GP surgery with a wonderful doctor with an unusual set of skills: he was qualified to carry out minor surgery, and he'd treated patients with haemochromatosis before. Once my new address was confirmed the medical appointments came thick and fast: with the gastroenterologist consultant at the Borders General Hospital; with nurses for blood tests; and eventually with my GP, who was to run my treatment for the next several months.

My body, I learned, had been absorbing more iron than it could use from the moment I was born. Most people have genes that regulate the production of hepcidin, a hormone that controls the absorption of iron from food in the gut. But I'd got two duff copies of the crucial gene, one inherited from my father, and one from my mother. The presence of these faulty genes meant that whatever iron was in my food my body took. This was only a bit more each day than my body needed to function, but it was always more, and the body has no way to excrete excess iron.

Iron is a crucial mineral: it plays a significant role in how oxygen moves through the body and is needed for healthy brain development in children. By the time I was diagnosed with haemochromatosis, though, iron had become for me a poison. Having run out of uses for it in my blood and muscles, and still receiving a little more every day than it needed, my body had begun laying down the spare iron in my tissues: in organs like my heart, and in my joints. My blood was stacked with iron, causing my blood cells to become enlarged in an attempt to cope with the excess. My body was literally saturated with it, and it had started to affect my brain. That's why I was getting so tired. The iron in my heart was why it had begun to flutter and falter. The iron in my joints was damaging too, leading to arthritis and pain. Each time I had walked up a hill, my body had been working not only against gravity but also the toxic effects of excess iron.

For some people with haemochromatosis the effects can be even worse. They can be fatal. Left untreated, the iron builds and builds, slowly poisoning the body to death. If enough is stored and your skin is white, the iron will become visible under your skin and you will turn bronze. You might lose sexual function, and your joints may well completely seize. Eventually you will develop liver disease, perhaps hepatitis, probably eventually, cancer. From there, with the poison still seeping in, the only outcome is death. Your body may well look like you've been abusing alcohol, and indeed before the genetic tests for haemochromatosis were developed in the 1990s, this is how the deaths of many people with the condition were quietly remembered by their families.

I know that I am lucky to be diagnosed so young, when most people don't find out until they are in their fifties or sixties. I know I am lucky to have iron stores in the midrange, rather than the sky-high rates I hear of in some of the sufferers' groups I find in the wilder reaches of Facebook. And yet I seethe with resentment and frustration at the years of missed opportunities for a correct diagnosis from doctors who looked at my body and blamed me for its malfunctions. I want to scream at them that

I am a mountaineer: this body that you dismissed as being fat and unworthy takes me skywards, despite the iron weighing me down; this wonky heart drives my legs over and over again even as it struggles for a rhythm with all that metal clinging to it; that I have learned how to manage the pain in my joints to keep on climbing against gravity and against others' expectations.

For all that defiance, my sense of myself in this body has changed. I am relieved to have answers, but I am frightened too by the prospect of having a condition that can never be cured and which, without regular management, would probably kill me. I am angry at the doctors who dismissed me and yet I am enormously grateful for the care and support I receive from my GP, who goes quickly from Dr Cormie to being Dr Paul – familiarity probably coming faster for me nearly fainting in his waiting room after a painful bloodletting.

We meet every two weeks for months, the ritual the same each time. A double appointment is booked for me by the receptionists, who also look after me when the doctor has finished. I'm called into the waiting room and lie down on the bed. Dr Paul gathers the equipment: tourniquet to partially stifle the blood flow in my arm; blood bag to collect the half litre that's to be taken off; sterile needle inside its protective casing; apparent masses of tubing. Dr Paul swabs the inside of my right elbow where there is a good vein – the only good vein, it turns out, in my body – and inserts the disturbingly large needle. By now there are multiple pinprick scars from previous insertions, a pixelated X marks the spot. I turn away before the needle arrives and pretend I'm somewhere else. I take deep breaths, the kind a labouring woman might as she's about to give birth, and I know even as I'm doing it that I sound ridiculous. But the performance helps me stay calm, and so long as the needle insertion doesn't hurt too much I know I won't feel ill afterwards. With the needle relatively comfortable in my arm, Dr Paul and I get to chatting as the blood pours down the tubes into the bag. I wiggle the fingers on my right hand to keep the blood moving and listen to Dr Paul talk about his daughters – both doctors – and his cycling – intrepid. It's not long before a fat, bulbous bag is filled, and

Dr Paul moves to clamp the tubes. He slides the needle out and a cotton wool ball is pressed on the entry site. The cotton wool is taped to my arm and then – CLANG – the bag is dropped without any ceremony at all into the bright yellow contaminates bin, ready for incineration. After the fainting episode I'm now allowed to stay in this room for a while, lounging on the bed, and the receptionist brings me a glass of water to replace some of the fluids I've lost. Once I feel OK, I get up, go to reception, and make another appointment for more of the same in two weeks. Then I go home where, in an hour or so, I will experience a completely overwhelming need to lie down on the sofa and sleep. This post-bleed fatigue will last for a few hours, and for the next several days I'll feel a bit off. It's why I'm finding it so hard to get into the hills.

Eventually, the bleeds take enough iron from my body that I am no longer considered to be overloaded. Instead, I am in what is called 'maintenance'. This is the state of healthy levels of iron that the doctors and I will try to maintain for the rest of my life. This is done through regular blood tests to monitor two key numbers: the ferritin level (the amount of a protein in my body bearing iron); and the transferrin saturation (the amount of iron being stored on the main iron-transporting protein in the body). Both should be below 50. This would be low for a normal person, but higher is unsafe for me. Once I'm in maintenance I'm allowed to donate my blood, which means no more dreadful clanging of my useless blood into a bin and much better snacks – though I miss Dr Paul. Lying on a donation bed in Edinburgh rather than my local surgery makes my ego glow, though the feeling is tempered by the thought that ScotBlood are doing at least as much for me by taking my blood as I am for anyone else.

Back on the top of Brown Knowe I've been in maintenance for four years. Having two babies is enormously helpful when it comes to using up iron in your body, and between the children and the occasional blood donation, I've been able to keep my iron levels even. Now it is postnatal unfitness that leaves me breathless, though the ascent really was humanely gradual for the most part.

It's been a while since I climbed this route, and I'd forgotten just how much I love the way the Minchmoor Road climbs the shoulder of the hill, contouring and winding its way up to the high pass. I'd forgotten too that the summit is quite such a distance from this pass, along the Southern Upland Way, and I'm fooled by not one but two false summits before the true top appears. It bears a modest cairn, some tatty fences and a tumbledown dyke, but it has enough beauty and panorama for a far loftier peak. I sit and eat my lunch with my back to the wall, drinking in the beauty of this place that my body has carried me to.

It's a wonderful walk from here, the route dipping and rising before contouring round a bleak lump of a rounded hill that makes my heart soar. The grass is soft, the views spectacular, and I feel as though I could walk like this forever. I revel in the strength of my body and am grateful to find that my joints are less painful as I push up the slope. It is sobering to think that without treatment I would be well into brain fog, exhaustion and worse by now. Instead, here I am on a hilltop in blazing spring sunshine, with mountain bikers sweeping past and waving cheery hellos. I'm here where my body – my mighty, mutant body – has brought me. I'm here where I most belong.

Endometriosis and the Female Trinity in the Peak District

Rowan Jaines

❦ I would prefer to write about the North Norfolk coast. That seastruck landscape defined my adolescence, in that place the white sand and grey sea is backdropped by coniferous pining and confirms my idea of myself as a subject outwith history. There is space to imagine my thoughts and actions – my personal identity – as a location of singularity and permanence in my life's narrative. In my mind's eye I can see myself striding across an empty winter Holkham beach, towards Brancaster in a muted palette that renders me the most real and fleshy element in my perception. Marram grass moves with the wind, the tide rolls in and out and time moves separately to me. My sense of self on the Norfolk shore appears as immutable, distinct from the biological processes that enfold me in my body – that is to say, my family history and non-personal future in the form of procreation. On these duney beaches the sea, sky and land all flow in an uncanny reflection of light. The whole landscape is a moon, a simile extended so far as to create a parallel surface on which my life's narrative might unfold as a tangent – spontaneous and dislocated from origin.

*

But this is wishful thinking. My own narrative can never be dislocated. My body, my sense of self and my relation to my own historicised identity has more in common with the site I find myself in, blown by the winds of chance, at this time of writing. The valleys and plateaus of the Peak District near Sheffield – known by the alliterative moniker the 'Lakeland Landscape' – is the site that for the past six years I have walked and thought, and the place where I have nurtured a relationship, a thesis, a puppy and a small allotment. This landscape, like myself, is organised around fault lines and fails to adhere to a singular character. Like me, it bleeds across boundaries. The moon here is not stretched across the landscape, but sits on high spreading her pearly light over the insuperably beautiful limestone face of Mam Tor. This moon on high appears to me as the unattainable apple that seeps through time, appearing first as loss and later, as desire.

The topological formation of this cluster of hills occurred through a slipping kind of reproduction that brings to mind female lineages. As the land slipped away from the eastern face of this region, this 'mother hill' and her children were formed from the restless shale that founds and grounds this landscape. As with motherhood in the negative perfect tense – these slippages and accretions hint at something negated that began in the past and stretches beyond this present moment. This place mirrors my life's trajectory in the form of an unreachable mother and an unachievable motherhood. Like the bracken that curls its fronds around the undulations of the Peak District, I am an invasive species and a fruitless one. As I walk through this landscape, the endometrial tissue that breaks the bounds of my uterus and binds its stipules around my pelvic ligaments bleeds in bright blooms of pain. These rosy fingers flowered too in my mother and grandmother's bodies and through this visceral pain, I find myself tethered to them as though by an umbilical cord, though their presence in my life has long been lost. The ancient Greeks referred to pain as a *dripping* because of the way it seems to relentlessly splash upon the same spot. I feel I understand this as I feel my own physical and psychic sufferings splash unceasingly upon the 'black lava' that the psychoanalytic writer Julia Kristeva describes as erupting from the ambivalent bodily identification between daughter and mother – that dangerous and generative byproduct that banjaxes time and logical (phallic) order.

🌱 In October 2019, I was diagnosed with endometriosis, the proliferation of gland-like tissue – similar to that which lines the womb – outside of the uterus. Endometrial tissue is cyclically stimulated and atrophied each month by a symphony of hormones and, in most cases, is released in a flux from the vagina during menstruation. In my body, however, this tissue grows along pelvic ligaments, and around the dark recesses of my bowel, where it waxes and wanes just like the tissue in my uterus but without an avenue of release, causing inflammation and the painful accumulation of blood. This tissue, once activated, can migrate and grow anywhere in the body and no matter where it grows, it creates uterine ecosystems complete with oxytocin and vasopressin receptors as well as oestrogen and progesterone receptors. I think of this not just as tissue that grows around my body, but rather as the creation of a myriad of miniature uteri. My immune response refuses to maintain the regular numbers of endometrial cells within genetically predetermined limits and it seems to me to aim to reproduce by spores rather than seeds. Bracken-like, my own fertility colonises the inner landscape of my body producing fronds rather than fruit, a human cryptogam; a womb that has no faith in its own privileged location as the site of genesis. This disease is highly heritable and its symptoms yoke me to a lineage of female pain, each of these miniature uteri that litter my body is gravid with the pain of the women who came before me.

As I put one foot in front of the other and look down at the dirt, the nettles, the tree roots, I find myself enmeshed, not only with these female forms but also with the landscape itself. Arthur Conan Doyle described the Peak District as hollow, and imagined striking it with a great hammer so that it would boom. I myself do not believe that the phallic force of a bludgeon is necessary to coax a sound from this place, which is not hollow but rather endometriotic in nature, riven with myriad miniature uteri. A rush could brush this place and it would tinkle like a thousand chimes. Indeed, Conan Doyle's misattribution of the endometriotic form of the Peak District as hollow – defined by lack and desiring of a priapic agential blow – coalesces with one of medicine's most enduring dogmas surrounding endometriosis, namely that the endometriotic body is a body in need of phallic input; in other words, impregnation.

The notion that pregnancy can suppress or even cure endometriosis is deeply embedded within the historical constructs that envelop the disease. The earliest antecedents of the pathology of endometriosis stem from ancient Egyptian gynaecological theories, later popularised by the Greco-Roman studies of Classical Antiquity in which the uterus was conceived of, not as an organ, but rather as an animal for whom conception and pregnancy was a *sine qua non*. Encoded within this biological pretext is the axiom of the necessity of marriage and motherhood for female wellbeing. In the absence of these socially prescribed roles, it was thought that the uterus would be deprived of its intended purpose and would wander through the body, wreaking havoc. Women of Classical Antiquity were usually married within a year of menarche, raising an average of six children, which in relation to the high rate of infant and child mortality indicates women spent a large portion of their reproductive years pregnant or breastfeeding. These culturally normative behaviours are likely to have functioned as a natural suppressant of endometriosis, and supported the idea that pelvic pain was triggered by stagnated and spoiled seed in the belly of the unmarried or infertile woman.

The dirty voluptuousness of female form appeared to take on malignant qualities in absence of impregnation and it was no great leap from the conception of female pelvic pain arising from putrid menstrual blood to the concept of endometrial tissue, and flux, as the host of demonic forces in the Middle Ages.

Endometriosis is still characterised as an occult phenomenon. The detection of this endometrial tissue remains beyond the powers of today's medical imaging technology as it is ghostly in its aspect, it has no real mass, only colour and thus does not show up on ultrasound. While **MRI** can pick up dense clusters of deep penetrating endometriosis, it cannot pick up smaller areas, which can cause as much pain and inflammation as some deep infiltrating lesions. The diagnosis of this disease can only be performed by invasive surgery, specifically a laparoscopy under general anaesthetic. As I awoke after my laparoscopic procedure in the autumn of 2019, I heard myself crying for my mother, an unconscious wading in the 'black lava' of my continued entanglement with my mother's absent body.

❦ My parents referred to me as the 'child who came too easily'. Like many women with endometriosis, despite pain and heavy bleeding with menstruation, my mother's fertility appears not to have been compromised in her early twenties. My mother described that upon deciding to cease the contraceptive pill, she discovered that she was pregnant with me – serendipity here appears as a hieroglyph for an accident, an act of god or chance. When I was eighteen months old, my mother experienced a late-stage miscarriage and this trauma was followed by years of infertility. In her trauma-soaked relationship with this daughter who came too easily, my mother regained a sense of her own early aggression towards her mother's body and split it from herself, transferring it onto me and, in doing so, continued a long-standing cycle. I have no access to my own infant aggression because I was drowning in her transferred lava, just as she before gasped for breath in the mire of my grandmother's infantile rage. She described to me later that she experienced my feeding as an act of violence on her body and felt that I had literally corrupted her insides. In this deadening rage, she created an external uterus to protect her from this destructive byproduct of maternal enmeshment. She purchased a bunk bed on which she placed me when I cried, removing the ladder – the birth canal – locking the door, splitting off her own pain and aggression through entombing my infant body in an empty womb.

I was seven when my sister was born. I remember clearly my shock at her body which was long and pink like a skinned rabbit. By this time my mother's conviction that I was the living embodiment of her split off pain and aggression was so strong that I was not allowed to touch the baby, lest I contaminate or destroy her, as my mother felt I had her own body. After this second child, my mother elected to have her uterus removed in order to free herself from the pain that I am now so familiar with. This hysterectomy was performed when I was eight years old, the same age at which my mother experienced menarche. Like a relay racer, I grabbed the baton and began a monthly cycle of vomiting and agonising stomach cramps, which kept my weight too low to menstruate and which the family doctor attributed to jealous hysteria over my infant sister's arrival. My pain further marked me out as a site of corruption in the family, the child who came too easily and destroyed my mother's fantasies of her own motherhood, instead implanting her at the heart of a site of repressed intergenerational female pain, in both her psychic and physiological landscape. It is no coincidence that my mother completed her rejection of me when I was twenty-four, the same age as she was when she gave birth to me. Her immune response refused to maintain the regular pattern of maternal expansion, instead driving back down and doubling, enveloping me in that deadened tomb of a womb without a birth canal, bleeding without a release.

The intensification of my pelvic pain without the provision of an infant onto which we might together displace these difficult feelings certainly contributed to my maternal rejection. It occurred in the course of a phone call in which my psychic and physical pain manifested in too much need, and too many difficult questions. My mother told me that she believed me to be actively psychotic and told me never to contact her again. After this I did not hear from her. She remarried two months later and I did not receive an invitation – Christmases and birthdays passed without a word. I bled, seemingly continuously, in a black, clotted transudation of pain. The mostly male doctors from whom I sought help for pain, anxiety, breathlessness and bleeding saw my peculiar admixture nature of symptoms as an indication of something suspicious, malignant in my personhood. I brought forth a curious anger in them, in one instance a general practitioner subjected me to a rough pelvic examination without lubrication and warned me: 'if you're lying about this, you should know that what they will do to you at the hospital will hurt much worse.' He was right. What they did to me at the hospital was more painful, not because I was lying but because they did not know what was wrong with me and gave me treatments and examinations that made me more ill. They inserted a copper IUD that caused garrulous floodings and vomiting, inserted tubes down my throat, and prescribed me SSRIs. When none of this worked, a psychiatrist suggested that I might have a personality disorder.

In this treatment I find myself linked to an alternative heritage to that of my biological maternal line, in the wider aspect of childless women who have been deemed mad, bad and nocuous as a result of disorders of the reproductive system. The difficulty in catching sight of endometriosis, even using the most modern of medical technology, seemingly re-animates old narratives about the childless female body in pain. In recent years, medical historians have hypothesised that the pathogenesis of hysteria – the ungovernable emotional excesses of women – emerges from endometriosis, particularly in unmarried and childless sufferers. Greek medical theory developed its conception of the wandering womb to postulate that the symptoms now associated with endometriosis were signs of a 'suffocating womb' that affected lascivious women and those who used drugs to prevent contraception. This understanding of the female body goes some way to explaining the harsh treatments that were suggested for sufferers of 'suffocating wombs' which involved suffocation and strangulation, as well as prescriptions to adhere to social norms of marriage and child bearing. Over time, this ideological position twisted topologically with wider cultural norms, and endometriosis sufferers, particularly those who were unmarried and childless, appeared as demonically possessed, as witches, as morally depraved. Later, in the nineteenth century, the condition was subsumed wholly into the psychiatric discourse and asylums across Europe sported wards devoted to the incarceration of 'hystero-epileptics' – young females, abandoned by their families often as a result of the confluence between endometriosis symptoms, mental illness and moral depravity. In my endometriotic body, I find myself entwined with multitudes of other abject women whose bodies were also considered a site of corruption.

I find this new narrative the meeting point of Derbyshire, South Yorkshire and Nottinghamshire, where the dissolution of limestone has given way to a gorge called Creswell Crags. This landscape is not the parallel surface of a Norfolk beach, on which my life's might appear dislocated from origin, unfolding as a tangent, but rather a deepening place where a walk can lead you from familiar paths into flutes, runnels, sinkholes, shafts, disappearing streams, and reappearing springs. In the nineteenth century, this gorge was home to Mother Grundy, a childless older woman accused of witchcraft and driven from the village. Legend has it that when a village child fell ill after eating a poisonous plant, she healed the child and the villagers in return invited her back to the village. Mother Grundy refused the villagers' offer and remained in the crag, which is now known as Mother Grundy's parlour.

In many ways Mother Grundy's parlour appears as Mam Tor's dialectical twin, the location of a non-fertile womanhood defined not by the uterus, but by more than-biological and social maternal action. The Peak District has granted me an understanding of my place in the world that was not available in other landscapes. When I married last year, I was thirty-five and – at least temporarily – infertile, having elected to be put into a 'medical menopause' in the summer of 2021 in order to alleviate the pain that clusters in the lower right-hand quadrant of my stomach and blooms out up past my kidneys and down to my feet. No family were present at the wedding – though some were invited – and without the Peak District and its lessons, I might have felt abject, rootless and without a feminine future or past; lacking in both a mother and potential motherhood.

❦ I am unlikely to become a mother in the biological sense without the aid of invasive medical procedures. Even if I decide to cease the hormone injections that I receive each month to shut down my ovaries, I am well past my fertile prime. Further to this, endometriosis has a serious effect on fertility, which means that I am more likely not only to struggle to become pregnant but also more likely to suffer miscarriages. As a result of the hostile environment that endometriosis and its associated inflammation cause for sperm and embryos alike, fertility treatments such as IVF have a reduced efficacy. In short, my marriage – the socially sanctioned start to 'family life' – resulted in the realisation that I will never have my own baby who 'comes too easily' on whom to continue the cycle of displaced pain and infant rage. I can never reclaim my lost girlhood as my mother took mine from me in exchange for the one she lost, in turn, to her mother. In coming to terms with the fact that there is much I will miss in not being able to 'naturally' fall pregnant, the Peak District materialised as a previously unarticulated narrative of painful womanhood and aggressive motherhood in my own family. The Peak District is split across a fault line. In the Dark Peak, Mam Tor gave birth to her daughters, who always threaten to themselves to diminish her through displaced material or to themself diminish through reproduction; on the other, in the Light, or White Peak, these processes are underground, the slippages and deterioration of limestone giving way to a honeycomb of internal spaces. The Dark Peak was formed by Mam Tor and her children from a loss, a slipping away of material from her form that casts shadows over the landscape. In turn the White Peak is endometriotic, riven with the integration of loss, matter that has fallen away to make secret worlds underneath the surface.

The White Peak is neither a daughter nor a mother, and yet its submerged geographies are home to both life and concealed histories. In this image we find the necessity of the allegorical figure of the crone, the childless woman in the trinity of womanhood. The mother–daughter dyad cannot be completed into a magical triad by the grandmother or the sister, since these are repetitions of the original dyad. Only the crone, the woman without a child who is cast out can perform this role – the hysterical or endometriotic woman. We might also call this figure Lilith. In the *Alphabet of Ben Sira* (c.700–1000 CE) Lilith appears as Adam's first, less compliant wife. Created from the earth like Adam, Lilith refuses to lie below him and flies away. It is only after this that Eve is created from Adam's rib, much like Mam Tor's loose shale cascaded down to cast shadow upon the Dark Peak. Lilith, the submerged landscape, is the exilic female in whom I find my narrative, as well as that of Mother Grundy and the abyssal topography of the Light Peak. Where Eve cares for her children, Lilith creates disruption that prevents entrenchment of power and facilitates the living of all things. As such she, and women like me can be understood as playing a vital role in the feminine trinity. The name Lilith means 'of the night' and in Jewish folklore, she appears as a lusty feminine night demon who brings storms, sex, and miscarriages. Pregnant women would wear amulets to protect themselves against Lilith, and though her stories predate and coincide with the Bible, she is alluded to only once or twice as the undoing of patriarchal civilisation.

Like Lilith, in my Mother's landscape I was the first born, a natural or God-given first experience of power over another being. As such, I took on magical qualities. I could understand her and make her feel seen and understood, worshipped. But in my corporeal earthly babyhood, my distress or rage manifested in this fantasy landscape as punishment and aggression. Psychoanalytic theory understands biological motherhood as a crucial stage in a woman's development, where she might consciously encounter her own experience of being mothered. In my mother's painful body and psyche this caused a fissure like the one I walk across now in the Peak District – my infant body physically manifested as the cut-off parts of her that her cruel superego would not let exist within her. The 'child who came too easily' manifested as a proliferation of fertile tissue where it shouldn't be.

As I walk the Rivelin valley, or along the Loxley river, or as I replay these walks in my mind from my bed to which I am still cyclically bound – pregnancy, the menopause, hysterectomies do not cure endometriosis, they merely suppress symptoms to a greater or lesser extent – this landscape offers me a sweetbitter gift. The integration of the loss of daughter and motherhood and the opportunity to sublimate rather than to project or transfer my pain – not only into writing, but into mothering relationships with those who are not biologically bound to me. The exile from my own mother-daughter relationship means that I am in a position to view these bonds not as lesser to my own lineage and socio-biological unit. Any children that I mother in my home will not be born of me like Mam Tor's dark daughters rather they will be like Mother Grundy, offered sanctuary in my riven heart – distinct from me and the intergenerational pain that proliferates in painful tissue accreting, fusing and bleeding. Their problems will be their own. I no longer wish for a 'child who came too soon' of my own. The Light Peak has given me an alternative maternal narrative.

Beats Per Minute

Feline Charpentier

You swear you have a handle on this. You're not going to let a little setback send you crazy. Everyone has shit to deal with, right? Especially now, with the world going to hell in an especially rickety handcart, at full tilt. Just because it's taking a few years to get over a virus doesn't mean you have to reassess your whole life and every decision that got you here.

Except, of course, that's what you do, with all that time you have, lying in bed, unable to read, or watch reruns of terrible TV. Even doom-scrolling Twitter is off the agenda on bad days. Instead, you take to doom-scrolling your own life, the catalogue of things to regret or become wistful about becoming one long infinite scroll behind your closed eyes – your mental thumb cannot help itself. Eventually, you run out of imagery and the adverts pop up, fine-tuned to your own particular hell.

You bought a cheap watch that gives you data about your failing internal system. Instagram told you it was the best one for the price. It's aimed at those who want to get fitter, thinner, better. It doesn't have a function for barely surviving. But you're only interested in the pulse rate, anyway. Apparently, if you stay within your envelope, work out your maximum bpm, then you'll be fine.

You do complicated calculations, set alarms, tick a box to agree that your data can be sold to the highest bidder. You are strapped in, suddenly a measurable entity. You work out that climbing the stairs too quickly can take you way above your envelope, which means there'll be payback tomorrow, maybe the day after. Your resting rate is an ordinary human's catatonic state.

You have ME/CFS. The virus that brought it, not the one everyone else was so afraid of, the timing terrible, ironic even. You are bed bound. Bed – bound. Your bed holds you, keeps you safe from yourself, from your brain that works all the time to sabotage your body. You exercise willpower, all day long, against a body that wants to move and exist, and be in the world.

Your brain, your nervous system, what a word, what a thing, Nervous System. Something has gone wrong, and you must lie still. You must lie there, and think, and rest, and resist the urge to move. Make your system less nervous. If you could bind yourself to this bed, bind your hands, stop yourself from moving, you would. A type of bondage you did not consent to.

They say it might be a year or two, maybe less, maybe more. As if this were nothing, as if this was not a lifetime in itself, the not knowing, the patience required. It will take time, far longer than you want it to. It will maybe last forever, though you are not allowed to think like that. To admit defeat is not allowed, not healthy. You must be chipper, positive, keep looking forward, not down.

You can't really listen to music. Your brain is over-stimulated, the receptors that send messages to and fro frazzled and frayed. Music is too exciting, it sends you loopy, brings with it nausea, headaches, the pain inevitable. You cry at the drop of a hat. The loss too great, the pain of wanting that which is past. A version of yourself so far from your present, it is unbearable.

Your son asks, 'Are you strong today, Mummy?' The answer is not always clear. It depends on how much you are willing to ignore your body, override the urge to say 'yes, of course, your mummy is the strongest'. Instead, you say 'no, I can't lift you; not today.' The tears don't help, and make people sad.

Beats Per Minute

Your heart has started acting strangely. Some days your system is switched to ON, and your heart races and thumps and thwacks against your rib cage, the little watch going crazy. You lie awake at night feeling the blood course around your veins, can almost hear it gurgling, rushing through your tired limbs.

And then, somewhere, a switch is flicked, and everything slows to a trickle. You are OFF. Your heart can barely bring itself to beat at all, the muscle tired, you feel your chest ache. Your blood takes shortcuts, ignores your extremities, pins and needles taking its place. Your brain makes cold calculations, which parts of you it needs to keep alive. You are catatonic, knocked out, in an altered state.

You have no control about the course of this, your system running on some alternative programme, no rhyme or reason to any of it. A virus got in and messed with the hardware, and you must wait it out. You don't even know if it is still in there, this tiny viral saboteur, or if this is just your hibernation state, your body and brain learning how to recover the system. There is no reboot, no hard reset, there is only slow, painstakingly slow rest, and gentle acceptance.

The internet says this condition means your heart might shrink a little, the cavities underworked, the heart unable to cope with the swings, the changes. Your heart is getting smaller, and you must lie still and sit it out. You must hope, without being hopeful, without relying on the inevitability of change. The only constant you ever had now obsolete, nothing changes, everything is different. It is a process of slow adjustment, this, your failing body filled with rage and meek acceptance. An adaptation to a new reality, one that may yet change, and leave you reeling, yet again.

*

Deepest winter, Snowdonia, somewhere high up, early nineties. A long drive, in the dark, being thrown about in the back of a long van, your shoulder slamming repeatedly against a speaker taller than you. Someone hands you a spliff, you juggle a can of Red Stripe, squeezing it between your knees as you brace yourself against the soft cushion of the speaker, strapped against the sides of the van with thick ratchet straps. You smile at the girl who hands you a joint. You can't remember her name. It doesn't matter. There's you, and her, and your best friend, and the guys driving the van, laughing and talking loudly, the driver swerving to keep the van on the narrow track that leads up the mountain. You're late, the sound system will take a few hours to set up, the rig already up there too quiet, something wrong with the leads, you're not sure, it is important, the guys in front are stressed, but you don't care, not really.

This is your turf, your comfort zone, the baseline that was set in your heart, against which you measure all that comes after. Can it make you feel like this? This free, this vital, this connected? The music, the repetitive beats that course through your veins and make you feel whole, the people, those who exist on the fringes, you find yourself here and you are home. This mountain, this Welsh air, the slate rock beneath you – you are an interloper and yet it welcomed you; it told you you were safe. Your mother worries about you, any mother would, but you don't care. This is your tribe, and always will be.

Despite the dodgy characters, the men you will sleep with even though you'd rather not. The ketamine parties where everyone thinks they're dying. The parties where people really do die. The geezers over from the city, who nick everyone's stuff. The drug-fuelled fights, the police cars that arrive, silently filming everyone at dawn. Despite all this, your heart is gone, given to this music, to these freaks and weirdos, to a life on the margins, in the liminal spaces where life happens in all its Technicolor beauty.

You arrive, the looping, crumbling lane up the side of the cliff survived. The lay-by where the rest of the vehicles are parked sits like a discarded bottle-top, dropped on the ridge, the mountain sliding vertiginously away in all directions. You lie on the hillocks of moss and rushes, a few minutes wobbling walk from the sound-system, boots slopping in and out of pools of brackish moor water. You and your best friend, staring up at the stars, marvelling at the way the sky wraps itself around you.

You are tiny creatures stuck on a spinning ball, staring up at the velvet sky.

The stars are fucking mind-blowing in Wales. You could almost stand on tippy toes and grab one, if you felt like it. In fact, you probably try, feel the tug as the vast canvas refuses to give up its crystal baubles, the ping as the star is returned to its rightful spot above you. The ground beneath you vibrates with the beat, a thrumming that invades your body. Your bones dance inside your flesh, you do not need to move your body to feel it.

'Fuck it, I'm dancing, you coming?' Your friend springs to her feet, you follow, and the two of you push your way through the small crowd that shuffles its feet, in a National Trust car park on the mountainside. By day this place is full of sensible estate cars and camper vans, couples in matching fleeces and walking boots, children gathering bunches of cotton grass to take back to their cul-de-sacs after half term has finished.

Your crew has got the leads working. The speakers curve themselves in an amphitheatre around you. The sound is coming from the ground itself, from the sky. The earth approves; it knows this beat. It feels it too. The moorland dances with you, it recognises the rhythm: 128 bpm. Thump thump thump. It travels down to the core of the earth, is echoed back up, the sky a giant speaker reverberating, mirroring you back to yourself. You are loved, you belong, you are one.

You don't believe in God. But if he did exist, he'd be a DJ. He'd be the one playing the beat you all dance to, keeping you afloat, keeping you alive. Without that beat you'd all be dead, you'd be nothing. What would life be? This beat connects you, makes you part of something far greater than you are, or can be.

You have your tribe. You found them here, on this mountain, in this wild, wild country, a guttural, earthy sense that you are all right, OK, no longer lost or drifting, but connected to the earth, a dance floor full of freaks and weirdos, lost kids and strange folk, all connected by this thread of music. The earth sees you, and it approves.

*

You have not eaten for three days. This is when it starts to pinch, when the hunger is replaced by something more profound, the hallucinations replacing the gnawing emptiness inside. The trees are watching you. It is a test. They want to see if you can show up, if you can stay the course, if you will make it. They don't care either way, of course, but they're starting to pay you a little stray attention, this strange woman sitting in a clearing in the midst of them.

You came here with no idea what to expect, just before you got sick. Looking back, it was the cusp, the peak of the seesaw, before the virus that made your life a before and an after, a black and a white, a singular moment that changed everything. You are still blissfully unaware. You have no idea what's coming.

You signed up when you read the word 'vigil'. Four days, no food, no shelter – you have always loved a challenge. There are six of you, all of you here for different reasons, a restless searching underpinning the nervous laughter the night before you wind your separate ways up the hill into the ancient rainforest. Your camps are separated enough that you are alone, the only connection a little rock with which you pin down hand-scribbled notes for one another once a day, a hundred metres from your patch. You receive a letter, on day two, from your neighbour, a note that makes you cry, the strangely deep connection in this lonely, guttering, beautiful place bringing you back to a version of yourself you thought lost forever.

You have raised your children, earned enough money to survive, become respectable enough to make your father vaguely proud. At least he now tells people what you do, knows what to say when they ask, rather than waving a hand vaguely overhead, as if to say, she's still working it out, I'm not really sure. You joined the throng, the society you felt separate from, became a part of the bigger picture, and in doing so lost something integral to what being 'you' is.

You are entirely insignificant in that forest. You lie in the moss, stare up at the canopy of oak and beech, watch the wind play with the chewy green leaves. See a mob of blue tits flit daily from tree to tree, the occasional seagull soar past, high up, through gaps of pale blue. Observe the progress the ants make in a line around your silent, still body. Watch the tiniest spiders crochet their silvery webs in between the leaves and ferns. You spend an entire day watching a spider the size of a pill rebuild the web she spent all night making, after a rain shower destroys it. She does it again the next morning, and the next. You marvel at her resilience, then wonder whether resilience is the right word. She just exists, she does not question the destruction, or rail against the rain. At least, this is what you assume.

A beetle the same vibrant green as a glow-stick watches you from the edge of your tarp for an hour or two. You wonder if it is real. Time bends itself into shapes, tricks your mind into seeing stars in the afternoon. The sun pauses at midday, immediately above you, for what feels like days. The nights go on forever.

On the third night, you hear drumming. A steady beat, then singing, a strange eerie tune you tell yourself must be kids, gathering down by the swimming spot at the bend in the river below. Except what kind of kids listen to strange folk music in the middle of the night? Later, your fellow vigilers will tell you they heard it too. Voices singing, in harmony, a drum beat, insistent, yearning, as if calling them over the edge, into the deep.

You dream and wake, and sleep, and dream again. Of salt-crusted islands and boats and talking trees and ants, so many ants, busy with their tiny lives, never stopping, never looking around.

The trees tell you things. They whisper, they impart their knowledge. You remember acid trips, mushroom-fuelled adventures where the plants in the fields spoke to you of the wisdom of ancient things.

The earth rises up from beneath your quiet body, creaking and groaning and whispering, enveloping you, trying to pull you down within it. You, but in slow motion, time-lapse, a creaking, rumbling, juddering, as the earth sucks you down. Life slows to a rhythm your body cannot keep up with. Except you catch a glimpse, a fleeting sight of something beyond, a deep, ancient time, where your heart rate keeps tempo, for a fleeting moment, with the rhythm of the forest. The trees keep watch, unmoved.

You realise how far you have come, how adrift you are from what, or who, you thought you were. The baseline is still there, the yearning, it is lost amongst the chaos of wanting to do things right, to find approval, fit in. Except you are more lost than ever. You are adrift, you do not belong – this is not the life you thought you would live.

You had no intention, you are intention-less, the joy is not there, there is no dancing. There is no dancing in your life, and what are you going to do about it? You can hear the forest asking. What the fuck are you planning to do about it?

*

You buy another gadget, your thumb's answer to everything, a click and it's yours, the solution to all of life's problems. A small, black, round little thing, it is the latest science. The internet says maybe this will help. Everything now is about management. You are no longer looking for a cure. Sweet relief, if only momentary, from your body's constant clamouring for attention. This is all there is. Your boyfriend buys it for you. You have given up looking for solutions.

The packaging is shiny and covetable: it comes with a strap, a little velvet bag, an app. It is the size of a small fist, pebble-shaped and smooth as a conker. It looks like a particularly anodyne sex toy. It crosses your mind that you've accidentally bought a vibrator, the language of sensory stimulation and deep relaxation suddenly sounding like code, wink wink, nudge nudge. You connect it to your phone, sign away more of your not-so-precious data.

When placed against your chest, it vibrates and buzzes against your vagus nerve. It's supposed to be doing deep, emotional things. Bypassing hours of work, one click, ten minutes a day, for enlightenment. There are different settings, short and long sessions, chanting and rainforest noises and the sound of rain on leaves.

The tiny boom and fizz of it instantly takes you back to standing in front of giant speakers, watching the soft fabric covering vibrate as the bass explodes out, enveloping your body and mind. The blasts of air with each drum beat, your heart opening a little more with each tap of your foot. The techno cleansing you of everything that you couldn't take, of every thought that kept you trapped inside your own body, grounding you solidly within, and removing you completely, all at once. Each beat per minute raising you a little higher, keeping you on your toes. Except you're lying in your bed, a marble martyr, perfectly still, your eyes covered as you wait for salvation.

You must lie still, and all the while hope that your envelope will grow, that your baseline will shift.

The rhythm has gone. There is no longer a beat to follow. You're free-styling in the mud, the cold light of dawn on the horizon, the trees still exactly where you saw them when the party started, silently watching. The party's over, and you're still shuffling your feet to the echo of a beat you remember, a miniature version of who you were. Maybe someone will turn the generator back on, the beat will pick back up, and you'll still be dancing in time.

Birdwoman VII

Earth

Moving Close to the Ground: A Messy Love Song

Eli Clare

Crossing Beaver Brook in August: The water flows, eddies, gurgles amid a tumble of boulders. I morph into a quadruped, some combination of hands, feet and butt always touching the moss-covered rocks. Surface of the water wrinkles, smooths, wrinkles again. I linger, let my body cool; the ripeness of decaying leaves, dirt and fungi surrounds me. When I start moving again, my body lifts, reaches, inches sideways, the boulders smearing my hands with muck.

*

In disability community, we rarely talk about sliding, scooting, crawling, crab-walking. We appreciate the speed of power-chair users on smooth, firm ground, admire the broad shoulders of manual-chair users. We trade mobility techniques, talk mechanics, support each other through the bureaucracy of acquiring new gear. We relish gimpy ways of walking: the rhythm and sounds of forearm crutch-users, the pure loveliness of how we decorate our canes and accessorize with them. In contrast, we seem loath to talk about, much less admire, modes of mobility that bring us close to the ground.

When we've been forced to drag ourselves up or down a flight of stairs—either in public because of outlandish inaccessibility or in private because we simply want to be with friends—we will tell stories about feeling humiliated, embarrassed, or enraged. But we don't exchange tips about sliding, when and where we scoot, how we protect our hands and wrists while crab-walking. We've not shared and accumulated decades of community know-how about crawling. Those of us who move close to the ground for pleasure or utility do so mostly in isolation.

As an unsteady walkie[1] who has a lifelong history of using these modes of mobility, I feel alone and lonely amid this disability community absence. My aloneness began early: at two, well after my non-disabled peers were exploring the world on their own two feet, I stumped around on my knees, discovering treasures and mysteries tucked under beds and into corners. I didn't have playmates. At six, when my family and I lived for a summer in a basement apartment, I perfected a scoot-slide, bumping myself down into our living room on my butt. Frustrated and half angry, my parents insisted repeatedly that I stand up and walk, even though I was petrified of falling on the stairs. At twenty, I started reading my poetry in public and had to crawl off of more than one stage because the steps were too steep. Mortified, I never stuck around to hear the other poets.

Now in my fifties, when I face a craggy trail, a lip of rock, or a narrow bridge without handrails—my balance more precarious than usual—I often drop to my hands and knees. Neither a protest against ableism nor a performance of disability, moving close to the ground offers me so much possibility and connection. Muscles loosen. Pace slows. Eyes, ears, nose focus. Yet I am still alone.

I want to share these experiences with folks who will understand them both viscerally and politically. I yearn for a disability love song to scooting and crawling.

*

Kettle Pond in October: walking over roots and rocks, slick from the morning's rain, I slow down. I concentrate. I brace myself through a stumble. My sweetie, long familiar with my pace and rhythm, offers me a hand. He knows that on this terrain, I need a third point of contact to steady myself. Before taking his hand, I hesitate, feel a moment of conflict. A slew of ableist lies reverberates through me—*burden, clumsy, ugly*. And then, as palms slide together, his solid stance bolstering mine, I remember: not *burden* but *love*, not *ugly* but *the quivering of aspen leaves*, not *clumsy* but *slow* and *intimate*.[2] Our creation of access makes the roots and rocks less treacherous but still difficult—terrain that I simply need to cross.

But when I decide to stop walking and instead lower my center of gravity and scoot, these roots are no longer a barrier. Rather, they form tributaries, crevices, miniature caves cushioned in moss, calling out to me. An orange-brown newt catches my motion, holds stock-still.

*

I have developed many strategies to gain access in the world. Certainly, moving close to the ground excels as one of these strategies. But just as importantly, it leads me deeper into intimacy with the more-than-human world. Access and intimacy don't always work in tandem; the wheelchair ramp into the post office or double time on timed tests isn't necessarily created through close and abiding relationships. Likewise, access doesn't guarantee familiarity and affection. But when the two come together—access creating intimacy and in turn intimacy fostering deeper and broader access—I feel tremendous ease and belonging. The pair strengthens my closest relationships, both with humans and with trees and rocks, chipmunks and maple leaves, trillium and lichen.

*

Lake Champlain at winter solstice: sculpted ice lines the shore. It coats the Monkton quartzite slabs that extend into the water and enshrouds the scruffy eastern red cedars growing out of the crevices. I walk, and then, after losing my balance, scoot into this winter magic. Soon my lower back and hands ache with cold that grows more intense by the minute. I slide among the cedars, absorbed in the fantastical frosted shapes, inching my way beneath the tree branches. I end up lying on my back, cradled by the winter rawness of frozen stone, chilled to the bone.

*

Moving low to the ground—through mud or snow, across puddles, over gravel—can be a messy affair. In the best of conditions, my hands get scratched; my wrists, elbows and shoulders ache from bearing my body weight; sharp rocks stab my hamstrings. Even so, I adore scooting. It slows me down, distance no longer measured in miles but rather in yards. I creep, inch, and linger. This pace creates intimacy and space for the tiniest details: mushrooms pushing up through pine needles, spores dotting the underside of ferns, miniature icicles hanging on the tips of cedar branches.

Actually, for me, the most difficult part of moving close to the ground has little to do with the physicality of scooting and more to do with ableism and the ways it privileges strong, steady, unassisted walking. The sheer amount of prurient curiosity, fawning infantilizing, and outright hostility I encounter when I move close to the ground is exhausting.

*

Second Beach north of La Push in May. Faced with a tangle of driftwood between me and low tide, I start clambering. I leverage myself up onto a log thirty feet long. I sit, trail my fingers along the salt-scoured ridges, swing my legs over, squirm my way to the trunk tossed against the one I'm currently on, lift myself over it. Scoot sideways some more. Reach across a gap, take hold of the polished remnants of a branch, lean my weight onto the next log. The people ahead of me tightrope across this tumble. I do not covet their balance, nor can I imagine their agility. I keep lifting and leveraging, admiring the bone-white wood, the ocean-sculpted rootballs—tentacles, lion heads, sun bursts. A middle-aged white woman stops and hovers over me. I brace myself. She smiles, takes off her sunglasses, enthusing, 'You're so brave. I just don't know how you do it.' Thankfully, she doesn't try to hug me. Behind her, teenage boys keep their distance; my skin prickles and burns as their eyes bore through me.

*

I find a belonging in the more-than-human world that I rarely experience among people. Trees don't gawk. Boulders don't call me inspirational. Oceans don't believe that I and my communities might well be better off dead than disabled.

Certainly, ableism follows me into the forest and onto the beach. Humans impose all the forces of domination—white supremacy, colonialism, capitalism, patriarchy, and more—on the more-than-human world. These systems rip people from earth and sky. They disrupt air and water. They shape who has access and who doesn't. They create the conditions under which many beings experience violence, including environmental destruction, and struggle for survival. They corrode love and belonging.

At the same time, sitting in the woods or at the beach, I glimpse a world that relishes crookedness, wholeness and brokenness, an explosion of sizes and shapes. In the more-than-human world, my shaky asymmetrical body is just one among many. I find spaces and relationships neither saturated with nor defined by ableism.

*

Gale River Trail in July: Not yet at the infamous boulder staircase known as Jacob's Ladder, we – my sweetie, two non-disabled acquaintances, and I – approach our second stream crossing. The narrow wooden bridge doesn't have railings.

My companions navigate it without hesitation. I, on the other hand, pause for a long moment. Maybe I can walk across, but worry that I might trip, tumbling into the current. I contemplate crawling, but immediately cringe, imagining how my new friends might respond. I've already slowed them down significantly. I feel embarrassed, conflicted again. The logic that declares walking vastly superior to sliding and scooting rises inside me—ableism lodged not only in the external human world, but also internally in my body. Shame takes hold. But one step out onto the span, and I know I can't push it. I lower myself to hands and knees and crawl. Shoulder leads; hip follows. The pace and rhythm soothe me. I watch swirling eddies through the gaps in the planks; the motion of the water doesn't threaten my stability when my center of gravity is this close to the ground. Slowly my shame and fear of falling recede.

*

I wish the fierce and tender song I'm trying to write could be unequivocal. But in reality, I have internalized the logic of walking. Even without non-disabled people gawking and taunting, I judge my body ugly and awkward. I scoot and crawl mostly as a last resort, rather than as a joyful first choice, because I have swallowed the ableist lies, allowed them to become my own. They disrupt my love of moving close to the ground and fill me with ambivalence. They leave me alone and lonely.

These falsehoods—*burden, clumsy, better off dead, tragic, dangerous, not fully human, child-like, worthless*—reverberate not only through my individual body but also collectively through disability community. I want to turn for a moment to disabled and chronically ill people and ask: given the access, intimacy and beauty created by moving close to the ground, why don't we talk to each other about these modes of mobility? What are the connections between our internalized ableism and our silence? What do we need to begin this conversation about the joys, embarrassments, dangers, comforts and discomforts, utility, inefficiencies and access that accompany crawling and scooting?

Surrounding these tender questions is a larger query that I want to ask everyone—disabled and non-disabled, walkie and not—because the ableist logic of walking reverberates through all of us in some fashion or another. What do we need to dismantle this logic that many of us teach, practice, implement, and enforce in many different ways? I bring longing and curiosity to these questions even as I still feel alone and lonely inside my messy love song.

I've often found my way out of isolation through poetry, music, art, story. This time I turn to film. I watch Gregor Wolbring, an Ability Studies scholar and bioethicist, in the documentary *Fixed: The Science/Fiction of Human Enhancement*. With a rebellious glint in his eyes, he claims, 'Crawling is in, walking is out.' The camera follows Wolbring as he moves through his life—in his home, at an airport, around his lab—mixing different forms of mobility, sometimes using a wheelchair and other times crawling. He says, 'I ... love crawling. ... I crawl wherever I can. ...'[3] Watching him, I feel just how much my internalized ableism shapes when and where I move on my hands and knees. I yearn to be as rebellious and matter-of-fact as Wolbring.[4]

*

Long Trail north of Sunset Ledge in June: I scoot down a steep tumble of rock. Spots of gray green lichen prickle my hands. I become an inchworm, humping along. Butt lifts; body weight shifts; knees bend, the glacier-etched schist ridged and warm beneath me.

*

I dream plentiful disability-centered conversations about crawling – love songs, manifestos, guidebooks written by a multitude of disabled people who know and claim the joys and discomforts of moving close to the ground. I need layers upon layers of stories, analysis and politics to undo the ableist logic of walking embedded in my body, to make space for shunned modes of mobility, and to continue the work of resisting shame. But beyond words, I yearn to scoot, slide, and crawl with other disabled people; to share in community the pleasure and connection I find when I move close to the ground through the woods.

*

Gale River Trail in July: We arrive at Jacob's Ladder—1,000 feet of elevation gain in less than a mile. I look up at this daunting and beautiful stretch of trail, granite rocks stair-stepping up the mountain. To keep my balance as I climb, I bend slightly at the waist and place my hands three steps above me, a quadruped once again. I slow, feel the skin of boulder against skin of palm. I turn aside repeatedly to let hikers pass. I can't move any faster. I breathe the green humid air, settle into this particular rhythm of hands and feet, heart and lungs.

Several years earlier, a group of disabled people—three wheelchair-users and two crutch-users—along with a bunch of non-disabled companions and assistants hiked this trail up to the newly renovated and disability accessible Galehead Hut. I learned about their adventure from afar, reading about it on the internet. When they reached Jacob's Ladder, Craig Gray slid out of his wheelchair onto the stone stairs and climbed using a move he calls 'butt-up'. Nicole Haley started singing 'You've Lost that Loving Feeling'. The whole group urged each other on: 'Let's eat that rock.'[5]

Across the years, I can almost feel them. My quadruped rhythm merges with Craig's as he leverages his body weight from one step to the next. I hear their encouragements and Nicole's soprano voice belting out the lyrics. I imagine them teasing each other and laughing together as they problem solve. I swear I can feel their pounding hearts.

Birdwoman VIII

A Natural Force

Jamie Hale

When I write about nature as a disabled person, I am writing from a fundamental understanding of physical limitation as a creative impulse. This doesn't suppose that only disabled people face these limits, but that having an impairment has made me sharply and constantly aware of the limits of being a mortal human. It is a reminder that there are many forces in the world more powerful than the human body, shaping the ways I write about nature and connect to it. I explore a sense that the natural world is big enough to hold the human within it, but also that the human can be subsumed within it.

My connection to nature is complex. There's nothing that cleaves closer to an understanding of what it is to be part of natural forces than the failure of your own body to obey the expectations set out. This is the understanding of our own mortality as a part of nature that most of us will confront at some point in our lives. For me, the disabled body is a body that is profoundly natural. However, that sets against the pernicious ways in which disabled people are excluded from nature. I experience the outside world as a contested space that makes no room for my physically impaired body.

At the same time, what changes would nature require in order to be accessible to me? Some of the routes I am barred from are inevitable – I will never climb Everest, and to tarmac the countryside for my wheelchair would be, I think, a tragedy. At the same time, kissing gates and stiles are avoidable human barriers, without which I could trek the countryside in my off-road tank-wheelchair. What right do we have to impose access on nature, if any? Have humans not already imposed too much?

This exclusion from such a vital part of the world has very much formed my sense of how I relate to it poetically. It's no accident that I typically write about nature in the dual contexts of loss and mortality rather than writing it joyfully – because my experience of nature as a person whose disability has progressed – is an experience of being increasingly closed out. I become both increasingly natural – subject to the processes of the body – and yet also increasingly *unnatural*, dependent further and further on electronics and machinery to sustain myself. Writing into nature has been a route back into experiencing it – multi-sensorial, fulfilling, and inviting me to consider my place in the world again.

Roadkill

One of the big themes I grapple with is the idea of death as a natural theme – the horror and grotesqueness of nature – and of what humans impose on it. Roadkill is such a brutal word, for the devastation caused by a callous end to life, a corpse rotting under car wheels. I remember that sickly smell from childhood – and recognised it again when my nose started rotting, one summer. How do we inflict ourselves on the world?

> the smell of rotting flesh is sticky late
> summer when bones scatter the roadside
> lazed-grazing deer crushed by waves of
> day-trippers only now it's me rotting
> in the late spring sun my nose is an
> open wound the whole world smells sweet
> and sickly. maybe the early-burning summers
> dissolve into this. maybe the rain – later
> this year than the last – will beat the smell
> from the ground like pungent spring

Rope

A scar is a natural fibre – my ropey, branching scars are sinewy – and sinew was used as rope, and sutured wounds closed, and catgut – sheep or horse intestines – has been used in musical instruments. I wanted to write something with the tautness of scarring, the tensions of the ways in which the body is exploited and exploits itself.

> limp set, ill-fit to open places; knotted
> old scars like braided rope. this skin
>
> shifts, slick, slips, and i too stumble
> the gaze pounding me in place makes no land
>
> my own. sinews like catgut and mine
> are spastic stringing me along

I left mis piernas behind in Spain

This piece writes into the surreal – the idea of nature as horror, that choking sand, the danger of the sun, the slipperiness of worms, the reliable weight of stone – and the solid structure that offered me, at a time when everything else was shifting. I wanted to entwine the body, nature, language and space as impacting back and forth on one another.

> I left mis piernas behind in Spain.
> Swallowed el mar between mis pies
> off Cadiz. That day el sol scorched me,
> mi piel blistering and peeling.
>
> Or quizás I left them by el hospital abandonado
> at the end of la ruta del autobus en Córdoba.
>
> At night I was chased by feet.
> In my dreams, the grains of sand were running.
> Legs mutated into worms, crawled down my throat,
> choked me. At night, my body came alive.

They did not come back. No surprise,
el regreso is always hard. You can never go home.

It has always changed. Or maybe you, niño,
are not the same. You left a child
playing in shoes muy grandes,
who thought el mundo something to learn,
possess. You returned half man.
Half something more alien than that.

I'm replacing estas piernas con los arcos
de la mezquita, great red and white
splayed up to support the sky.
A stone-carved palm from home.
I replace them with palabras.
Los dientes, los dedos, el espacio.

I wish to be held by a river, please

I want to let myself be subsumed in a nature that is powerful enough to do so. I want to understand what it is to be taken away by something, to be part of something larger than myself. I am interested in the ways in which my body subsumes itself the same ways that broader nature might also subsume it.

    i wish to be held by a river please   drowning
    is something i do at night   waking choked

    only reminds me that air is precious   i wish
    to be empty   a river knows the void, carves it

    day on glimmering day   months later   her path
    has changed   i wish for rounded stones   my edges

    are raw and sharp   i wish for a dream woven
    of reeds   with which to sail the rivers   please

    i wish to remember this wish when i am floating
    in confusing seas   i wish to come safe to land

    then leave

The Fisher King

For Bedtime Stories At The End Of The World

I love the Arthurian myth of the wounded Fisher King, and here impose a trans and crip reading upon it. With climate change as a mass disabling experience, it refuses an individualistic healing, acknowledging the fundamentally entwined experiences of body and nature. It is a piece that carries within it a joy in resistance – a joy in saying that I will tie my body and my fate to nature.

This boat replaced my legs, long ago.
I never leave the water now, though
my oars are green with algae, and thick
slowly through the sludge. The fish I catch
and eat – still raw and wriggling – are long
and thin. More fragile bone than flesh. I choose
to stay amidst the water, not return to shore.
My wound, my body, my failing land – the
acid rain has drenched the trees and lakes.
I will not be healed – my legs – my wound.
Watch me turn away Perceval – his lance
can make whole only me, but I am hurt
as the land is hurting and I would rather die
as the land itself is dying. But come the grail
and its devastation shall be healed – I shall stay
like this, from choice, but not be barren, bear
daughters from my womb, my hidden wound
and stay off shore, and over days the land
itself regrow, refresh. Friend, there will be
a place where we can start again, my wound
a badge, the land, not sore but healing,
our love, not sore but healing – please – bring
only the holy grail – and yourself. Please,
come to me alone and let us heal the world.

the poet limps *in words* as a balance *for worlds*[1]

Alec Finlay

Join my endurance walk experiment. We set off, sceptical medics in white coats either side of me, or ME, politely encouraging. A tartan blanket's draped over my shoulder. We continue together – I continue between them – across hills, through pinewoods, fording burns, until the moment comes. Is it on day one? Do I walk on into the night? Did I go impossibly far? Wherever we are, I can go no further.

The medics nod. There's no denying my effort and, in their minds, the experiment proves I can walk some distance, so I must be well.

Wait, I say: *stay a while, this is my experiment; we need to parley*. After so many years, I'm determined they see the *Lag* take hold.

Day two, they become impatient. *Of course you're stiff. It was a long walk.* Day three, bastard lactic, joints agony, cleugh across my diaphragm, mother-waves of fatigue. *Stop*! I insist: *you're not leaving yet*, laying across the doorway like a draught excluder.

Peak pain on day four, spindleshanks stuck with pins, shadowed eyes, feet cramping into gnarly roots.

Pain forms its zone of exclusion.

I can't describe the end of my fantasy walk. The medics crept away while I slept fitfully.

Long after a walk is over, my cells collapse in a mitochondrial fizzle. Such alien pain insults the signature of medical care, which imagines fatigue, and its temporal slippage into Post-Exertional Malaise – what I call *Lag* and Marion Michell terms *The Aftermath* – as '*an extreme response, born of health anxiety*'.[1] If their conception of *Lag* were benign, we could have held its strangeness together and formed a description in scientific terms. Instead, tens of thousands with ME, millions with Long Covid, experience these energy crashes and are met with similar disbelief.

§

my doctor told me I wasn't ill,
my doctor said it was anxiety,
my doctor said it was depression and lack of motivation,
my doctors said there was nothing wrong, all in my head,
my doctor blamed me for not getting better,[1]

§

The distribution of pain is never even.

When an illness is 'invisible', or its social representations is stymied, there's a risk people's pain will be shackled to false narratives, intensifying their affliction. In the case of ME, a few jaundiced psychiatrists speculated the aetiology of the disease lay in erroneous patterns of thought. This loss of co-created reality, which doctor/patient relationships depend on, figured a wild dance of blame, anticipating the conflict between accusative and recuperative models of healing. This continues today, with Long Covid sufferers being accused of '*extreme behavioural responses*' and being '*health anxious*'.

§

constant muscular and neurological pain, shuddery, sore, aching all the time, every movement hurts, the pain, oh god, the pain! pain here, now there, now here, like acid eating through the skin, burning, blotchy, on fire, stung by nettles, pale fine porcelain, drained of life, cold to the touch, pain an enemy within stabbing repeatedly, every muscle severely bruised, every cell in my body being ripped apart,[2]

§

Gossip fills a vacuum. Lacking a medical explanation, ME was fit for caricature.

I thought ME was a form of burnout,
I thought ME was about being lazy,
I thought ME was Yuppie Flu,
   an illness Del Boy coveted as a badge of honour,
I thought people were faking, putting it on,
   (to my shame),
I thought ME was my failure[3]

I hold the twin realities of trauma and illness, or I can dream one within the other: this doesn't permit others to fantasise my pain as a spectre.

No disease is 'mysterious', except that it lacks adequate description.

No illness is 'invisible', except we fail to see it.

The targeting of ME is an early episode in the war on vulnerability, foreshadowing today's culture of accusation. '*I won the internet*' is a proxy for hunting, not healing. Those who deny others' pain, demand exclusive rights to suffering, or presume an inalienable right to accuse, have been allowed to trump complex reality. '*They keep a list of names*'.

Representing pain requires us to translate our experiences empathically. What is lost in GP consultation rooms, or online Committees of Public Safety, is access to a common ground of healing. When realities are permitted to co-exist, and there is good faith, we can parley, making pliable the terms of reality, and this allows bodily, social, or political healing.

The pandemic produced a collective awareness that healing must include access to nature, good food, clean air, safe working conditions and the absence of domestic violence. These are inalienable rights. Now the left-behind are being left behind, leaving millions in poverty, grieving, cold, hungry, or with symptoms of pain and *Lag* that are denied care. Now the vulnerable must navigate a world in which the mask has slipped.

after The Hologram[4]

being broken
my teaching

asking for help
my gift

Elaine Scarry's profound account of chronic pain and torture proposes pain as a metaphysical test. Our pain is felt as an insistent reality; pain in another is beyond our nerve-endings and, thereby, elusive.[5] For us to believe in someone else's pain requires the translation of our innermost experiences into those of another, as if we walked by their side or, if necessary, walked for them.

Affirming the validity of pain remains an act of love.

§

The medical coterie who foisted a diagnosis of anxiety on ME took advantage of gappy knowledge to perform their own hysterical fantasy, framing the disease as '*a cultural phenomenon and metaphor of our times*'. Whenever a disease is framed as symbolic in this way a falsehood is being fomented. Rather than believing people's descriptions of their symptoms and investigating the mechanism of *Lag*, psychiatrists perceived '*culturally sanctioned expressions of distress*'. With a parasitic opportunism they revived the diagnosis of neurasthenia under a new term: *'healthism'*, conjuring up an *'illness of modernity'*, fingering the work-shy and faddy types over-anxious about toxins.[6]

No disease is a projection of the cultural imagination.

No disease deserves to be read as a symbol or punishment.

No vulnerability deserves to be targeted with disbelief.

Their ideological kingpin, Professor Simon Wessely, has applied the proposition that unexplained illnesses are expressions of anxiety to a dizzying range of healthcare crises, from ME and Gulf War Syndrome, to the Camelford disaster and illnesses suffered by those in proximity to Ground Zero. Blaming people's justified fear of toxicity erases the real impact of toxins. Here he is, riffing wildly about ME:

> *In a previous era, spirits and demons oppressed us. Although they have been replaced by our contemporary concern about invisible viruses, chemicals and toxins, the mechanisms of contagious fear remain the same ... To the majority of observers, including most professionals, these symptoms are indeed all in the mind.*[7]

In his mind, Wessely blamed the *'ideology'* of Environmentalism for encouraging a culture of angst, in which *'our physical environment is responsible for most of our bodily discomforts and ills'*.[8] But our concept of Nature *is* in crisis precisely because we recognise ecosystems are vulnerable, sensitive to toxic stress, and subject to chronic exhaustion. Polar bears are presumably guilty of being anxious about the melting ice cap.

Wesselyianism is not listening to today's talking wood, in which trees signal distress and fungi seek reconciliation between conflicting species. This dismissal of environmental toxicity and stressed immune systems crunched into the irrefutable reality of Covid-19, a virus which locks onto toxic particles and proves pollution deals death.

The numbers of healthcare workers with Long Covid created an angel of suffering, dowsing the Wesselyian fantasy of ME in a cold rain of reality. Many who had stood by while ME was targeted are now sadly aware how it feels to fall into *Lag*.

How was this collective erasure of lived experience maintained for decades? Why are some descriptions of reality believed and others not? Only patient-led medicine can prevent future scandals.

I've listened, helpless with frustration, as experts hypothesised *Lag* or allergies don't exist, candidiasis isn't real and the efficacy of medicines I was forced to purchase illegally was a placebo.

Despite Wessely's scepticism, the passage of time affirms patient-led activism and environmental campaigns are largely accurate in their depiction of ill bodies and degraded landscapes.

If people with ME had been listened to years ago, we may have treatments available for Long Covid now. Until medical science cracks these genetic puzzles, we require models of recuperation that are closer to rewilding than graded exercise. Is the ecological remediation of bogs and montane scrub so different to the treatment of post-viral diseases? Studies of the gut biome and mitochondria confirm symptoms discussed by ME support groups for years. Patient descriptions of medically unexplained diseases are oracles of future cure. Long Covid message boards shiver with descriptions of sensitivities to foods, histamines and moulds, which, setting aside anxiety, we may recognise as the natural responses of a frayed immune system. Our communal immune system is bolstered by peer-to-peer solidarity – the *our-illness-is-real* of ME campaigners, the historic *don't-dare-ignore-us* activism of the HIV/AIDS movement and the *radical-healing-gentleness* of Maggie's Centres.

§

With good reason, the Long Covid community fears the stain of ME – of being, as one clinician put it, '*consigned to the wastepaper basket*'. In a response to a plea for support for children with the disease, the government response refers to mental health services fifteen times and Long Covid once. A recovered professor succumbs to a messiah-complex, asserting that '*the belief that #longcovid fatigue is biomedical reinforces the symptoms*', as if his rare good fortune could erase the pain, breathlessness, myocarditis and allergic reactions experienced by two million people.[9] This fantasy is why medical staff with Long Covid demand their disease, '*be treated with a scientific methodology without bias*'.[10] Translation: don't walk away; don't presume to know more than the person in pain describes; don't disbelieve Post-Exertional Malaise; don't batten psychological explanations onto biochemical causes; don't devise forms of care which are harmful; don't pressure people to undertake fantasy walk experiments.[11]

a common delusion
*   is that one great walk*

will heal the ill when
*   cure lies in minor walks*[12]

Lag may point to the persistence of micro-clots and thrombogenesis. Despite the accumulating evidence, the prejudice against post-viral diseases still enables some NHS regimes to revive graded exercise, encouraging Long Covid patients to exercise beyond what their symptoms will allow, as if walking alone could cure a malfunctioning autoimmune system.[13] The obvious danger of the psychiatric fantasy that *Lag* is caused by aberrant patterns of thought, rather than exhausted cells – as if a river was responsible for flooding, not rain and loss of trees – is that it imagines someone with ME or Long Covid slipping into a storm of anxiety because they went for a walk. This, in turn, produces an ideological determination to retrain their aberrant mind, as if walking further – which is walking too far – could undo the relapses that such walks cause people. What form of magic is this?
'*Come in Mr Kafka, the psychiatrist will see you now.*'
No matter how joyful I am to take a walk – further than the brick wall, on to the three birches, to the end of the beach – the psychiatrists fantasise that tomorrow, or the day after tomorrow, my mind decides, arbitrarily, to punish my body. Why the delay? Why did I not collapse during the walk, or immediately after: surely that is when I'm imagined to have been anxious, even

though I was, in fact, joyous to feel the air on my face and meet a friend?

It is by walking, or not-walking, that this chronically ill community stands apart from the category of disability. Being unable to walk qualifies someone as disabled. It is the very variability in the ability to walk that characterise ME and Long Covid, making them unacceptable. Explaining to a PIP assessor – twenty-something years old, in a call centre, no medical expertise – that I'd once walked 250 metres, but relapsed for 6 days, they noted, '*can walk 250 metres*'.

In the early months of Long Covid I tried walking an extra yard each day, as if I could outwit *Lag*. After each walk, a day of hope, then day two and relapse, lasting days. There was no anxiety, only a desire to be one of the walkative.

Walking is fundamental to our understanding of human nature. No matter how Nietzschean someone aspires to be, *Lag* cannot be undone with sheer effort. The human will cannot walk us fitter. For hundreds of thousands of people who find themselves unable to return to their walking norm, graded exercise amounts to benevolent and dangerous taunting and, for those who can't walk out of Long Covid, there's the *waste-paper-basket* diagnosis of ME.

Sadly, walking remains a provocation to my disease. If my body fails to walk back to fitness, it is not because the mind cannot support the exertion my walking requires. Walking, or simply being vertical, we seem to relive the mechanism of the virus over-and-over-and-over again.

Gains in healing are gifts of the Goddess Rest, not the God Exercise.

§

This is a response to one NHS regime for Long Covid: 'every mind matters', which I have translated – redeemed – into a manifesto of recuperation and 'radical rest'.

Aim for a daily walk. Do walk with someone until you feel confident going out on your own. *Aim for a daily rest. Do ask someone* to settle you, if you feel exhausted or anxious, as being reassured by others is an intrinsic part of healing.

Try making a walk part of your daily routine to give your day structure. *Try making a rest part of your daily self-care, to give your recuperation the comfort of a daily rhythm. Choose where to rest carefully: maybe you can use a day-bed, or rest by a fire. Make your place of day rest as comfy as possible – cushions, blankets, a restful view, daylight, flowers and sunshine.*

Don't worry if you need to stop and rest. That's a normal part of recovering and getting strong again. *Don't worry if you need to do something that makes you tired; fatigue is part of your life, for now, and you will recuperate, in time.*

If you have an exercise bike at home, this might be a good alternative to walking, particularly on wet days. *Resist the natural urge to use an exercise bike, weights or to walk too far, and please never go to the gym; it's far more healing to take a very gentle walk and rest in the sun. Don't waste money on a personal trainer – instead, choose a practice that is gentle and meets your needs. Never exceed your limits. Allow your energy to heal your body.*

What should I be aiming for with my walking? *What should I be hoping for as I convalesce?*

You should aim to build up to thirty minutes of activity at least five days a week, but this is not going to happen at the beginning of your recovery. *You should learn 'radical rest', for as long as you need to, every day of the week; rest more than you ever imagined you'd require – but accept that this is not always going to be possible.*

Take your time and build up as you feel you can and aim to do a little more each day. *Take all the time you need to rest and aim to conserve a little more energy for healing each day.*

Choose a good time of day (when you are not too tired) to go for a walk. *Choose a good time of day to rest. Learn to rest without any stimulus if you are able; leave your phone or computer in the other room and try to rest without music or radio.*

You might want to think about times when routes are a little quieter (early morning or evenings). *You will gradually learn to rest at the right time of day, and anticipate when you need to recuperate, before you become exhausted.*

Wait an hour after eating a meal before you exercise and take a drink with you. *Rest after you eat; your body uses energy to prepare food and digest. Take the opportunity to rest whenever you have a warm drink; try to have water as often as tea or coffee.*

Walk with someone until you feel confident to be out on your own. *Rest alone. When you have to go out, consider whether it's really necessary – could you ask someone for help, or have something delivered instead?*

If you live alone, you might want to walk with a friend, but you must maintain distance between both of you. *If you live alone, you must learn to ask people who you can trust for help, and not mind if some friendships fall away for a time.*

Start with just walking for five minutes without stopping (or less if you feel breathless and tired). *Start by resting longer than you ever imagined you'd need to (you will need to rest for longer if your fatigue is severe).*

Gradually build this up, by one or two minutes. *Gradually reduce the things you do which are not necessary; learn to allow yourself to use energy for healing.*

Once you can do ten minutes without stopping, aim to do two ten-minute walks a day. *Never try to push through or go further than you actually can. You will only relapse.*

Once you can achieve three ten-minute walks, aim for two fifteen-minute walks. *Accept that sometimes you will overdo things, whether because you forget to rest, or something had to be done.*

Gradually progress to a thirty-minute walk. *Don't measure your recovery in terms of distances or duration; notice how intentionality and 'rest with purpose' gradually make it possible to adapt to your new life, and allow healing.*

Once you can walk for thirty minutes without stopping, you can begin to build up your speed. *As you adapt to your available energy and learn to prioritise recuperation, your understanding of healing will alter.*[14]

Italics by Alec Finlay with Jenny O'Boyle

§

After thirty-five years of *Lag*, I *still* have that innate urge to walk out of illness. I've watched the Long Covid community go through the same shocks I did, age twenty-one: legs no longer functioning, pain bringing waves of grief, fatigue abrading sense of self, lack of medical care and loss of friendship exiling one from a cohesive reality. When I first became ill, I experimented with a walking stick as a signifier of what had befallen me. It didn't help. Now I make poem walking sticks for community walking groups. It doesn't matter that my furthest safe walk is 200 metres, or the length of a station platform. I can still love the idea of a walk.

§

As a self-protective measure, Long Covid support groups propose an alternative to graded exercise: *radical rest.*[15]

Together, we share the urge to walk further.

Together, we walk too far.

Together, we learn to limit walking.

Together, we avoid the relapse cycle, which damages our health, demoralises our spirit, deepens our sense of exile and risks suicide ideation.

I always feel I can walk further than I do.

I can always walk further than I do on any day.

The temporal *Lag* always trumps the spatial walk.

§

The Gospel of Rest preached by the ME Community to their Long Covid brothers and sisters

> *stop every single thing you can, stop trying to do anything at all,*
> > *take time to rest or you'll make yourself worse*
> *stop running from the pain,*
> > *resting now really is your best chance*
> *let it all go and you're more likely to get it all back,*
> > *just stop, stop and rest, give in to it, and completely rest*
> *believe yourself, what you're feeling is real,*
> > *you need to rest, rest completely, total rest*

don't try to push through like the doctors advise,
if you don't rest now, it's much less likely you will recover[16]

§

No one wishes to play the role chronic illness foists on them.

No one wants to be distracted by pain and know worse is coming.

No one wants to find a response to well-intended *are you better now?*

No one wants to conceal the impact of invisible illness.

No one wants to need help or know none is forthcoming.

No one should be tempted by the elect role of suffering.

No one wants to hide their yearning to join the walks others make.

No one wants to say, for the hundredth time, *I can't do this, eat that, walk there.*

No one should have to feel the shame of rejection.

No one likes to hear their limits referred to as a 'lifestyle' choice.

Care, being so longed for, can become hard to accept. Pain makes us, briefly, children again, longing to have our head stroked, be reassured by fingers, never fists, and feel entirely safe.

Love witnesses someone's pain, but sees the person separate from its imprint.

Love strokes sore knees, soothes temples, brings tea.

Love uses the experience of pain to affirm the reality of another's pain.

Love dreams a figure of light at the side of a person in anguish.

Love goes back in time, to a landscape before pain arose – even, if required, to the moment of someone's birth.

§

On my thirtieth birthday, David suggested carrying me up Arthur's Seat on an old wooden chair with broomstick handles. The bearers were to arrive for breakfast and off we'd go. The promise of access was kind, lifting me above my limits, but I blushed. How would it feel to be *seen* as helpless as a king raised on a throne? Hungover, the bearers never turned up and I still haven't been up the hill my window looks out on.

Twenty-five years passed between the onset of ME and my standing on a mountain top. Why on earth do I make so many projects in wild landscapes when I'm unable to hike? Why sing bare beautiful places in which I struggle to belong?

I grew up at the back of a heather moor, sheep fanks and blind burns my familiars, explored on wee adventures with Mum, Ailie and our ridiculous donkeys, Serpolette, Artemis and Maus. Gifted a cottage retreat, my father created an island garden, then declared 'war' on the world agoraphobia exiled him from. His walks kept the chimney tops of home in sight. Stone aircraft carriers patrolled the ponds. His imagination adapted this little world to his illness in an act that was therapeutic and belligerent.

How could such a home not be fraught with conflict – an idyll broken by thundering rages? The postman delivered accusations and collected denunciations. A helicopter fly-by and the joke went they were '*spying for the Scottish Arts Council*'. Did the clicks on the telephone line mean it was tapped? A starting pistol was kept by the receiver.

My mother, exhausted with ME, further swelled the post bag, responding to desperate letters from poorly strangers, sending out reams of photocopied advice. I was formed by these crises of representation, each arising in illness, one physical, the other psychological. For a time I was attracted to the volatile and charismatic, setting out to make safe and pacify. His dominating mode of conflict made our lives often terrifying, with public rows, legal cases, press rammies and raging arguments.

My solace was a walk up the hill to see peewits zig-zag, or over to Anston Burn, where there were magical hazels and a pool long enough for two swim-strokes. It was safe beyond the border, where the only traces of humanity were ruined fanks, the outline of an old croft and the craze for shooting butts.

§

Is pain wild? If I walk too far – not far at all, almost nowhere – a black sun appears.

    To relapse in a beautiful place accentuates the physical hurt. When I could walk, I always tried to save the one expedition for the last day, to take pain home with me and leave the image of the landscape untainted. A childhood yearning for wild nature made me long, in my art, to heal the tensions between distant memories of walking without constraint, and the pain walking in wild places has caused me since. Later in life, being outdoors became, again, a refuge from violence, where indoors was sometimes unsafe.

§

Slow to admit I was disabled, stupidly long walks with pals left me with *Lag* and no adequate picture to convey the pain. My poetry and art in wild places created an impression of vitality. A lover admitted, '*I'd no idea you were so ill.*' An artist accused, '*You will never belong in nature*' – a bitter gift that inspired the determination to do just that.

    How to represent pain without being hemmed in by shame, or snared in the struggle to assert its reality in the face of hostile medical authority? How to avoid being a victim of erasure? How to belong in wild places, as norm walkers do? I found others would walk for me – they will for you, if you ask.

    The injustice of illness became bearable through practices of imaginative adaptation in the forms art and poetry allowed. Creative viewing offered access to wild places I couldn't walk to or over. Poeming the landscape modelled a recuperative way of life. Mould became a metaphor for gossip and the toxic impact of social media, which has its own cliques.

    I understood that the poetic imagination was a machine for creating a sense of belonging – one that needn't be armed or tribal. Unable to walk, collaboration was a way to co-create representations of wild nature, in the same spirit as characterises patient-led care, sharing eyewitness. Immersing myself in toponymic metaphors and vulnerable ecological realities, I perceived human recuperation could align with natural remediation, wounded landscapes with wounded bodies, community conservation projects with patient-led healthcare.

Why shouldn't fatigue and energy injustice, or radical rest, offer adaptive models for climate breakdown?

Despite my own wabbit condition, I could even hymn energy landscapes, watching blades turn on Eigg or Rousay, creating a score for the ebb and flow of tidal languages from the ancient elements of coastal place-names, and imagining the evolution of the mill from Neoltihic quernstones to Oyster marine renewable devices.

§

the human body
frames topography

My poetics was an attempt to recover a sense of belonging. Traditional cultures of viewing guided my imagination, through hills I couldn't climb, to viewpoints where I found meaningful alignments with the skyline. When I couldn't walk further, I lay by a burn and allowed Gaelic place-names to reveal breasts, clefts, shoulders that are noses, relict pinewoods, peaty pools imagined as eyes and caves where wolves were heard, or could be again.[17]

Names provided innumerable images to look up to, explore from counterpane, or ask a friend to walk to and photograph. Ecopoetic translations of names revealed past, present and future ecological and social realities, proposing remediation to heal the map's ancient cache of metaphors. Names dramatised landscapes, revealing places of energy, dwelling and desire: shieling, pùball, tainchell – summer-huts, hunting-benders, deer-drives – recording the ways people of different classes enjoyed or inflicted their sense of belonging on the land. Thrill-seeking hunters or, in modern times, daring climbers, engaged in what I term The Crazes, scattering names for shooting butts and pitches over the hills. Hunting overlaid a vast network of names over the Highlands. To *drive* wild animals to slaughter is a term Freud would approve and, today, despite the C-word, *conservation,* the reality of hunting remains blood and status, totemic meats and feasts and a plague of deer leaving hills denuded of woods.[18]

§

Creag an Chanaich, *Bog-cotton Crag*
Ciochan a' Chop, *The Foamy Tit*
Cnoc nan Aighean, *Hind's Knowe*
Coire an t-Suidhe, *Hunting-seat Corrie*
Dùn Coillich, *Wood Hillfort*
Tom Phobuill, *Bender Tom*
Meall Damh, *Stag Tump*
Meall Tairneachan, *Thundering Lump*
Tom nam Braoileag, *Whortleberry Knowe*[19]

§

an out-
  look

is a land-
  mark

Using creativity to adapt to the limits of my disability, rather than endlessly pushing into relapses – there were still plenty of those – changed my life, for a time. It dawned on me that this disabled perspective wasn't niche: it offered new insights on human and ecological vulnerability for everyone.

In the old ways, toms and knowes were preferred to mountain summits as places to see from and be seen on.[20] Lumps and bumps offered pre-modern people semi-accessible views, some of which were sacred and most likely access to these was limited.

Place-names taught me to recognise dùns, suidhe and sìthean, hillforts, seats and fairy knowes – which played the

the poet limps in words as a balance for worlds

role of crowns, theatres and mythic subterranean chambers, conferring status on the landscape.

Names transformed some views into mytho-poetic hunting poems, others into the domains of early saints. Associations with kings, saints and the aristocratic hunting cult were no obstacle to repurposing these landforms as sites for poetic viewing – a kind of Gaelic Shan Shui – where huts of healing could flower. This contemporary Hutopian revolution already exists on one island and down a few narrow glens.

The short climb to the cathaoir on St Fillan's Chair, near the hillfort of Dùndurn, or the flattie-stane leac on the summit of investiture, at Dùnadd, where the king of Dál Riada stood in a stone footprint, were life-changing. Although the worsening Long Covid has affected my health, making these hillocks inaccessible to me, seats, chairs, dùns, and fairy hillocks remain dear to my heart.[21] They are a body of found natural architectural landforms, in which mounds set within mountains compose poetic views. These outlooks had alleviated my lack of walking. Thanks to Gaelic names, I found their embodied knowledge was everywhere.

There were Neolithic beacon dùns, like Dùnan an Aisilidh and Dùn Liath, recalling signal fires, like those that relayed the fall of Troy to Mycenae.

The bloody theatre of the Gaelic hunt was revealed in deer-traps and hunting seats, at Invercauld and Glenmoriston. 'Fiannscape' land-poems set down the names of deer, stag, roe, boar, and heroic Fingalian hunters on the Glenshee hills.[22]

There were sìthean fairy hillocks with imaginary chambers to comfort my loss of velocity, going under the earth into the darkness of pain.

At Acharn and Dunkeld, there were Ossian-inspired follies and fog houses expressing an eccentric culture of viewing, adaptable to disability perspectives. At Bruar, the waterfalls were out of reach, but Lady Emily Percy's sketch shows a 'view-house' in which Basho and his pals could have composed renga.[23]

There were new follies, such as the Hutopian hut at Inshriach and viewing platform at Outlandia.

G. F. Dutton's marginal garden was a masterly ecopoetic reinterpretation of the eighteenth-century wild garden.[24]

Healing was written into the planning of Victorian asylums, which had viewing mounds and 'airing courts' in their grounds, like the model Mount Fuji in the Suizen-ji garden, Joju-en,[25] or the shale bings of West Lothian, where the spoil has healed with meliot and saplings.

Walks to these inspiring landscapes often led to crashes, but compared to the craze for mountain summits, they were all, in a rough manner, accessible. These found landscapes helped define a practice of place-awareness and, with it, new approaches to disability access.

Rewilding ecologists, innovative factors and gamekeepers led me to understand how landscapes can heal passively, over time, like someone recovering from chronic illness.[26] As land management shifts from the grip of Crazes towards rewilding, hybrid roles emerge, and prestige transfers from prestige antlers to collective pines.

Place-awareness and creative disability access are a means to parley between conflicting versions of environmental reality, furthering a culture of recuperation as an alternative to one of blood and thrills. In each of these projects, vulnerability is an expression of nature. They ally the aspiration that those with chronic illness should be supported to heal in wild places with the ecological remediation movement.

§

word-mntn

S
C H I
E H A
L L I O N

fairy mountain of the caledonians

§

the poet limps in words as a balance for worlds

BEN GULABIN
CÀRN AN DAIMH
LEABAIDH AN TUIRC
CRAIG OF RUNAVEY
BAD AN LOIN
MEALL RUIGH MOR THEARLAICH
MEALL A' CHOIRE BHUIDHE
BEN EARB
CREAG AN DUBH SHLUIC
CREAG AN UAINE
MEALL UAINE
MEALL BHINNEIN
CREAG NA BRUAICH
MEALNA LETTER
MOUNT BLAIR

conspectus (Tom Darmaid)

§

*a path is a way
   through the land*

*a view is a picture
   of the world*

Turning the skyline of sorrow, I found creative ways to repurpose these ancient cultures of viewing. Notating hill names as 'word-mntn' and 'conspectus' visual poems that defined a horizon in the round, composing viewing in a turning circle as an alternative to the dotted lines made by walkers. Viewpoints which held spiritual and social significance could regain meaning as portals of access.

I helped to revive Japanese renga as 'shared writing', composing poems collaboratively in the landscape, sat all day on a flat-pack larch platform with four-square posts that compassed the view.[27]

These practices evolved, over years, into a version of ecopoetics reframed by disability. I found I could define poetic forms that were available to the walking constrained and walking norm alike.

§

My most far-reaching access project was realised in a wild landscape where estates under the stewardship of John Muir Trust, Forestry Land Scotland, a community woodland, and privately owned land, share a fence post. 'Day of Access' was an act of solidarity. Ecologists, foresters, gamekeepers, and landowners drove disabled people up Meall Tairneachan, a pyramidal lump among lumpy hills.[28] To the west was stand-alone Schiehallion, a skyline so distinct it gave birth to the contour line.

'Day of Access' is an experimental reintroduction of vulnerable ecologies into vulnerable ecologies, as proof that the meaning of a landscape can be reimagined – which is to say, can be healed. The experience of that ascent made real the imaginative confluence of human and ecological vulnerability, environmental remediation, and human recuperation. It also reaffirmed the genius of the Gael for conceptualising natural forms as architecture. On a rushy plateau, overlooked by a suidhe, we felt the presence of Schiehallion anew in a sacred hunting landscape.

§

happy she'd come
  home afraid

to hear the door-
  handle turn

Walking defines agency. By walking we arrive, take our leave, demarcate the boundaries of our reality, enact choices and access the people and places we love.

When I lived with a partner who was subject to episodes of anomie and occasional violence, being outdoors was a way to be safe, sharing gentle walks, or lying on a blanket beneath apple trees. Indoors, her wildness could erupt as suddenly as a stag breaking cover pursued by hounds. The arc of memory traces those tight, flailing fists.

for the violently enraged
  their violence lasts a moment

for those exposed to their violence
  every moment is alive
  with fear of that rage

What is physical pain compared to fearing someone you love? The first blow can be explained away. When the second comes, wariness settles over you as any moment can become fraught. Love was shadowed by a new kind of *Lag* – '*I never hit you, except that time when I hit you and anyway, there was always a reason I hit you.*' Though I could describe the handful of events – how the blows fell, on head, shoulder, arms, or shins – I was told, once again, that I would never be believed and that such events could never happen. And so another intense experience of pain was denied reality.

After the worst assault, I met someone whose crisis of belonging was as deep as my own, and that alone gave me the courage to walk away. There was the hope of being safe, hidden away together, healing like lions. We walked by a sea wall in which the older and old stones met in a precarious marriage.

Art is the saying of unsayable realities. When reality is denied its commonality, or worse, bodily experience is kettled by erasure, or false accusation, then recuperation is made that much harder. What is vigilante culture or Wessleyianism but the targeting of vulnerability? What use is the urge to forgive, the ability to affirm trauma, or agree that violence passes down generations, if people claim this right to distort reality?

As Denise Riley says, in *Time Lived, Without its Flow*, the possibility of description and the kinds of temporal experience we inhabit are '*intimately allied*'. Illness schooled me harshly: being believed is the ground upon which shared social reality stands or falls. Confronted by disbelieving cliques, we depend on the solidarity of a few empathic friends who are willing to translate from their own experiences of pain, fatigue, or violence. From my experience, being subject to a falsified reality is more hurtful than any punch.

This targeting of vulnerability guided me back to the writer's task: to describe complex reality and trust the reader to translate from their own experiences without being tempted by accusation or blame.

§

The imagination can be transformative or totalising. My father's garden was a magical place, entrancing for those who enjoyed a brief walk. The intensification of the imagination that agoraphobia provoked impelled his landscape from an idyllic retreat towards Jacobin fury. The garden was not a work of parley, but a theatrical clash of values with the desire for violence. The poet threw lightning bolts but, when the weather turned to thunder, his face blushed and took shelter under the covers, reliving the Clydebank Blitz.

Exile fathers exile. The family walked away from (our) home after his death. Is it a duty to tear away camouflage nets, or leave that very human rage concealed in stone frigates and bronze guillotines? The realities each of us can speak to depend on whether we have a gang at our back or we're in the company of people we trust to parley. The gift of the garden, and the conflicts that the family endured, need not be in conflict. Acts of violence can be forgiven, but only if they are permitted to exist.

§

It took me half a lifetime to make a hut of healing. I began with the dream of a view-hut in the Hebrides, its walls lined by 10,000 feathers, inspired by mad Sweeney. It was made real by a gentle man who raised the thorn-high bed and set the wide window before a graph of jaggy mountains. The hut gifted a sense of belonging to those with constrained walking – the walk to the door was mostly doable, the view spectacular. Sweeney's hut offered artists and writers the opportunity to dwell, briefly, in a healing Gaelic landscape, among native whips and bluebells, where they could allow wildness to gently reconfigure their thought.

But I went there with my tender and enraged love. A malevolent voice called her into madness, provoked by wooden boards, the hut's wild sense of permission, and, sadly, because it was my dream of healing. I'd imagined Sweeney's wound-shock as a figure of recuperation, but she alleged that the island refugia lured her into madness. I've never felt more afraid than I did that week. Her spirals of self-hatred coiled and sprang with manic intensity. Once again, vulnerability had its fragile permission to belong in a wild place ripped from its grasp. It hurt that a place of such serenity should have this mental anguish imposed on it. Worse was the knowledge that, had the hut been a projection of her own imagination, she would have embraced it.

I couldn't bear the burning brand of conflict being dragged up the path into a space intended for healing. Sweeney's myth felt like a curse. My own need for healing was forced into exile. I'd been dreaming of this refuge for years as a place the partially disabled could rest within a jagged view.

Later she returned without me, taking on Sweeney's mad persona, making a beautiful film that eulogised their dual descent into the underworld, redeeming the land in her own image, a Fingalian narcissus gazing at her bearded reflection in the lochan, filling the entire horizon with a woman's profile. She gathered the island and the Sweeney myths that I'd collected and renewed into herself, entirely erasing my authorship, in a gesture I was to become familiar with. Here was that animus towards vulnerability all over again, this time like rock-paper-scissors engulfed by flame.

For me, the film's allure was a further disassociation, translating the madness into that old Scottish aspect of the wounded psyche, *glamour*, a cast enchantment. Her stylised dramatisation veiled the desperate, chaotic reality of that week in the hut and the episodes that followed.

In the same way, my father's garden was lovely and, for those who lived there, haunted by rage and episodes of anomie. I would have given anything for the garden to have remained a public marvel *and* a family idyll, with a wee fifie bobbing on the lochan. But my father's riven nature made that impossible and the result is an inevitable exile. I would have given anything for the Sweeney myth to have proved a cathartic resolution of my partner's rage, for the hut to have been allowed to be a refuge, and for her film to have healed the threat of madness and violence that hung over us. Nothing changed. Nevertheless, the achievement of his garden and her film remain: beautiful, enchanting, available to all, except the intimates who bore witness to the sometimes fraught conditions of their creation. I speak of these realities now out of a belief that art can parley lived experiences and disarm fantasy, if truth be told.

The vulnerability of illness remains integral to my creative journey. I was guided away from the disbelief of the fantasy-walk the poet limps in words as a balance for worlds experiment, towards huts of healing, days of access, and a cottage hospital. My evening walk around the four corners of a tiny garden is, for now, a world.

>*the convalescents*
>   *are breakfasting*
>
>*in the convalescence*
>   *garden*

this is my body

Kate Davis

    this is my body a body of evidence
a body of evidence /of wrong doing?
a wrong body? – You look all right to me
an imagined wrong body?   – Do I look all right to you?
is it just my imagi . . .
aren't we all a
like
under   the   s   sss
under the s   s   s
un
der
the

    this is my body mass indexed
and filed under Faulty
a body armoured against the gaze
of those whose jaws tighten for a second
before they can stop them

    this is my body and
sold under false pretences
a body sunk by the weight of iron-work they attached

this is my body

to calliper it up
right
and proper
this is my slap-dash
shambling
arse-over-tit
shameful
shame full ugly body

how do I know it's ugly?
because world
you told me
you repeated it every day until I got the message
it was you
not the earth
who is in any case far more trustworthy than you
whose fault-lines and erosion and subsidence
and tectonic shenanigans have never
made me feel as inferior as your pointing finger
your flapping lips
who is a close relative of mine
and who I will not be leaving even if I could
tied as I am to earth by my stumbling feet
my inability to
skim
skip
balance
stand to attention
stand
at ease
tied too by the dead weight of my own skin which is
a kind of carapace that holds me here beetling on my back
a stuck insect easy to pin in place for
examination by specialists and display to the public

it was not the earth
it was you world

with your sharp intake of breath
your whispered asides
you stared at me
and stared at me
until you found me wanting
until you found me wanting
to look
like you
to look all right to you
to look right

this is my body
and for too long world
you have
body-pierced it with your stares
body shaped it with your princesses your dolls your stories
of angels and the whole shebang of good-loveliness
you pushed in my face until I understood that it was my job
to do better
that you were never going to wait for me to hobble over
that those of us who are not Beauty must be
The Beasts

this is my body
a body of knowledge
a body of work

and I am making with it
a body of language

After Raymond Antrobus, 'Dear Hearing World'
and Danez Smith 'dear white america'

I should apologise here for such a bad-tempered start and for what might seem like direct and unfounded criticism. I accept the sincere assurances that no one out there has anything against me personally — that no one thinks less of me because I have a disability, because I look different. Someone does, not you obviously, but someone out there stares, turns away, calls out names I can't repeat.

When I think about how people see my body move, I see a clumsy thing without grace hobbling along, tied to the earth. That word, 'hobble' has taken me decades to say – it's dangerous, one of what I think of as my 'snake words.' I remember the first time someone used it about me – a school rounders match and my team won by half a point. I'd scored half a rounder and a team-mate said 'if it hadn't been for you hobbling round we wouldn't have won.' I didn't know I hobbled. I was so shocked I couldn't speak. After that, I could only walk in public by making spells to get me somewhere safely and hide my limp, my wasted leg, my stumbling, shameful body. I'm seventy years old and I still use a spell when I'm walking outside the house.

I was born in a wild place between a wood and hills littered with limestone boulders. Trees, plants and animals crept relentlessly into the garden. That world to belong to us – to me – I moved through it like a native. There was little that separated me from it – I owned the places I played, owned my body, could push it through hawthorn hedges, over walls and up trees. After I caught paralytic polio, I lived my life much nearer the ground and always looking down in an effort to avoid tripping up.

My walking was poor and my range limited, sometimes to the distance I could hop. That got me as far as the small field in front of our house where in summer I'd sit on a tiny area of exposed limestone. There, lady's slipper flowers clung and crawled towards me from the margins and grass was turfy and short. I could worry at those growing edges, peel them away to discover what was underneath – a dusty, greyish powder, ants, various little armoured things, red mites and, best of all, minute snails. I could see that the leaves and flower spikes of lady's slipper grew from stems in a particular, predictable way, that the flower clusters looked random but that each individual flower had a way of curving itself open and arcing back so that one side mirrored the other and streaks of colour were symmetrical.

The dramatic new faults in my body changed my relationship with the earth under my feet. In one way, for the better – the ground was now my close friend and most fascinating companion. At the same time, it became my nemesis – to look up while walking was asking for trouble – if I wanted to stay upright, I had to keep my eyes on the ground. Thus began a lifetime of knowing and naming plants, but failing dismally to recognise birds.

All that was a long time ago. Now I'm an old woman – surely I should have come to terms years ago with my asymmetrical body, my wasted leg, my limp – should have learned to be more body positive? So why haven't I?

In some ways I've done OK – it took a long time but I'm finally able to believe that my damaged body is not my fault. I don't love my crippled leg but I've stopped regarding it as a cold dead thing attached to me at the hip, stopped imagining plucking it from my body and laying it somewhere mossy and dark from where it will never find its way back to me. Now I take better care of it, try to protect it from cold and the injuries it can't feel, check it for signs of damage, put extra factor 50 on the thin, mottled skin.

Yet when I go outside, I still choose to hide it most of the time. I'd like to point out here that I consider hiding to be a valid coping strategy. Partly, it's to protect it from cold – it has no capacity to warm itself or to keep warm and manifests a deathly cold I've never experienced anywhere else in my body. But more than that, the world still stares with that look of shock –> confusion –> distaste –> pity I know very well. I definitely need to do more work on my response to such looks – work harder at developing my self-esteem.

And if the starers could make it less obvious – that'd be great too.

Physalis Protectus Seriflorum

Acknowledgements

Thank you to everyone who has been involved in, and supported, this project. From the early notion of such an anthology coming into being with Deirdre O'Byrne at Five Leaves Bookshop, to Arts Council England who awarded me an ACE grant, and to Caro Clarke and Footnote Press for bringing the work into being, thank you all.

Thanks go to Jan Kofi-Tsekpo from Arts Council England, Jon Woolcott, Paul Scully of Kendal Mountain Literary Festival and Andrew Willan of Wealden Literary Festival who responded so positively to the prospect of such a project early on.

A special thanks goes to Polly Atkin for her enthusiasm, support and encouragement, for suggesting and connecting me with some wonderful writers and for generally being brilliant. To everyone who has contributed their words and images, an anthology is made up of so much more than can ever be translated. For the time and energy, thought and sensitivity that each and every writer, poet and artist has given to this project, and for the trust and generosity that you have shown me with your work, I am enormously grateful. You have made this book far more than I could have ever hoped or imagined.

Thanks go also to Arts Council England, who supported me with a funding grant to be able, most importantly, to pay contributors for their work and to run a series of workshops

Acknowledgements

throughout 2022 which enabled more than a thousand writers to explore their own connection to nature and the more-than-human world around them. Thanks to all the organisations and groups that have supported the project, the literary, nature and disability charities and organisations who hosted and supported the workshops that have run while the anthology has been in process: Arvon, Chronic Illness Inclusion, Festival of Nature, Healing Justice London, ME Action UK, POTS UK, Resting Up Collective, Society of Authors – Authors with Disabilities and Chronic Illness Group, Sussex Wildlife Trust, Wealden Literary Festival, and everyone else who has cheered and championed us along the way. To everyone who joined us for the workshops and wrote about their connection with the more-than-human world for the first time, who were seasoned writers, and those who connected with each other through shared experiences and diagnoses in conversations in the chat function of Zoom. You have all been a part of this process and fuel for me in making sure this book sees daylight.

A special thanks go to my own writing and artists' community, who have cheered me on, read early drafts of my work, and shared their own words of encouragement. You have all been brilliant and I'm very grateful for your friendship, creativity and writerly advice: Aly Fixter, Helen Meller, Fran Springfield, Anna Stratford, Sue Tangney, Nicola Wilson, Alex Woodcock, and Nicole Zaaroura. Thanks also go to my friends and family, my mum and sister Jo.

Enormous gratitude particularly to Caro Clarke, who has been a supporter throughout this project and who found such a thoughtful and ambitious publisher in Footnote. To Alice Marwick who has made such a beautiful job of the cover design, and to Rose Green, Dhruti Modha, Grace Harrison, Vimbai Shire and Chloe Johnson who have been sensitive readers, editors and enthusiastic supporters, and all at Footnote, thank you!

Contributors

Isobel Anderson is a musician with a PhD in Sonic Arts and a passion for creating supportive music tech education spaces for women. Her four solo albums have amassed over 25 million Spotify streams and her sound works have been performed on international stages. She has published in journals such as *Organised Sound* and the *Journal of Sonic Studies*. Threaded throughout her work is a fascination with how we make sense of ourselves, the world around us and the process of creative exploration itself. She is proud to produce and host the critically acclaimed feminist music tech podcast, 'Girls Twiddling Knobs'.

Kerri Andrews is Reader in Women's Literature and Textual Editing at Edge Hill University. She is the author of *Wanderers: a History of Women Walking* (Reaktion, 2020), and is the editor both of the anthology, *Way Makers: an Anthology of Women's Writing about Walking* (Reaktion, 2023), and the first ever edition of Scottish nature writer Nan Shepherd's letters (Edinburgh University Press, 2023). Her current work in progress is a non-fiction book about walking and motherhood.

Polly Atkin (FRSL) is a poet and non-fiction writer. She has published three poetry pamphlets and two collections – *Basic Nest Architecture* (Seren, 2017) and *Much With Body* (Seren, 2021). Her non-fiction includes *Recovering Dorothy: The Hidden Life of Dorothy Wordsworth* (Saraband, 2021), a Barbellion-longlisted biography of Dorothy's later life and illness, and a memoir exploring place, belonging and disability, *Some Of Us Just Fall: On Nature and Not Getting Better* (Sceptre, 2023). She works as a freelancer from her home in the English Lake District.

Khairani Barokka is a writer and artist from Jakarta, based in London. Her work has been presented internationally, and aims to centre disability justice as anticolonial praxis. Among her accolades, she was a UNFPA Indonesian Young Leader Driving Social Change, a NYU Tisch Departmental Fellow, and an Associate Artist at the National Centre for Writing. Okka was co-editor of *Stairs and Whispers: D/deaf and Disabled Poets Write Back* (Nine Arches Press, 2017) and is currently editor of *Modern Poetry in Translation*. Her first book, *Indigenous Species*, was published in 2016, followed by *Rope*, in 2017, and she was shortlisted for the Barbellion Prize with *Ultimatum Orangutan* (Nine Arches Press, 2021). She has two books forthcoming in 2024.

Victoria Bennett is a poet and author. Her writing has previously received a Northern Debut Award, a Northern Promise Award, the Andrew Waterhouse Award, and has been longlisted for the Penguin WriteNow programme and the inaugural Nan Shepherd Prize for underrepresented voices. She founded Wild Women Press in 1999 to support rural women writers in her community, and since 2018 has curated the global Wild Women Web project, an inclusive online space focusing on nature, connection, and creativity. *All My Wild Mothers*, her debut memoir, is published by Two Roads Books (2023).

Feline Charpentier was born in Germany but grew up halfway up a mountain in Snowdonia. She has three children, and recently moved to south Devon. Feline has had many jobs, from river surveyor to baker, but recent chronic illness and needing to care for her youngest son, who has Cystic Fibrosis, means she is currently able to write more than before. She is working on a novel and has a number of shorter fiction and non-fiction pieces due out this year. Feline was shortlisted for the inaugural Curae Prize, and her short story is to be published in the print anthology with Renard Press (2023).

Cat Chong is a poet, publisher, PhD student at Nanyang Technological University, Singapore, and visiting PhD fellow at the Institute for Medical Humanities at Durham University. They're a graduate of the Poetic Practice MA at Royal Holloway, co-founder of the Crested Tit Collective, and digital editor at Osmosis Press. Their work has been published internationally by presses such as Bad Betty, Flint, Ache, Permeable Barrier, Singapore Unbound, Experiment-O, The Polyphony, and Ethos Books. Their most recent publications include the pamphlet *Plain Air: An Apology in Transit*, '—I'm writing my way out – and this is a place of refuge—' a chapter in *Not Without Us: Perspectives on Disability and Inclusivity in Singapore*, as well as installations such as *The Kindness Connection* which was commissioned by Singapore General Hospital. Their debut collection *712 Stanza Homes For The Sun* was published by Broken Sleep Books in April 2023.

Eli Clare is white, disabled, and genderqueer, living near Lake Champlain in unceded Abenaki territory (also known as Vermont in the United States) where he writes and proudly claims a penchant for rabble-rousing. He has written two books of essays, the award-winning *Brilliant Imperfection: Grappling with Cure* and *Exile and Pride: Disability, Queerness, and Liberation*, and a collection of poetry, *The Marrow's Telling: Words in Motion*. Additionally he has been published in dozens of journals and anthologies.

Eli works as a travelling poet, storyteller and social justice educator. He currently serves on the Community Advisory Board for the Disability Project at the Transgender Law Center and is a Disability Futures Fellow (funded by the Ford Foundation and the Andrew W. Mellon Foundation). Among other pursuits, he has walked across the United States for peace, coordinated a rape prevention programme and helped organise the first ever Queer Disability Conference.

Dawn Cole is an award-winning artist based in Kent. Her research led practice centres around memories and memorialisation. Her work is included in the collections at the Victoria and Albert Museum and she was artist in residence at Canterbury Cathedral in 2018. Her work has been exhibited internationally.

Lorna Crabbe is an artist, curator and researcher living and working in Hastings Old Town. Her artwork spans artists' books, painting, drawing, costume and collage, all with a link to archives, obsessive collecting and a re-imagining of the past. Crabbe co-directed the Coastal Currents arts festival from 2009–2015 and is a trustee of the Hastings Storytelling Festival. She often works on research based projects that explore local heritage in creative ways, most recently a celebration of the fortieth anniversary of Hastings Jack in the Green.

Kate Davis is a poet based in Cumbria. Her work has been published in Iota and Butcher's Dog, implanted in audio-benches, sung throughout a 12-hour tide cycle, embroidered onto clothes, remixed by a sound artist and printed on shopping bags. In 2013 she received a Northern Writer's Award, New Poets Bursary. Her first collection *The Girl Who Forgets How to Walk* was published by Penned in the Margins (2018) and her second will be published in March 2024.

Carol Donaldson is a writer and conservationist. Originally from Essex, she has worked for many of Britain's best wildlife charities and currently runs her own environmental consultancy. She has written for *Wanderlust*, *BBC Wildlife Magazine* and the *Telegraph*. She was *BBC Wildlife Magazine*'s Travel Writer of the Year in 2011 and her first book, *On The Marshes*, was published by Little Toller in 2017. Her second book, *The Volunteers*, is due to be published by Summersdale in 2024.

Alec Finlay is a Scottish artist and poet whose work crosses over a range of media and forms. Finlay was awarded the 2020 Cholmondeley Award for services to poetry. Recent publications include the Scottish Design Award's best publication winner, *a far-off land* (2018); *gathering*, published by Hauser & Wirth (2018); *th' fleety wud* (2017); minn*mouth* (2017); *ebban an' flowan* (2015), and *Global Oracle* (2014). Sweeney's Bothy, on the Isle of Eigg, was co-conceived with the Bothy Project; it still hosts artist residencies.

Jamie Hale is a queer/crip artist, curator, poet, writer, screenwriter, playwright, director, policy analyst and charity CEO, a cyborg kept alive by multiple machines. Their poetry centres on queer/crip perspectives of embodiment, nature and mortality. They were a 2021–22 Jerwood Poetry Fellow and in 2021 won the Evening Standard Director-Theatremaker of the Year award for their solo poetry show, NOT DYING, which has been performed across the UK and screened internationally. Their critically acclaimed pamphlet, *Shield*, was published in 2021 by Verve Poetry Press, and they are working on their first full collection. They also founded CRIPtic Arts, an award-winning organisation committed to exploring, developing and platforming the creativity of disabled people, and in 2023 co-founded the UK's first Disabled Poets' Prize, which was awarded in 2023.

Jane Hartshorn is a poet and PhD candidate at the University of Kent, writing about the lived experience of chronic illness. Her pamphlets include *In the Sick Hour* (Takeaway Press, 2020) and *Tract* (Litmus Publishing, 2017). Hartshorn's work has been published by Boudicca Press, Dostoyevsky Wannabe, Lucy Writers and SPAM, and she is an editor at Ache Press and founder of CHASE Medical Humanities Network.

Hannah Hodgson is a writer living with a life-limiting illness. She has been published by BBC Arts, *The Poetry Review*, *Magma* and *Mslexia*, amongst others, and has edited for both *Poetry Wales* and *The Butcher's Dog*. Her first full collection (*163 Days*) was published by Seren in 2022 and adapted into a play for BBC Sounds, and was highly commended in the Forward Prize for Poetry (2022). She won Northern Writers' Awards for Poetry in 2020 and 2022. In 2021 she won the Poetry Business's New Poets Prize, as well as The Diana Legacy Award in recognition of her advocacy and social action work. As well as her first collection, she has three other pamphlets: *Dear Body* (Wayleave, 2018), *Where I'd Watch Plastic Trees Not Grow* (Verve, 2021) and *Queen of Hearts* (Poetry Business, 2022).

Sally Huband lives in the Shetland Islands and is the author of *Sea Bean* (longlisted for the Wainwright Prize for Nature Writing, 2023). Her writing can also be found in *Antlers of Water*, an anthology edited by Kathleen Jamie and *Archipelago – A Reader*, edited by Nicholas Allen and Fiona Stafford. She is a recipient of a Scottish Book Trust New Writers Award and holds a PhD in ecology and anthropology from the University of Edinburgh.

Rowan Jaines is a lecturer in Human Environmental Geography at the University of Sheffield. Originally from North Norfolk, her PhD thesis focused on the agricultural landscapes of the drained fenlands that arc between Boston in Lincolnshire and Kings Lynn in Norfolk. She is a quarter of the four womxn team that have authored *Nature's Calendar*, a look at the UK natural world through 72 'micro seasons', published by Granta in 2023. When Rowan is not reading or writing she likes to hang out with her best friend, Astrid the golden retriever, border-collie cross. They share a love of sitting in sunbeams and eating dairy-based produce.

Dillon Jaxx is a queer writer with disabling chronic illness living in Sussex. Dillon's work is published both online and in print, including in *Poetry Wales* and *Ink, Sweat and Tears*. Shortlists include Nine Arches Primers 2021 and Creative Future Writers' Award 2022. Winner of the Rebecca Swift Foundation Women Poets' Prize 2022, they are working towards that debut collection.

Contributors

Louise Kenward is a writer, artist and psychologist. Working for the NHS for much of her career, she set up ZebraPsych in 2020 with the aim of raising awareness and understanding of energy limiting chronic illness. Her writing has been widely published, and is included in: *Women on Nature* (2021), *But You Don't Look Sick* (2021), *The Clearing*, the *BMJ*, *The Polyphony*, *The Unwritten* and the *Bookseller*. In 2020 she co-produced *Disturbing the Body* (Boudicca Press) and her essay commissioned for BBC3, *Landscapes for Recovery* ('The Ocean as Mirror'), was broadcast in 2022. Between 2021 and 2022 Louise was writer-in-residence with Sussex Wildlife Trust. Currently undertaking a practice-led PhD with the Centre for Place Writing at Manchester Metropolitan University, Louise's research explores post-viral illness through the landscape of the Romney Marshes. She is preparing her first full-length book, *A Trail of Breadcrumbs*.

Abi Palmer is a writer and artist. Her work often explores ideas around queerness, chronic illness and multisensory intervention. Her debut book, *Sanatorium*, was published by Penned in the Margins in 2020 and was shortlisted for the Barbellion Prize. Her writing has been commissioned by the *Guardian*, Wellcome Collection and BBC Radio 3. In 2016, she won a Saboteur Award for her poetry installation *Alchemy* and in 2020 she was awarded a Thinking Time grant by Artangel. Palmer has exhibited at Tate Modern, Wellcome Collection and Somerset House. Her most recent work is *Abi Palmer Invents the Weather* (2023), a series of four short films that show her creating boxes for her indoor cats to experience the changing seasons.

Louisa Adjoa Parker is an RSA Fellow and writer of English-Ghanaian heritage. Author of four poetry collections, including *Salt-Sweat and Tears* (Cinnamon Press, 2016), *How To Wear a Skin* (Indigo Dreams, 2019), and *She Can Still Sing* (Flipped Eye, 2021), and a short story collection *Stay With Me* (Colenso Books, 2020), her work has appeared in a wide range of journals and anthologies. She has been highly commended by the Forward Prize, twice shortlisted by the Bridport Prize, and her poem,

Contributors

'Kindness', was commended by the National Poetry Competition in 2019. Her memoir of life as a mixed-heritage teenager in the southwest of England is to be published by Little Toller Books.

Alice Tarbuck is a writer and academic based in Scotland. Winning the Scottish Book Trust New Writer's Award for poetry in 2019, her first poetry pamphlet *Grid* was published by Sad Press in 2018 and her first book *A Spell In The Wild: A Year (and Six Centuries) of Magic* was published by Two Roads (Hachette) in 2021. Her work has been published widely, and she has appeared at StAnza, Belfast Literary Festival and Literary Dundee.

Nic Wilson is a writer and a *Guardian* Country Diarist. Her work has featured in anthologies, journals and magazines including *Gardeners' World*, *The English Garden*, *The Garden* (RHS), *The John Clare Society Journal* and *Women on Nature*, edited by Katharine Norbury (2021).

Supported using public funding by
ARTS COUNCIL ENGLAND

Resources

Chronic Illness Inclusion	www.chronicillnessinclusion.org.uk
Dysautonomia International	www.dysautonomiainternational.org
Haemochromatosis UK	www.haemochromatosis.org.uk
Healing Justice London	www.healingjusticeldn.org
Hypermobility Syndromes Association (HMSA)	www.hypermobility.org
Long Covid SOS	www.longcovidsos.org
ME Action UK	www.meaction.net
POTS UK	www.potsuk.org
Resting Up Collective	www.stillill.uk/resting-up-collective
The Wren Project	www.wrenproject.org

Endnotes

Introduction

1. Eli Clare, *Brilliant Imperfection: grappling with cure* (Duke University Press, 2017) p. 25.
2. Eli Clare, 'Notes on Natural Worlds', in Sami Schalk and Jessica Smartt Gullion (eds), *Disability Studies and the Environmental Humanities: Towards an Eco-Crip Theory* (University of Nebraska Press, 2017), p. 255.
3. McPhail, T. (2023) Allergies and the Microbiome. *Start the Week*. Radio 4, 5th June. https://www.bbc.co.uk/programmes/m001mlg2
4. Anna Kafer, 'Bodies of Nature: The Environmental Politics of Disability' in Sarah Jaquette Ray and Jay Sibara (eds), Disability Studies and the Environmental Humanities: Toward an Eco-Crip Theory (University of Nebraska Press, 2017), p. 204.
5. Elspeth Wilson, 'If you want diverse books you need to change your definition of commercial', *Inklusion Guide*, 2023. Available at: https://www.inklusionguide.org/blog/elspeth-wilson [accessed on 16 May, 2023].
6. Climate Reality Project, 'Climate denial: why it happens and what to do about it', 2022. Available at: https://www.climaterealityproject.org/blog/climate-science-denial-why-and-what-to-do-about-it [accessed 28 May 2023].
7. Dr Fergus Brown, 'The WHO Has Not Declared The Covid-19 Pandemic Over', *Full Fact*, 18 May 2023. Available at: https://fullfact.org/health/who-covid-pandemic-over/ [accessed 22 May 2023].
8. Kathleen Jamie, 'A Lone Enraptured Male', London Review of Books, Vol. 30, No. 5, 6 March 2008, pp. 25-27, [Online] Available at: https://www.lrb.co.uk/the-paper/v30/n05/kathleen-jamie/a-lone-enraptured-male.
9. Polly Atkin, 'Field Notes: Open Mountain', *John Muir Trust*, 25, 2019. Available at: https://www.johnmuirtrust.org/whats-new/news/24-field-notes-open-mountain [accessed 28 May 2023].
10. The term 'more-than-human', was coined by David Abram in the 1990s, specifically to refer to 'earthly nature'. It has since been broadly adopted as a way of distinguishing humans from the rest of the natural world.

Endnotes

Field Notes

1. An earlier version of Hyper-oceanic appeared on the *Lone Women in Flashes of Wilderness* website: https://www.lonewomeninflashesofwilderness.com/
2. Marjorie Hingley, 'Microscopic Life in Sphagnum', *Naturalists' Handbook 20* (Richmond Publishing Co., 1993).

Under a Wide Blue Sky: Chronic illness, Nature and Me

1. Vincent J Felitti MD, FACP A, Robert F Anda MD, MS B, Dale Nordenberg MD C, David F Williamson MS, PhD B, Alison M Spitz MS, MPH B, Valerie Edwards BA B, Mary P Koss PhD D, James S Marks MD, MPH B, 'Relationship of Childhood Abuse and Household Dysfunction to Many of the Leading Causes of Death in Adults: The Adverse Childhood Experiences (ACE) Study', *American Journal of Preventative Medicine*, 14(4), (1998), p. 245–258. Available: https://www.ajpmonline.org/article/S0749-3797(98)00017-8/fulltext (summary: APA PsycNet https://psycnet.apa.org/record/1998-04002-001).
2. According to Wikipedia, female hysteria was once 'a common medical diagnosis for women, described as exhibiting a wide array of symptoms, including anxiety, shortness of breath, fainting, nervousness, sexual desire, insomnia, fluid retention, heaviness in the abdomen, irritability, loss of appetite for food or sex, (paradoxically) sexually forward behavior, and a "tendency to cause trouble for others".' Though is no longer recognised by medical authorities as a medical disorder, its diagnosis and treatment were routine for hundreds of years in Western Europe.

Things in Jars

1. Mark Schonbeck, 'An Ecological Understanding of Weeds', *eOrganic*, 2009. Available at: https://eorganic.org/node/2314#:~:text=Pioneer%20plants%E2%80%94what%20we%20call,feed%20and%20restore%20soil%20life [accessed 16 May 2023].

Threatening Rain: On Bodies, Bad Weather and Bad Clothing

1. https://www.nature.com/articles/s41746-019-0180-3
2. Arthur Guiterman, *A Poet's Proverbs: Being Mirthful, Sober, and Fanciful Epigrams on the Universe, with Certain Old Irish Proverbs, All in Rhymed Couplets* (E.P. Dutton, 1924), p.5.
3. Alfred Wainwright, *A Coast To Coast Walk* (Francis Lincoln, 2017), p. vii.

4. Wainwright, p.7.
5. <http://tohatchacrow.blogspot.com/2015/04/obscured-by-clouds wainwrights-bad.html>
6. Dorothy Wordsworth, *Rydal Journal*, 21 November 1834.
7. Dorothy Wordsworth to Anne Pollard, 12–17 April 1834.
8. Greg Freeman, 'Sarah Doyle on transforming Dorothy Wordsworth's journal into poetry', *Write Out Loud*, 24 April 2021. Available at: https://www.writeoutloud.net/public/blogentry.php?blogentryid=114011
9. Dorothy Wordsworth, *Rydal Journal*, 7 April 1834.
10. Dorothy Wordsworth, *Rydal Journal*, 1 May 1830.
11. Dorothy Wordsworth, *Rydal Journal*, 5 May 1834.

Foraging and Feminism: Hedge-Witchcraft in the 21st Century

1. Law, Donald. *The Concise Herbal Encyclopedia* (St. Martin's, 1976), p.81.
2. Clark, Sarah, 'Forage for your supper', 4 June, 2015. Available at: https://www.visitscotland.com/blog/scotland/foraging/
3. http://foodanddrink.scotsman.com/food/wild-scottish-and-frees-guide-to-summer-foraging-in-scotland/
4. http://www.snh.gov.uk/planning-and-development/economic-value/rural-enterprise/foraging/
5. Carell, Severin, 'Wild harvest reaps big rewards in foraging rush' in the *Guardian*, 27 April 2009. Available at: <https://www.theguardian.com/environment/2009/apr/27/wild-food-foraging-reforesting-scotland [accessed 12 December 2016].
6. Ibid.
7. http://www.ryerson.ca/~meinhard/sampson.html
8. Wear, A., *Knowledge and Practice in English Medicine, 1500–1800* (Cambridge University Press, 2000).
9. Ibid.
10. For more information, see: http://www.shca.ed.ac.uk/Research/witches/introduction.html
11. https://www.deveron-projects.com/rhynie-woman/
12. https://www.deveron-projects.com/rhynie-woman/
13. https://www.deveron-projects.com/rhynie-woman/
14. See: https://grumpyoldwitchcraft.com/
15. https://www.youtube.com/watch?v=h77DjKOZ3Z4
16. Robert Macfarlane, 'Introduction', in Nan Shepherd, The Living Mountain (Canongate Books, 2011).

The Thing I Fear Has Found Me

1. https://www.hopkinsmedicine.org/health/conditions-and-diseases/headache/how-a-migraine-happens

Endnotes

Moving Close to the Ground: A Messy Love Song

1. *Walkie* is a disability community word to describe people who walk rather than roll. It isn't intended to create a walking/rolling binary. Disabled people know there are thousands of ways to walk and thousands of ways to roll and many of us do both. Rather *walkie* makes visible a privileged mode of mobility that is entirely taken for granted.
2. For more on access intimacy, including a foundational definition, see Mia Mingus, "Access Intimacy: The Missing Link" in her blog *Leaving Evidence* (https://leavingevidence.wordpress.com/2011/05/05/access-intimacy-the-missing-link/).
3. *Fixed: The Science/Fiction of Human Enhancement*. Dir. Regan Brashear, 2014. In contrast to Wolbring, transhumanist engineer Hugh Herr declares later in *Fixed*, "I mountain climb. I trail run. I play tennis. I do everything I want to do. If you remove the technology from my body, all I can do is crawl. I'm completely crippled." His blunt words reflect an intense connection between crawling and the devaluing of disability.
4. In her review of *Fixed*, feminist disability studies theorist Alison Kafer uses the contrast between Wolbring and Herr to think about the tension that surrounds crawling. She writes: 'I admit to a thrill of recognition here. Herr's comments explain why we so rarely see images of disabled people crawling—other than for purposes of protest or performance—but ... *here's hoping Wolbring's appearance sparks more documentation of this everyday (yet spectacularly stigmatized) modality*.' [emphasis mine]. (Alison Kafer. "Fixed: The Science/Fiction of Human Enhancement" *Disability Studies Quarterly*, 35:4 (2015).) Her call sparks me to write specifically and frankly about my experiences of moving close to the ground.
5. Carey Goldberg. "For These Trailblazers, Wheelchairs Matter," *The New York Times*, 17 August 2000. Available at: https://www.nytimes.com/2000/08/17/us/for-these-trailblazers-wheelchairs-matter.html

the poet limps in words as a balance for worlds

1. See 'Health Education England removes Long Covid video after scientific evidence supports complaints', Doctorswithme, 2021 https://doctorswith.me/health-education-england-removes-long-covid-video-after-scientific-evidence-supports-complaints/ [accessed 7 June 2023].
2. Alec Finlay, *descriptions: a patient-led description of ME, composed from the words of people with ME* (Action for ME/morning star, 2022).
3. Ibid.
4. Cassie Thornton, *The Hologram: Feminist, Peer-to-Peer Health for a Post-Pandemic Future* (Pluto Press, 2020). See also: https://www.youtube.com/watch?v=Qv4qv1YJYQo
5. Elaine Scarry, *The Body in Pain* (Oxford University Press, 1987).
6. Evidence suggests that every pandemic – Spanish flu, to MERS, SARS, and COVID-19 – produces a community of 20–27 per cent of people with

Endnotes

long term autoimmune dysfunction. The recent All-Party Parliamentary Group on ME report, 'Rethinking ME' today, accuses this 'long-term disconnect between the treatment deserved by people with ME and what they experience in reality'.

7. Simon Wessely, M.D.: 'Responding to Mass Psychogenic Illness', *New England Journal of Medicine*, 13 January 2000.
8. Ibid.
9. Professor Paul Garner: https://twitter.com/PaulGarnerWoof/status/1521467617697046529?s=20&t=84orPxd7jEYw1Pmw8HPQsg
10. '1. Research and Surveillance – persistent symptoms of COVID-19 should be dealt with using a scientific methodology and without bias. People experiencing them should be counted; 2. Clinical services – services need to be timely, tailored to individuals' presentations, and involve investigating and treating pathology, as well as the functional recovery of individuals; 3. Patient involvement – patients must be involved in the commissioning of clinical services and the design of research studies ("no decisions without me"); 4. Access to services – clinical services commissioned should not unfairly discriminate against those with negative tests and a clinical diagnosis should be adequate for accessing any appropriate services." From 'doctors as patients: a manifesto for tackling persisting symptoms of covid-19', quoted in Phillip H. Roth and Mariacarla Gadebusch-Bondio, 'The contested meaning of "Long COVID" – Patients, Doctors, and the Politics of Subjective Evidence', *Social Science & Medicine*, Vol. 292, January 2022.
11. See, for example, advice given by Professor Trudie Chalder, a proponent of CBT for ME and Long COVID, and literature produced by The Oxford Health NHS Foundation Trust, which warn against long periods of convalescence: https://babcp.com/Events/Event-Details/eventDateId/275, and, https://www.virology.ws/2020/04/16/trial-by-error-oxford-nhs-recommends-get-cbt-for-post-covid-cfs-patients/
12. The term 'minor walk' refers to the very short or recuperative walk. See: https://www.artwalkporty.co.uk/footprint-alecfinlay.html
13. GET: graded exercise therapy. See: https://me-pedia.org/wiki/Graded_exercise_therapy
14. See: https://www.yourcovidrecovery.nhs.uk/your-wellbeing/getting-moving-again/
15. The term was first referred to on Body Politic in Spring 2020: bodypolitic.slack.com
16. Ibid.
17. The names these effects refer to are discussed in my place-aware mapping of the Cairngorms, *gathering*, published by Hauser & Wirth, 2018.
18. Red deer herds are around ten times larger than is ecologically supportable.
19. The place-names are from the landscape where the first 'Day of Access' was held; they were translated with help from Peter McNiven.
20. Tom: Gaelic, knoll, mound, hillock.
21. St Fillan's Hill, Perthshire: 170m; Dùnadd, Argyll: 54m. An inaugural rock may have had a cloth laid over it or temporary canopy added. There were also seats of judgement and hillocks of the laws.

Endnotes

22. *Fiannscape*: my term for mytho-poetic landscapes in which place-names project Fingalian hunting ballads.
23. Sketch is in the collection of Blair Atholl castle.
24. *Wild garden*: concept defined by Christopher Dingwall, with reference to Bruar, and similar sites, where '*the revelation of astonishing natural scenery*' was paramount; see 'Gardens in the Wild', *Garden History*, Vol. 22, No. 2, (Winter, 1994).
25. Information from Christopher Dingwall.
26. Some pioneering restoration ecologists were formerly gamekeepers, most notably, Dick Balharry.
27. The renga platform, co-designed by David Connearn, toured the British Isles for many years.
28. Rather than focusing on the transportation of disabled people, 'Day of Access' encourages dialogue between those that care for the land and those with limited access to it.